If These WALLS *Could* TALK:

NEW ENGLAND PATRIOTS

Stories from the
New England Patriots Sideline,
Locker Room, and Press Box

Scott Zolak and Jeff Howe

TRIUMPH
BOOKS

To Caitlin, Avery, and Taylor
—J.H.

Library of Congress Cataloging-in-Publication Data

Names: Zolak, Scott author.
Title: If these walls could talk : New England Patriots : stories from the New England Patriots sideline, locker room, and press box / Scott Zolak and Jeff Howe.
Description: Chicago, Illinois : Triumph Books LLC, [2018]
Identifiers: LCCN 2018004259 | ISBN 9781629374420
Subjects: LCSH: New England Patriots (Football team)—Anecdotes. | New England Patriots (Football team)—History.
Classification: LCC GV956.N36 Z65 2018 | DDC 796.332/630974461—dc23
LC record available at https://lccn.loc.gov/2018004259

This book is available in quantity at special discounts for your group or organization. For further information, contact:

Triumph Books LLC
814 North Franklin Street
Chicago, Illinois 60610
(312) 337–0747
www.triumphbooks.com

Printed in U.S.A.

ISBN: 978-1-62937-442-0

Design by Amy Carter

Page production by Nord Compo

Photos courtesy of AP Images unless otherwise indicated

CONTENTS

FOREWORD

I remember sitting in the locker room before Super Bowl XXXVI. On Tuesday of that week, I was informed that Tommy was going to start the game after I'd helped us win the AFC Championship Game against the Steelers. It was the very definition of bittersweet. I was fired up for my teammates but extremely sad I wasn't going to get to play. Willie McGinest came over to me as we were getting ready to take the field. He leaned over and grabbed the back of my neck and said, "Never forget man, we started this shit."

It was a cool moment, and it crystallized how I feel about the transition the Patriots went through with those teams I was so privileged to be a part of. We all took a lot of pride in being there when the team went from being fairly irrelevant to a contender. From there, of course, the Patriots have gone on to become the most dominant franchise in professional sports. All of us who were part of those teams in the 1990s deserve to take a lot of pride in that we left the organization better than we found it. We all have a certain degree of ownership in the amazing success the Patriots have had since we left.

When I was drafted by the Pats back in 1993, I only knew the names of two guys on the team: Andre Tippett and Irving Fryar. I never even got to play with Irving. This was back in the dark ages when the only games you could watch were your local team's, one national game, and then the Monday night game. That meant I ended up watching the Seahawks and then one or two other games. The Patriots just weren't on national television much. I was fairly unaware of much of anything regarding the Patriots other than the fact that they hadn't been good for quite awhile.

That rookie year—that was a crazy year. It was hard. I went from being a small-town kid from Walla Walla, Washington, to school in Pullman, which was an even smaller town, to being the figurehead for a struggling NFL franchise in the most passionate sports market in America. It was pretty heady stuff for a 21-year-old kid. We proceeded to lose 11 of our first 12 games, and I was on the sidelines for the only game we won. It wasn't much fun. I had success at Washington State during my last year and had grown accustomed to winning football games. Going through a stretch like that where we couldn't get out of our way and couldn't win was pretty rough. Thankfully, it ended the right way. We won our last four games and knocked the Dolphins out of the playoffs in the season finale. There was a lot of optimism going into the offseason, but I remember in the middle of that season thinking, *Man, are we ever going to win a frigging game? Where is the upside here?*

I felt like things were turning around in 1994. We were 3–6 at one point, but scoring a ton of points. We were just having trouble stopping people. We opened the 1994 season against the Bills and Dolphins. Both games were shootouts. I think I threw eight touchdown passes to eight different receivers in those first two games. We felt like we were hitting our stride offensively, but we were giving up too many points. It seemed like we were getting better. I really felt like something was happening.

At halftime of the 10th game against the Vikings, we were down 20–3. Warren Moon was lighting us up and things weren't looking good. That's when they finally decided to let go of the reins a little bit and let me sling it around. Scott Zolak was awesome for me, especially in the early part of my career. He had some success the year before I got there and probably wasn't ecstatic to see the team go draft some kid to take over the QB spot.

Zo swallowed his pride and was supportive of me that whole time we were together. At halftime of the Vikings game, Zo went to Ray Perkins or Bill Parcells, maybe both, and said, "Hey, why don't you let the kid go?" Shockingly enough, they listened to him. We threw it 53 times after halftime, and we came back to win that game 26–20 in overtime. I'll never forget the feeling of watching my buddy Kevin Turner cradle the ball in his hands for the game winner! We went on to win our next six to sneak into the playoffs. All of a sudden, it looked like we had a chance to beat somebody.

I remember talking to Pat Harlow late in my second season in 1994. I probably won't get his exact words right, but he grabbed me and said, "Man, this is fun. We haven't had hope since I got here, and now we've got a squad that I think we can win with." It was pretty cool to be with some of the guys who had been through it and hadn't won many games.

Our team was really young those early years with the exception of Tippet, Bruce Armstrong, Pat Harlow, Vincent Brown, et al. There were a few veteran leaders, but those teams were really young. There was a nucleus of us who stuck around for a number of years. There was a real sense of camaraderie on those teams. Part of it was the "us against the world" mentality. We were practicing at Wrentham State School, which was an abandoned mental hospital five miles from our locker room. Every day we would dress in our practice gear, get in our cars, and drive over to the field. Our facilities were the worst in the league. We had a tiny little weight room. It rained in the training room. We were the perennial underdogs and we embraced that role. We spent a lot of time together off the field socially. We would get together for dinner at least every other week, and we would usually stop to have a beer or two after games. It was fun to be around a bunch of guys I was really close with as we started to get better and more competitive. Looking back, it felt more like a high school or college atmosphere than the big business NFL. It was a special thing to be a part of.

We didn't have a place to hang out after games, so my wife and some other wives found us a tent where we could get together after games with friends and family. We were all friends, and we liked to get together off the field.

There was another time when Zo pulled me aside—and this was pretty cool. Bruce Armstrong and I had developed a really good friendship. I love Bruce to this day, but he was not the easiest guy for most guys to talk to—big and kind of angry most of the time. I remember Zo grabbed me and goes, "Man, Bruce talks to you. He never talks to rookies." I thought that was a cool badge of honor.

One time in practice my rookie year, I stepped into the huddle and Bruce was talking to somebody about something. I looked at Bruce and said, "Shut up." Bruce got quiet, and I called the play. I remember looking around the huddle and some guys were startled that I said something to Bruce. He grabbed me after that practice and said, "I know you're trying to take control of the huddle, but don't ever tell me to shut up." I was borderline afraid for my life so I said, "You got it, Bruce. Yup, you got it." Ray Perkins came to my defense and said, "Hey, Drew has the huddle." Bruce just put a hand on Ray and said, "We got this. We're good." It was a cool moment because I don't think Bruce was very happy about it, but he knew what I was trying to accomplish. I didn't tell him to shut up again.

It's a little bittersweet when I get together with some of those guys now. A lot of us got right to the point where it was ready to take off and then we moved on. Guys either retired or moved to different teams and had to watch from afar. There's a tinge of regret that we didn't get to see the mountaintop, but there's definitely a sense of camaraderie in knowing that we weren't part of the machine; we were the ones who actually built it. There is a sense of pride in building something. If you come into an organization that is already successful and rolling, you just become a cog in the machine. We were the guys grinding it out as underdogs to really affect change. That's a much harder task. Winning in the NFL is always hard, but cultural change within an organization is particularly difficult. We were part of changing that culture.

When I got the call in 2011 to be inducted into the Patriots Hall of Fame, I was extremely flattered. It was an amazing honor because it was voted on by the fans and the people who watched our transition. There was then, and still is to this day, an appreciation for what we accomplished in the '90s. Getting the call and being inducted into the Hall of Fame was really meaningful to me. The ovation I received at halftime of that game was so loud and long it was a bit overwhelming. I'm proud I kept it together and didn't start bawling on stage. It was important to me, but I think it was even more meaningful to my family. My parents, my brother, my wife, I think they all harbored more resentment than I did about how things ended. I didn't, and still don't harbor much resentment about that. I understood it. But it was really important for my family to see the appreciation from the organization and the fans. It was a cool moment for my kids, too. They were too young to remember much about my playing days with the Pats. The boys were born in Boston, but they were too young to know what was going on. It was really touching and meaningful for them to see the appreciation from the organization and the fans.

One thing I enjoy when I come back to New England is the reception I get from fans and people in and around Boston. It's really different from my playing days. When I was playing I was the star player and people wanted autographs and that kind of stuff. Now I get the sense that people feel we're friends; just buddies catching up. If I'm walking down the street I'll end up talking with somebody and catching up on my wine business, my kids, etc. There's still a genuine interest in what's going on in my world and a genuine appreciation for what we were able to accomplish. My son, Henry, and I went to Celtics and Bruins games in November 2017. The genuine appreciation from so many fans was both fun and meaningful. People are genuinely thankful for what our teams did in the '90s.

My relationship with Mr. Kraft has grown since I left. We have a true friendship. What he's done as the owner of that franchise is truly amazing. It all starts at the top. He is a guiding force for that organization and really for all of New England. To be able to call RKK a friend and to keep in touch with him on a regular basis is important to me. He is always very kind. Mr. Kraft grabbed Henry when we were flying on his plane to Denver for the Patriots-Broncos game and told him, "Hey, you need to know that your dad was probably the biggest force in changing our organization." Henry looked at me and smiled, and Mr. Kraft put his hand on his shoulder and said, "I mean that. Nobody was more important than your dad in helping this thing change." His words, from his mouth to my son's ears. It was really meaningful and impactful for both me and my son. Thanks, RKK.

I will always consider myself a Patriot. I will always consider it a great honor to be a part of the teams that changed things for New England. Go Pats!

—Drew Bledsoe

CHAPTER 1

WELCOME
TO THE JUNGLE

Scott Zolak had arrived, or at least that's what he had believed. His initiation with the New England Patriots was during a darker time, three years before the dawn of Robert Kraft's reign as owner and nearly a full decade before Bill Belichick's arrival. And when the Patriots selected Zolak with the No. 84 overall pick in the 1991 draft, quarterback Tom Brady was a few months shy of his 14th birthday. The Patriots, to put it bluntly, were an embarrassment, and visions of a dynastic era that would push two decades and be led by a castoff coach and sixth-round pick would have been delusional. But that was the state of the organization in the early 1990s, and Zolak was thrilled to fulfill a lifelong dream of reaching the NFL.

Zolak was the first pick of the fourth round and the fifth quarterback off the board, following first-rounders Dan McGwire and Todd Marinovich and second-rounders Brett Favre and Browning Nagle. And head coach Dick MacPherson, who tried to recruit Zolak to Syracuse before he committed to Maryland, excitedly called his new quarterback to bring him to Foxboro, Massachusetts.

MacPherson couldn't snag Zolak the first time around. After all, Zolak was ranked as one of the top two high school quarterback recruits in Pennsylvania along with Major Harris, and he needed three feet of snow in upstate New York like he needed a hole in the head. Plus, Syracuse was running an option-style offense at the time, and Zolak wanted to sling it.

"I'm like, 'Holy shit, I'm not going to Syracuse,'" Zolak recalled.

But when MacPherson shared his admiration the second time around, Zolak was ecstatic. He didn't know a lot about the Patriots, although he had immense respect for former quarterback Steve Grogan, and he was a big-time Larry Bird fan. He loved the tight shorts, the Celtics' aura, everything about them, and he couldn't wait to see some games at the old Boston Garden. And since Zolak wore short shorts and sported a mullet, he figured he'd fit right in with that crowd.

Aside from all that, Zolak was in the show. This was the NFL. This was big time, the dream, the arrival. So when he got the draft call from MacPherson, chief executive officer Sam Jankovich, and vice president of player operations Joe Mendes, Zolak was ready to make the short trip up north.

"Mac was like, 'Jesus Christ, you've got to come play for me now. I'm drafting you, so you've got no choice,'" Zolak said.

The excitement tempered when Zolak soon learned why the Patriots of the early 1990s were among the worst organizations in professional sports, and why the weather in New England can drive a man crazy, and why the traffic in Boston could transform Mother Teresa into Charlie Sheen. The Patriots had one intern, Aaron Salkin, who greeted Zolak a day after the draft with a sign with his name on it before they retreated to a white Ford van at Logan Airport.

But Zolak landed during rush hour and it was sleeting, so the traffic was borderline apocalyptic. At the start of the ride toward Foxboro, which in theory should only take half an hour, Zolak remained amped up over his first trip through Boston, particularly when they passed the Garden. Then they slowly crawled south down I-93 through Quincy and the remaining towns that acted as a buffer between the state capital and Foxboro Stadium, and the excitement turned into natural frustration throughout a ride that spanned two and a half hours.

"I was like, 'Where the hell are we going?'" Zolak said. "I'm miserable at this point. You have no idea where you're going, so it feels like five hours. We pull up past the stadium, and he's like, 'There's the stadium.' You can't really see it because it's dark at that time of night."

Alas, the Foxboro Stadium sign rubbed right up against Route 1, so that was all the proof Zolak needed. Salkin then informed Zolak that offensive line coach Rod Humenuik was waiting for him at the Endzone Motor Inn a few miles south of the stadium. Nowadays, the hotel is merely the butt of a joke of how to stay near the stadium for a game without spending more than your lunch money. But that's where Zolak and his fellow draft picks would be holed up for the week during the Patriots' rookie camp.

Zolak was delighted when the hotel clerk informed him that he had a deluxe suite waiting upstairs, although that was mostly because Zolak was surprised the place even had a deluxe suite. Zolak was overcome by the smell of chlorine on the way to his room, so he excitedly asked the clerk where the pool was located. As it turned out, the pool didn't exist, but the hotel staff was certainly diligent with their efforts to maintain a clean hot tub. Lo and behold, Zolak opened his door and found an outdoor hot tub smack dab in the middle of the room.

"So I called my dad and said, 'I think I've made it.'"

Started from the Top, Now We're Here

A hotshot athlete in Monongahela, Pennsylvania, Scott Zolak was the son of a high school athletic director and the grandson of steelworkers, so he was practically starring in the real-life version of *All the Right Moves*. The blue-collar town was rife with tradition, too, as Joe Montana, Ken Griffey Sr., Stan Musial, Freddie Cox, and Deacon Dan Towler all hailed from the area. The residents worked in the mills during the days and lived through the high school teams at night, particularly under the Friday night lights.

Zolak was like every Pennsylvania kid who desperately wanted to play football for Penn State, and the Nittany Lions began recruiting Zolak by the time he was a freshman at Belle Vernon High School. Zolak's father, Paul, was the athletic director at Ringgold High School and had sent a handful of players to Penn State. During his own recruiting process, Scott Zolak ate spaghetti and meatballs at Joe Paterno's small, nondescript State College house that had a red and white checkered tablecloth in the former coach's kitchen.

But in typical Penn State fashion, they wanted to turn Scott Zolak into a linebacker, which they also tried to pull on Jim Kelly and Jeff Hostetler. Zolak had never played defense in his life and wasn't sold on the idea of bulking up his 6'5", 222-pound frame to head to Linebacker U. Zolak passed on the offer to flip sides, and Penn State wound up with quarterback Tom Bill in the 1986 recruiting class.

Along the way, Zolak reveled in the high school scene. He started as a sophomore and junior at Belle Vernon and transferred to Ringgold to play for a better program during his senior year, which was a major deal for a local star to uproot for a rival program. To do that, his parents put their house on the market for an exorbitant price—about double its value—that they knew wouldn't draw any offers and moved into a "shit box" down by the river to get him into the district to qualify for Ringgold.

"My family sacrificed a lot to watch me play," Zolak said. "We ended up winning a lot and going to the playoffs, so it was cool."

They played every Friday night in front of at least 10,000 fans at Ringgold. The stadium had a press box due to all of the attention that had been heaped upon the team, and the field was encircled by lights because the idea of playing Saturday afternoon football was absurd. The loyal, passionate town shut down and engulfed the stadium. Paul Zolak pioneered the use of Astroturf at the facility and his wife, Daryl, was a popular teacher in the area, so Scott Zolak was a household name, even a celebrity, in the district.

"It was steel town versus steel town, and everybody knew everybody," Zolak said. "It was about pride, man. You didn't want to lose for your hometown. You didn't want to lose for your neighbors."

After games, high school kids got to act like high school kids. Zolak played a starring role then, too, especially after he cashed in on a bet with his father. They had a deal: if Scott earned a college scholarship, which was as sure of a thing as the sun rising every morning over their Pennsylvania town, Paul Zolak would buy him any car he wanted. So the star quarterback with the mullet who wore tight shirts and listened to Def Leppard, REO Speedwagon, and Styx made the obvious choice. He scored a silver IROC-Z with the T-tops. Zolak and his teammates would pack it after games and head to McDonald's to eat French fries and drink sodas.

"That's what kids did back then," Zolak said. "We'd drive around, crank tunes, and cruise the mall, what any other high school kid would do."

Prior to his senior year, Zolak played in the Big 33 Football Classic, a recruiting bonanza for the best high school players in Pennsylvania at Hersheypark Stadium. His offensive teammates included future Broncos Super Bowl champion wide receiver Ed McCaffrey, and Zolak recalled seeing Michigan coach Bo Schembechler and Louisville coach Howard Schnellenberger among the 30,000 in the stands.

The recruiting element was like a game of dominos for the quarterbacks, as Zolak, Major Harris, and Browning Nagle jockeyed for the right program. Zolak obviously wanted nothing to do with the Syracuse weather or Dick MacPherson's option system, and it was even more unappealing to convert to linebacker to play for Penn State. Schnellenberger, who gained fame at the University of Miami, told Zolak he could start for four years at Louisville, but Zolak admitted "that kind of scares you as an 18-year-old kid." So that's where Nagle wound up.

Zolak was really drawn to the University of Maryland for a host of reasons. As much as anything, he fell in love with head coach Bobby Ross, but Zolak also had a family connection to the area. His uncle, Chuck Zolak, who was the quarterback for Delaware's co-national championship team in 1963, lived near Maryland's campus, and he could serve as Scott's father away from home. Not to mention, it was only a few hours from home, so Zolak's parents could drive to his games. It all made perfect sense to commit to one of the better programs in the country.

Maryland endured a bout of tragedy and turmoil around the time of Zolak's arrival in 1986, however. Zolak, a huge basketball fan after also starting on the hardwood for all four years of high school, joined the rest of America that became infatuated with Maryland star forward Len Bias, and Zolak relished the opportunities to watch Bias play during his recruiting trips and then again in summer league games when he arrived on campus prior to his freshman year. But Bias died of a cocaine overdose two days after the Boston Celtics drafted him with the second pick in June 1986. As part of the fallout, men's basketball coach Lefty Driesell resigned in October, and Bobby Ross bolted after the 1986 football season.

Meanwhile, Zolak had to wade through a stacked quarterback depth chart, and he knew he'd redshirt as a freshman. But his first target was Gary McIntosh, a decorated high school All-American who was viewed by the Terrapins as the eventual starter. Zolak didn't give a damn.

"I remember being on my official visit there after I committed, and a couple defensive backs go, 'Oh man, you aren't coming here, are you?' I'm like, 'Yeah, why?' They're like, 'You're never going to play. We've got this guy Gary McIntosh.' He ended up transferring to Navy because I beat his ass out for the job my first year there. I had no fear of anybody."

Zolak had far greater respect for starter Dan Henning Jr. and fellow backup Neil O'Donnell, who started Super Bowl XXX for the Pittsburgh Steelers. Henning's father, Dan Henning Sr., was a Bill Parcells disciple and a brilliant offensive coach who taught the spread offense to Charlie Weis and served a number of roles in the NFL and college for more than four decades. He also raised a hell of a competitive son.

Henning could relate to Zolak's toughness, too. Perhaps Zolak's most memorable play at Ringgold High occurred against, of all teams, Belle Vernon, when he took a wicked blindside shot on a heavy blitz but still delivered a pass that traveled 60 yards and went for a game-winning touchdown. So Zolak shared an appreciation for players with a similar level of intestinal fortitude.

"I learned a ton from Henning," Zolak said. "This kid was a small, undersized kid, but he had guts and balls, and got the shit kicked out of him, but he stood there and threw it."

O'Donnell beat out Zolak for the backup job and ultimately became the starter until Zolak took over in 1990. Despite being the fulltime starter for one season, Zolak left Maryland ranked fifth in school history with 270 completions and seventh with 3,124 passing yards, and he was a four-time Atlantic Coast Conference Offensive Player of the Week.

Zolak flourished under the tutelage of head coach Joe Krivak, and the quarterback really benefited from his chemistry with tight end and H-back Frank Wycheck, who in 2000 delivered the key lateral in the Tennessee Titans' "Music City Miracle" comeback victory in the playoffs against the Buffalo Bills.

"Frank really carried me my senior year, kind of put me on a national stage and got me noticed," Zolak said.

Zolak orchestrated the spread offense at Maryland, setting a school record with 29 completions against Michigan, and he took that skillset to the Blue-Gray Game on Christmas. Houston coach John Jenkins led Zolak's team, so they operated with the run-and-shoot. Zolak was the MVP of the all-star game to further open eyes of NFL scouts.

"We threw the shit out of it," Zolak said. "I think I threw it 45 times in the first three quarters. And we had no plays. We held up signs and that was the name of the play. We'd hold up a rat trap, and that was a trap play. That was cool. Everything at Maryland was so rigid like it is here with the Patriots. It was simple like that, and it works. It shows you that you don't have to complicate things to make it work."

Northward Bound

The 1991 NFL draft was a crapshoot, and Scott Zolak was told he could be taken off the board as early as the second round or as late as the sixth. The New York Giants showed plenty of interest, and Zolak met with general manager George Young on a couple of occasions. Even though Bill Parcells was gone by that point, it was an appealing landing spot given the Giants' recent history with a couple of Super Bowl victories, and Young left a significant impression on Zolak.

But the Giants didn't take a quarterback. The Pittsburgh Steelers and Washington Redskins, who also took a liking to Zolak, also ignored the quarterback position in the draft. And the Atlanta Falcons, who were undoubtedly taking a quarterback, turned to Brett Favre in the second round, so there was no argument there. Patriots vice president of player operations Joe Mendes worked Zolak out at Maryland, but the quarterback thought little of it. Really, Zolak just never envisioned himself in New England until head coach Dick MacPherson summoned him in the draft.

The aura of being in the NFL quickly wore off during those two and a half hours in a white van that methodically worked its way south on the most frustratingly congested highway in the state while also meandering through the sleet that would be out of season if it weren't dousing New Englanders who are used to exchanging shorts for snow boots on a daily basis in April. And for an out-of-towner who was getting ready for his orientation in a new area of the country? Nightmarish.

"You're in East Bumbfuck," Zolak recalled. "It was the worst first impression. You're like, 'This is the league? This is the NFL?'"

But if the hot tub in Zolak's hotel room felt out of place, it merely prepared him for the glorified high school stadium that housed the Patriots from 1971 to 2001. During his initial tour of Foxboro Stadium, Zolak was taken aback by the locker-room's metal benches and steel-cage lockers. Really, if someone didn't know any better, it'd be easy to convince them the locker room facilitated a junior varsity team. As the tour moved to the equipment room, Zolak remembered asking for the location of the weight room, and he was shocked again when the coach who guided the tour told him they had already walked through it.

That's when it started to click. Maybe this was why the Patriots were basement dwellers, coming off an embarrassing 1–15 season in 1990, because they sucked the winning culture and professional lifestyle out of the players the moment they walked into the building.

"Things only got worse the next day when you saw the facilities," Zolak said. "You walk in to see the locker room and you're like, 'This can't be the NFL.' Sure as heck enough, it was the NFL. But hey, man, it was a paycheck. It was cool. You're in the league."

Zolak was humbled in another way during his first day at Foxboro Stadium. He met linebacker Andre Tippett, who was enshrined in the Pro Football Hall of Fame in 2008, and that was an intimidating encounter to say the least. Tippett didn't talk to rookies until they earned his respect, but he was truly a remarkable teammate who eventually became close with Zolak. But that first day? That was a wakeup call.

"You think you're going to get there and these veterans are going to be nice to you," Zolak said. "It wasn't that Tippett was a dick. Tippett was Tippett. He wasn't going to deal with any rookies."

Into July, Zolak briefly held out during the start of training camp due to a technicality with his draft slot. The 84th selection would have typically been the final pick of the third round, but there were only 27 first-round slots in 1991 because the Jets used a first-rounder on Rob Moore in the 1990 supplemental draft. So Zolak's agent, former Patriots linebacker Ralph Cindrich, lobbied to get him money that would have been earned if the 84th pick was still in the third round.

It all worked out, and Zolak put the money to use. He knew he wasn't going to beat out quarterbacks Hugh Millen or Tommy Hodson during his rookie season, so he was on cruise control while basically redshirting. Zolak bought three gold chains and a red Ford Explorer when sport-utility vehicles started to take over the roads. He immediately threw some bass tubes in the new whip and cruised the area wearing his patented tank tops and cowboy hats, shouting, "Sun's out, guns out!" And there was a sound chance everyone on the street heard the Guns N' Roses blaring from the speakers. Really, he was Rob Gronkowski before Rob Gronkowski was Rob Gronkowski.

"[I was] just a Midwestern hick from Pennsylvania coming to play in the big city, and I really didn't think I was going to play," Zolak said.

From Montana to Foxboro

Like Scott Zolak, Pro Football Hall of Famer Joe Montana hailed from Monongahela, the petite coal-mining town in southwest Pennsylvania. Montana was a no-doubts-about-it type of star at Ringgold High School where Paul Zolak coached and served as the athletic director. There was an obvious air of greatness about Montana early in his football career, as was his "Joe Cool" personality that made him both popular and beloved by his community. He was a big-time Huey Lewis and the News fan (they actually played at his NFL retirement party), and Montana's friends called him Joe Montanalow due to his resemblance to Barry Manilow.

Scott Zolak was seven years old in 1974 when Montana was a senior, and the young kid was also already well-known because of his father's involvement with the Ringgold program. So Zolak was in charge of darting onto the field after kickoffs to snag the orange tee during games, and Montana and the team took an easy liking to him.

Montana did it all, from playing quarterback to kicker to punter and defensive back. He prepared well and was consistently calm and collected in tight situations, and Zolak watched him intently, wanting to model his game after Montana with every noticeable detail. But the thing that stuck out to Zolak was the way Montana competed, and that showed when Montana waded through a crowded depth chart to win his job at Notre Dame. Years later, in a comparison that reached extraordinary levels, Montana's situation at Notre Dame reminded Zolak of Tom Brady at Michigan and again with the New England Patriots.

Years later, when Montana was already halfway to his quartet of Super Bowl victories, he had a gift for Zolak when the younger quarterback was heading off to Maryland. Montana gave him a football with a handwritten message: Good luck at Maryland and see you in the NFL one day. Considering Montana was Zolak's idol growing up, the ball meant everything to him, a prized possession that he always held in the highest regard.

Zolak wore No. 13 at Maryland and hoped to keep the same number with the Patriots when he arrived in 1991, but it belonged to Tommy Hodson, who was a year older and someone Zolak respected while even watching his games at LSU. So Zolak took No. 16, "because Joe wore 16."

Depth Charge

There was an interesting dynamic in the quarterback room during Scott Zolak's rookie year in 1991. Starter Hugh Millen was anything but a franchise-caliber quarterback, so he was understandably in it for himself and never helped Zolak or backup Tommy Hodson. Millen was also a social misfit. He was smart and well-read, and had some ideas for some business ventures, but he wasn't all that relatable. Millen got into a huge fight with his fiancée, cheerleader Lisa Coles, after he bought her a fax machine for Christmas because he genuinely believed it was a practical gift for their business plans.

Hodson and Zolak had an instant connection, though.

"I remember watching Tommy as a four-year freaking starter at LSU," Zolak said. "He was the galloping gray ghost, married the homecoming queen, just a great guy. He helped me the most. Tommy was a good dude and was happy for me when I got my chance."

Zolak didn't play in 1991 when the Patriots went 6–10 in head coach Dick MacPherson's first season, and they limped to an 0–9 start in 1992 before Zolak got his first career start. Millen suffered a gross, third-degree separated shoulder, and he tried to play because it was his left, non-throwing shoulder. But it was also sticking out about 2 inches more than his right shoulder, and the pain was clearly too intense to endure. Hodson temporarily took over but broke his wrist against the New Orleans Saints when the Patriots succumbed to their ninth consecutive loss.

So it was Zolak's show for the Patriots' Week 11 trip to meet the Indianapolis Colts. But first, there was a reunion. Paul Zolak brought Joe Montana's signed ball to his son as a way to reflect on the journey from Monongahela to the NFL. Zolak appreciated the moment, and he rubbed the football 16 times before his starting debut.

Zolak completed 20 of 29 passes for 261 yards, two touchdowns, and an interception, and he was named AFC Offensive Player of the Week for his performance in the 37–34 overtime victory. He uncorked a 65-yard touchdown pass to wide receiver Greg McMurtry, hit receiver Irving Fryar five times for 65 yards, and delivered a pair of passes to running back Jon Vaughn for 32 yards on the game-winning jaunt in overtime. And Zolak remembers the details of the day with the utmost clarity.

"We got in a little bit of a shootout," Zolak said. "Things just move so fast at that level. That was the biggest thing for me. Your head is on a swivel. You really don't know what the hell you're looking at half the time, and of course, you have no reps in practice. So you're just thrust into it with a pretty shitty team. The only guy I really had was Irving Fryar. Ben Coates was making one of his first starts. I threw Ben his first touchdown in the first quarter. It was a play-action pass, '137 X Corner,' and Ben was the X tight end on that. So he made a hell of a catch for a two-yard touchdown and kind of got us going in the game, and that was the only thing I really remember reading correctly. When I say 'reading,' I mean seeing the secondary.

"I remember we had the ball right before the end of the first half, and all I remember is seeing the safeties split. Greg McMurtry was running an inside skinny post. I was getting ready to get hit and I closed my eyes and threw it as hard as I could, just a 30-yard bullet right up the middle. I remember hitting the turf, and all I hear is people cheering and booing. And I see McMurtry running down, and I'm looking around for flags and I don't see any. I see Freddy Smerlas over on the sideline, and I take my helmet off and I bow. And I turned around and I bowed again, and I'm pointing.

That was it. That was the moment like, 'I got it.' It stuck, and I started having some fun.

"We moved the ball well in the second half, and they ended up taking it to overtime. I remember getting the ball in overtime, and Jon Vaughn was our tailback. They were watching Coates so closely, so all I said I was going to do was, 'Hey Jon, sneak through the line. I'm just going to keep hitting check-downs to you. We had like five check-downs and got Charlie Baumann down in range and he ended up winning it for us in overtime."

After the game, Zolak was asked by a reporter if he did anything differently or had any types of superstitions, so he mentioned that he rubbed the Montana football 16 times. Because Zolak led the Patriots to their first win and Montana's standing in the NFL, the story took off locally in New England to the point where UPS wanted to get involved with the shipping duties of the ball.

The Patriots were humbled two weeks later on the road against the Atlanta Falcons, and Pro Football Hall of Fame cornerback Deion Sanders was particularly problematic during the 34–0 loss.

"Deion Sanders picked me off twice," Zolak said. "Both picks were throwaways. I intentionally tried to throw both away deep, and he ran them down and started showboating. I was trying to overthrow Irving Fryar twice. I actually got two personal fouls for hitting Deion late out of bounds because he was doing that showboating, high-stepping shit. I speared him twice out of bounds. Irving Fryar pulled up on both routes. I thought he was going to run through it, and I just tried to throw the ball away. Deion, that son of a bitch, ran them both down. That was the fastest guy I've ever played against."

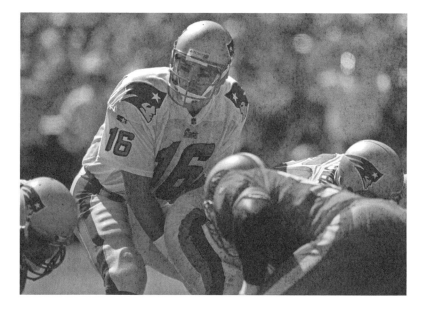

Zolak loved Fryar, though. Fryar, the first pick of the 1984 draft, wasn't very popular with Patriots fans because of a domestic violence incident in 1986 that caused him to miss the AFC Championship Game victory against the Miami Dolphins, and then a gun charge in 1988. But Fryar helped Zolak when few would, considering he was a third-string quarterback during his first two seasons.

"Irving got a bad rap here," Zolak said. "He was one of my favorite guys to play with. I got Irving at the end of his career, so I think I got the good Irving. Irving really taught me a lot about how to get ready to play this game and play at this level just as far as working out. He, Ty Law, and Curtis Martin were probably the three hardest-working guys, and I'm talking about what they did beyond what they were required to do. That's what sticks with guys when you see them work out that way. Irving helped me a lot as a rookie and second-year guy because nobody else really did."

Millen was healthy enough to return after the loss to the Falcons, but Zolak replaced him during the 6–0 loss to the Colts in Foxboro and made his final start of the season a week later in Kansas City against the Chiefs. Zolak got rolled up from behind and suffered a serious high-ankle sprain that initially caused him to tell interim coach Dante Scarnecchia it was broken as he remained on the Astroturf.

The medical staff carted Zolak off the field and into the X-ray room where they confirmed the bones were intact, so Zolak and the trainers determined they'd try to give it a go. They stuck a 6-inch needle into the ball of Zolak's ankle to numb the pain, but he had no control over his foot and couldn't explode the way he hoped.

"It was the weirdest feeling having the numbing agent in there and you know you have no control over your foot," Zolak said. "It was pretty scary, actually. It was also kind of a realization that you play at all costs. That was the mentality of the league, and it still is to this day. And the guys who don't shoot it up, you get forgotten about."

Zolak wore a size-13 shoe, but they taped up his ankle so heavily that they gave him a size-15 to see if it would fit. Ultimately, Zolak had no chance to return to the field, and the Patriots placed him on injured reserve. The tissue spread too much between the bones in his leg, and the only way it would heal was through four months of rest. He couldn't play, couldn't go skiing, couldn't even dip his toes down to get them into a boot. It was a pretty crushing time.

The Patriots held their Christmas party a couple weeks after Zolak's injury, and the quarterback arrived on crutches with tight end Al Golden, who spent his only season in the NFL in 1992 before turning to a coaching career. Zolak said he drank so much that he didn't need the crutches on his way out the door, which led to an epic speech the next day from Dick MacPherson. The head coach was a lovable guy, like a grandfather and Gene Hackman's character in *Hoosiers* all rolled into one. But MacPherson laid down a three-rule system for Zolak.

"Son, you like to go out all the time," MacPherson told Zolak. "I'm going to give you three rules. I want you to enjoy the first, sip the second, and refuse the third. Your problem, Zolak, is you always get confused between rule two and rule three and start over at one."

Zolak remembers the conversation fondly, and it was one of their last talks before the Patriots fired MacPherson following the two-win 1992 season. That offseason led to quite possibly the greatest shakeup in the history of the franchise.

CHAPTER 2
REELING IN THE BIG TUNA

To the New England Patriots, or at least the players who resided in Foxboro Stadium's cagey locker room, Bill Parcells was nothing more than a mythological figure. He led the New York Giants to victories in Super Bowls XXI and XXV and rose to prominence as one of the greatest head coaches of his generation by restoring prominence to that proud franchise.

The Patriots, meanwhile, were a mess as they transitioned from Raymond Berry's strong teams in the late 1980s. They had a rocky mixture of aging veterans and young players who simply weren't that good and clearly weren't ready to carry a team into a new age, and the culture clash resulted in a string of embarrassing seasons. Under head coach Rod Rust in 1990 and Dick MacPherson from 1991 to '92, the Patriots were 9–39, including a scandal-ridden 1–15 season in 1990.

The players had a good idea MacPherson would be gone after the 1992 season. They adored MacPherson, but that was part of the problem. He was a lovable grandfather type, someone you'd want to have over for Thanksgiving to rattle off stories of the glory days. But MacPherson had some health issues that kept him away from the team for the final eight games of the 1992 season, and the Patriots needed a drastic culture change.

The 1992 Patriots weren't talented, and they were even less confident. Their two-game winning streak during quarterback Scott Zolak's first pair of starts was sandwiched between a nine-game losing streak and a five-game losing streak. It was all a product of failing to make the transition at quarterback after Steve Grogan and the combination of relying on aging stars to carry a group that was saddled with some poor draft classes from the late 1980s. Players didn't know their roles on the current team or their status for the future, even if they were under contract, so they just played out the string in 1992.

"Winning and losing are the same thing. They're both contagious," Zolak said. "You start to get into a rut, and it's like, 'All right, shit, we lost six games. What the hell is seven? What the hell is eight?' You just kept going. The stadium isn't even half full. The stadium is pretty shitty to begin with. It just wasn't mentally good. It wasn't mentally healthy."

Meanwhile, Parcells was trying to get back into the NFL after spending a couple years working in the media. He had retired from the New York Giants after the team's second Super Bowl victory in the 1990 season, ending an eight-year reign as the head coach. But Parcells got the itch again and hit the interview circuit, first being turned down by the Tampa Bay Buccaneers before focusing his attention on the New England Patriots.

Parcells was building a reputation as a great head coach who reveled in the idea of breathing life into a franchise on life support, hence the inclination to take over the Buccaneers and Patriots. But the Giants were mired in a far more tenuous situation when Parcells was promoted from defensive coordinator to head coach in 1983. After the Giants went to five NFL championship games from 1958 to '63, they were stuck in a two-decade funk under five different head coaches. They had missed the playoffs 18 times in the 19 seasons prior to Parcells' takeover, and they only had three seasons with a winning record during that span.

So if Parcells could save the Giants, he could save anyone, including the bumbling Patriots of the early 1990s.

"We knew they were going to bring someone in. We just never thought it was going to be Bill Parcells," Zolak said.

There was a legitimate amount of excitement when the Patriots hired Parcells. The players knew football would be relevant again in a region where the Patriots struggled for attention against the Red Sox, Celtics, and Bruins. But more than that, the Patriots could play for something again. With Parcells, they could build a winner, and they recognized a drastically different demeanor right from the jump. The players were blown away, to the point where they wanted to start working out for the season as soon as Parcells was introduced.

"When Parcells came, everything was different," Zolak said. "Everything changed. Everything went from casual, having fun and just plugging away to, 'This is serious business now.' The game was big now. The game became big.

"Night and day, it was like losing one of the Beverly Hillbillies grandpas and then all of a sudden bringing in this world tyrant. You remember walking on eggshells. He'd make your life a living hell during the week so that you'd actually look forward to game day to get away from him. He couldn't track you down when you were out there on the field. All he could do was scream at you. But you were so much more ready to play the game, and you played with an edge. There was a different air of confidence with that guy. He changed the whole approach to football here, and just your whole mindset. Football became a 365-day job with him. You were in there every day, and it became a competition and trying to beat the other guy. He established that. With Mac, we were on cruise control."

Zolak's first encounter with Parcells was as unforgettable as it was routine. Parcells didn't change his approach with his players during their introductions. He was unequivocally the man in charge, and he let them know that he was smarter and far more connected than them. Parcells also had this way about him that forced the players to understand how much he knew about their background and personal lives.

Zolak was walking through the hallways by the coaches' offices when he happened upon Parcells, who was decked out in his standard garb alongside offensive coordinator Ray Perkins. Parcells was wearing a white New England Patriots T-shirt with blue bike shorts, tube socks, and golf shoes without the spikes. (He had bad feet, and the golf shoes offered the only form of comfort for a coach who was always on the move.) And Parcells was drinking coffee out of a Styrofoam cup, which was viewed as another sign of a cheap organization that wouldn't splurge for the superior paper products.

At any rate, that was Parcells' exterior getup. It was always more difficult to figure out what was ticking on the inside.

"What's your name?" Parcells asked Zolak.

"Scott."

"I know your name. Maryland, right? Five years at Maryland. From what I hear, you like to play your music loud, drive trucks, and wear tank tops. We're going to change all that. You're never going to refer to yourself in the third person. And remember this—I know you're single and you guys like to hang out and go out. I've got fucking spies everywhere. I know where you're going to be, who you're going to be with on what night, and don't ever lie to me. I won't lie to you, and you won't ever lie to me and we'll be fine. All right, honey, go pound some weights.'"

Zolak was geeked up: "I'm like, 'Wow, that's Bill fucking Parcells right there. That's awesome.'"

Parcells quickly took a liking to Zolak. The quarterback was a gym rat, and football was the most important thing in his life. As the son of a coach, Zolak grew up around the game and practically lived at the facility, always staying after his workout to shoot the breeze in the locker room with his teammates, coaches, or whoever else was in the area. That's partly how Parcells got to know the players. He liked sharing stories and relating with the players, and the best way to do that was by maximizing his time around them. It also helped him figure out how to push their buttons. But the key was they had to love the game enough to be willing to be around all day every day.

When Parcells was polling the Patriots for guys to keep, assistant coach Dante Scarnecchia's name kept coming up, so he was another no-brainer for the 1993 team. Quarterback Hugh Millen wasn't on Parcells' good side, though. Millen was a big-time brown noser, and Parcells saw right through it. Were you a football guy, or were you a salesman? Parcells wanted football guys, and he knew how to surround himself with coaches and players who would ultimately breed success.

Master Motivator

Bill Parcells boasted as great of a personality as there's ever been on an NFL sideline. He had an obvious New Jersey personality, and he was street smart. Parcells knew how to relate to anyone, even if he had to become their enemy to do it. But really, he had everyone's respect, and the love-hate element of his relationships was epic. The workweek was hell, but the players recognized they were as prepared for Sunday as they'd ever be.

They also loved to release a week's worth of pent-up aggression on the opposing team.

Zolak adored Parcells during their time together, and even he had a tough time describing the impact Parcells had on the locker room.

"He wasn't an asshole. He knew how to drive 53 different guys, and that was the best thing about him," Zolak said. "He didn't treat every guy the same way. He knew how to push your buttons, and he knew how it needed to be pushed. He knew how to be hard on you, but at the same time garner your respect. By the end of the day, you wanted to run through a wall for the guy. It was weird. It was a love-hate relationship, but it was more love. I don't know, it was the Jersey in him. He had a way of talking down to the guys' level where he didn't seem like he was the coach. He had a great way of explaining things, and he flat-out told you where you stood. There were never any mind games or mind tricks. It was, 'Hey look, you're making too much money. You better fix this or your ass is gone.'"

The stretching line prior to every practice was legendary. Parcells would saunter toward the players twirling his whistle and twisting their minds. It was a standup comedy routine, and he took his act to another level when the Patriots conducted training camp practices at Bryant College in Smithfield, Rhode Island. He'd yell at the players loud enough for the fans to hear the one-liners, and the roast master was captivating, unless you were the butt of the joke.

There was a time when Parcells shouted over to offensive coordinator Ray Perkins to shine the spotlight on Zolak and starting quarterback Drew Bledsoe, the No. 1 overall pick in the 1993 draft and the face of the franchise. The point? He wanted more accuracy out of their throws that day.

"Hey Ray, look at these two quarterbacks," Parcells shouted. "They've both got girlfriends. I'm sure Drew brought his girlfriend all the way out from the West Coast. Zolak, all you do is run around with Guns N' Roses in your truck trying to pick up girls. You guys go to the damn carnival trying to win a prize, and those girls come home crying. You guys can't hit a bull in the ass with a fistful of rice from three feet away.'"

And the crowd would laugh, and Parcells would get louder when he peered over at guard Todd Rucci.

"What are you looking at, Rucci? You look fatter than a stuffed kumquat today. What you eat last night, five pizzas or five calzones? Did you have your Italian mother come up and make meatballs?"

The players had to sit there and take it, but they kind of got a kick out of it, too. Whatever the purpose of the insult, it got the best out of his guys. Usually, they just wanted to shut him up for a day. They certainly didn't want the fans laughing at them, and the fans showed up in droves, often hanging from the fences, after Parcells and Bledsoe arrived in 1993. Parcells also had a habit of bringing friends to practice, whether it was Jon Bon Jovi or radio host Mike Francesa or an old high school coach. Parcells would play up the comedy routine around them, too.

"He would rip the shit out of guys, and this would go on for 25 minutes," Zolak said. "It was standup comedy for him. And the more people laughed, and the more fans heard it, the louder he got. He kind of dug it. But at the end of the day, it's, 'You know I'm only busting your balls, right?' That's how he was. He knew how to break your balls and then ingratiate himself with you."

Parcells got on his coaches, too. Charlie Weis, an offensive positional coach in the mid-1990s, would get edgy around Parcells, and the players could even see it. So if Weis' positional group wasn't having a good day, they'd go at it in the middle of the workout.

"Charlie Weis would get real nervous around him," Zolak said. "The coaches were like the players. They wanted to please him. So after a couple bad plays, he'd look at Charlie like, 'Charlie, really? What the fuck?' And he'd just stand there and stare at Charlie, and Charlie would look back like, 'Really? What are you fucking looking at? Don't fucking look at me. Coach your fucking team.' And this would go on and on."

Parcells had plenty of ways to control the chaos. He'd rattle the players' minds while they stretched, but he'd intensify the conditions between the lines as they practiced. That was another significant element to Parcells' preparations. He didn't want the players to encounter anything during a game that they hadn't already seen at practice, and he'd even amplify the distress level of the situations.

If Parcells wanted the quarterbacks to be more precise with their seven-step drops, he'd stand directly behind the huddle and then move toward the pocket before the snap. So as soon as Bledsoe or Zolak planted their back foot, Parcells would be perfectly stationed to be standing right behind their earhole. "Now, now, throw it, throw it, throw it!" he'd scream. Or if Parcells really wanted to drive the point home, he'd whip the whistle off their helmet or slap them after their seven-step drop.

"Next thing you know, you're throwing the ball right into the ground because he made you spaz out," Zolak said. "You'd look at him and start bitching, and he'd be like, 'Hey, I'm just trying to create the most hostile environment so when you get out there and see shit, you don't panic, okay?'"

During team drills, particularly a blitz period, Parcells had a different tactic to rattle his offense. He'd realign the defensive formation to create an overload or order an alteration to the blitz scheme to help spring a player off the backside edge. And then Parcells would order the blitzer to deliver to the quarterback's head. Remember, this was football in the 1990s.

The key components of the kicking operation weren't absolved of the treatment, either. After long snapper Steve DeOssie delivered the ball to Zolak, the holder, Parcells would sometimes throw an entire bucket of water on the ball to rattle everyone. There was another time when Parcells halted DeOssie before the snap, took the ball, dunked it in water, and covered it in mud before giving it back to the snapper. Then he doubled down by telling kicker Matt Bahr to make the field goal or the team would have two extra sets of meetings that night. Bahr missed.

"He'd make every single play of practice competitive," Zolak said.

Hell hath no fury like a Big Tuna scorned, and there were no excuses for low-energy practices. It was obvious when Parcells got mad, too, because he'd get quiet. The players knew if they were having a bad day, but they didn't want to reap the consequences of a sluggish effort. Those days are unavoidable at times, though, especially a few weeks into training camp or a couple months into the regular season.

So the angry stages of Parcells started with his quietness, and then it'd progress to him stopping and staring a hole through a player. They didn't want it to worsen from there, because Parcells had no issues with forcing them to start over a period, and that's if they were lucky. Every now and then, Parcells would blow his whistle and tell everyone to start over, so they'd get back into the huddle. And then he'd interrupt and say, 'No, the whole practice from the stretch.' There was nothing worse than being two hours into practice and having Parcells order them to start it again, leaving them on the field for four and a half hours.

Actually, there were times when it got worse. During the season, Parcells wanted the players to eat lunch in one of the club sections in Foxboro Stadium because they were able to overlook the game field. So if a tight end had a bad practice in the morning, Parcells would bring in four tight ends to work out on the field while the players were eating lunch. After a kicker had a lousy practice, Zolak noticed he wasn't eating during the lunch period because he was sick to his stomach while watching other kickers try out for his job on the field below.

"Bill was so good at bringing people in to push your buttons," Zolak said. "He'd audition people right in front of your face. The biggest thing with him was, 'Honey, never get comfortable.'"

Even the Friday weigh-ins were stressful. Parcells used to push Zolak to get down to 238 pounds, but Zolak could realistically only drop to 240 on his best days. Steve DeOssie always hated the weigh-ins, so he'd torture himself inside the sauna Friday before assistant coach Dante Scarnecchia took his weight. Afterward, Zolak and DeOssie would go to town on the gallon of milk and four dozen doughnuts that they had waiting.

After Parcells would beat them down physically and mentally, he'd become their friend, and that was a major element of his ingenuity and relatability. The players, and even the coaches, would hate Parcells on the practice field, and he'd scare the confidence out of them with his mind games over their perceived job security. In the back of their minds, they recognized Parcells' brilliance, as he used his unique means to maximize their prep work for games while drawing the best out of each player.

Off the field, Parcells revealed more of his human side, and that's how he ingratiated himself. He'd hang out in the locker room after their workouts and share stories of his New Jersey roots and his times hanging out with Eddie and the Cruisers and the E Street Band. Parcells was like the old offensive lineman who could find a way to talk with anyone in the locker room, regardless of their background or status on the depth chart. And then he'd bring it back to football, for better or worse.

Hey, you sucked today. We pay you too much money to suck.
You keep getting better, honey. Good job. Keep doing that. This is
why you lift all those fucking weights.

The players dug it. The compliments would carry them for
a week. The insults hurt, but at least they appreciated his hon-
esty. Compare that to other coaches who might sugarcoat a player's poor performance and then cut him, seemingly out of the blue.
For Parcells, if you needed to improve upon an element of your
game, he damn well made sure you recognized it. Parcells would
wear out his players, both mentally and physically, throughout the
long days, but it was reassuring to leave the facility with a proper
understanding of where they stood.

Take running back Curtis Martin as an example. Martin was as
talented as any back in Patriots history, evidenced by his enshrine-
ment to the Pro Football Hall of Fame in 2012. But Parcells had
a hand in prying out the best in Martin, who didn't always hit the
hole as hard as he should at the beginning of his career. Parcells
called him "Boy Wonder" if Martin's effort didn't match or exceed
his talent. And if Martin tip-toed around a tackler or perhaps
passed up yards in the spirit of self-preservation, Parcells would
yell, "Quit running around in your high heels!"

Martin always took it the right way, and all parties involved
knew Parcells' criticism was unleashed out of love. Heck, that's
why Parcells later brought Martin to the Jets in 1997. Martin was
a perfect example of someone who would get ruthlessly ridden by
Parcells and come out of it as a better player.

Really, wide receiver Terry Glenn was the only player who
didn't take to Parcells' snide remarks, but they had a strange working relationship from the start. The Patriots selected Glenn out of

Ohio State with the seventh overall pick in the 1996 NFL draft, much to the chagrin of Parcells, who preferred to take a defensive player. And when Glenn was slow to recover from a hamstring injury during his rookie training camp, Parcells famously referred to Glenn as "she" during an interview with reporters. That storyline cast a cloud over Glenn throughout his rookie season and much of his career, and Parcells' motivational tactics never hit home with the talented wideout the way they aided Martin and all the others.

"Nobody ever got offended by 'high heels' or 'she's doing all right,'" Zolak said. "The only guy who took it the wrong way was Terry Glenn, and that's a shame because I liked Terry. Terry was one of my favorites. He was cool to me. Parcells would take these subtle jabs that he knew would motivate Curtis. But if you'd do that to Terry Glenn, he'd go in a shell. It's amazing Bill couldn't connect with Terry Glenn. Parcells knew how to push every single guy's buttons.

"He'd never say anything to me, but he'd always bring in third-, fourth-, fifth-string quarterbacks while we were sitting in there eating lunch. They'd be out there working out. He'd do it with kickers, too. He brought in Phil Dawson with Adam Vinatieri, and Dawson had a great career. He knew how to push guys. He'd bring in guys to push them or he'd say something. Some guys, he could call out. Some guys, he couldn't.

"It's amazing he couldn't connect with Terry. He didn't do anything different with Curtis that he did with Terry. It's just that Terry took it differently and it's a shame. I feel bad about those days. Terry was an introvert. Curtis was hardnosed. The upbringing and the drive, Curtis looked at Bill as the father figure. I don't think Terry did. He looked at Bill as someone who was bearing down on him."

Parcells gained notoriety for his digs, but let's not overlook his supportive efforts. He recognized talent even in unnatural situations, and the best example involved Tedy Bruschi. The Patriots selected the 6'0", 250-pound defensive end out of Arizona in the third round of the 1996 NFL draft after his decorated collegiate career, tying the Division I-A record with 52 sacks, earning All-American honors twice and winning the Morris Trophy as the best defensive lineman in the Pac-10. He was ultimately enshrined in the College Football Hall of Fame, and Bruschi was later described by Bill Belichick as the "perfect player" when he was inducted into the Patriots Hall of Fame.

Bruschi was undersized and tumbled to the third round, but he had eye-opening talent at training camp with the Patriots. Parcells didn't care how Bruschi got on the field, but he ordered defensive coordinator Al Groh to find a way.

"We had no clue what Bruschi was going to be," Zolak said. "I just remember when he was drafted, we're trying to figure out what the hell he is. I remember being at one of those practices and Parcells screaming at Al Groh right behind the offensive huddle, 'I don't give a fuck where you need to put No. 54. I don't care if he's inside, outside, hand down. I don't care if you put him 50 yards deep in center field. Find a way to get 54 on the field each and every snap.' Al would always sit there and shake his head like yeah, okay. He never had a comeback for Parcells."

Parcells was also rare in that he liked to work out with the players in the weight room. That wasn't the most common practice in that era, and obviously, Parcells wasn't exactly a comparable physical specimen to the professional athletes who worked for him. But they admired that about Parcells, and it also gave the players a chance to bust his chops in return.

When players were on the treadmills, they'd typically run at a speed of 7 or 8 mph. Parcells would go at half that pace, and they'd laugh because he'd struggle to just hang on for his workout. He had that knock-kneed walk and the gimpy feet with a towel over his shoulder just caked in his own sweat, and he recognized when his players were paying attention.

"It was always funny watching him," Zolak said. "And you'd be peeking over and he'd say, 'Don't you say a goddamn thing.' He's just trying to be one of the guys, shower with us and everything. It was just funny because you're not used to that."

They loved to razz him over his golf shoes, too.

"So he would take the spikes out of the golf shoes, and we'd always break his balls because he'd sit back and cross his legs, and you'd look at the bottom of his shoes and there'd be holes in them," Zolak said. "We'd be like, 'What the hell is that?' And he'd say, 'Shut up, don't say a goddamn thing. You'll see what it's like.' It was funny."

That was the locker room. It's like that to a degree these days, but there's no doubt the high-stakes back-and-forth has tapered off due to the exposure on social media, the heightened gravitation toward political correctness, and maybe even other factors like shorter training camps and the greater degree of roster turnover that takes away from team camaraderie over the years. But even just eliminating the debate between then and now, Parcells' willingness to get into it with his players added a fun element to the workday. Football is a violent game, and these guys have testosterone to burn during and after practice.

"Nobody ever got offended," Zolak said. "Nowadays, you can't do a damn thing. That was locker room talk. It's a breaking balls thing. It's talk you'd never use with your family or your wife or your sister. It's a second language you develop because you spend so much time together. You're a second family with players at this level, maybe not so much now today because they're out of there earlier and don't have two-a-days. But when we went to camp, we went to fucking camp. Camp was camp.

"You're in Dorm 15 and you're wearing the same pads twice a day. You might be in shorts in the afternoon, but you've still got your shoulder pads and helmets on. There's no shells. There's no reversible jerseys. There's no walkthroughs. It was full contact in the morning, Oklahoma Drill, and it was two and a half hours and then in the afternoon it was two and a half hours. That was camp. This is bullshit, what they do now. It's a collision sport. I think we're educated more on how to deal with that stuff, but you made a living hitting people. I think that's why the product struggles a bit today. You don't hit. It takes you a little while to get going. Guys are getting hurt because when they get hit, it's like, 'Whoa, what the hell was that?'"

Crafting a Winner

Bill Parcells' first major decision as the New England Patriots head coach yielded monumental success, as he selected Washington State quarterback Drew Bledsoe over Notre Dame's Rick Mirer with the first pick in the 1993 NFL draft. He also nailed his picks in the second round with linebacker Chris Slade, guard Todd Rucci, and wide receiver Vincent Brisby. And even though wide receiver and special teamer Troy Brown didn't take off until Bill Belichick seized control in 2000, he was a nice way to cap off Parcells' first draft.

The 1993 Patriots opened the regular season with four consecutive losses, including an embarrassing 45–7 defeat to their archrival New York Jets in a home game at Foxboro Stadium. Make no mistake, Parcells was an outstanding head coach but he wasn't a miracle worker, and he wasn't going to turn a dismal roster into a contender in his first season. But he also wasn't going to sit around and watch his team display the same complacency that plagued their previous three seasons.

After their Week 5 bye, the Patriots traveled to Sun Devil Stadium to take on the Phoenix Cardinals, who hadn't fielded a playoff squad since 1982. So when the Cardinals built a 14–13 halftime lead, Parcells lost his damn mind.

"That was the first time Parcells snapped," Zolak said. "He goes, 'I haven't said anything in weeks. I'm sitting back and I'm watching. I can't sit back and watch anymore. I want to know when you guys are going to wake up. I'm tired of getting fucking pushed around.' He picked up a Gatorade cooler and threw it through a blackboard and shattered [it]. He had never done that. He was pretty controlled: 'We're going to do this. We're going to approach this. We're going to make adjustments.' He said, 'I'm sick of watching you guys getting pushed around and taking it. When are you guys going to fight back?' From that second half, we came back and won that game. That was kind of a point where everything turned for us. We got tougher."

The Patriots rallied for a 23–21 victory, so Parcells liked the response. But the Pats lost their next seven games before closing the season with a four-game winning streak that culminated with Bledsoe's four-touchdown performance at home against the Miami Dolphins. The Pats went 5–11, and Parcells continued to get his guys in place through free agency and the draft.

Parcells' team building was a case study in football toughness. He signed safety Myron Guyton and guard Bob Kratch in 1994, when the Pats also drafted tackle Willie McGinest and offensive lineman Max Lane. In 1995, the Patriots signed guard Will Roberts and defensive tackle Reggie White, and drafted cornerback Ty Law, linebacker Ted Johnson, running back Curtis Martin, cornerback Jimmy Hitchcock, and center Dave Wohlabaugh. And in 1996, they signed safety Willie Clay, briefly employed cornerback Otis Smith, and drafted safety Lawyer Milloy and linebacker Tedy Bruschi. With Bledsoe in charge of the offense and the violent forces of fullbacks Sam Gash and Kevin Turner and tight end Ben Coates already in place, Parcells' Patriots got more hardnosed by the year.

"We're going to have tough fullbacks," Zolak said. "We're going to kick guys' asses on the edge. Bill would bring in his guys who would teach you how to work out, get with those certain groups. You know what's funny? Rex Ryan reminds me a lot of Bill Parcells but without the winning and the cachet. Rex had the actions and brashness. Bill was like that but it worked. We were good. Rex won at the beginning with the Jets, but his shtick wore off and got old. Bill never had a shtick. That was real. He was real. Bill was just a damn good leader."

The pendulum swung in 1994. The players didn't exactly know how to win yet, but younger guys gravitated toward Parcells' veterans. And even though the Patriots knew they weren't the most talented team in the NFL, they harnessed a great deal of pride in the idea that they'd fight everyone on every play. They wanted their opponents to remember they played the Patriots that day.

"That was the first year we really started getting tough. It's one thing to throw talent out there, but then you start getting tough and you start drafting guys who can knock some guys' heads off. You start to see it. You can start to see guys flying around. All these types of guys that Parcells brought in, they all wanted to knock your dick in the dirt."

The Patriots took a while to get rolling in 1994. They opened with a pair of losses against AFC East foes when Dolphins quarterback Dan Marino and Bills quarterback Jim Kelly out-dueled Bledsoe in a pair of shootouts. They responded with a three-game winning streak but then succumbed to a four-game skid, which was capped with a defeat in Cleveland against Bill Belichick's Browns.

The turning point came in Week 11 against the Minnesota Vikings at Foxboro Stadium. The Patriots had a 3–6 record and fell behind 20–0 in the second quarter before Bledsoe delivered three touchdown passes after halftime, including the overtime winner to Turner for a 26–20 win. It sparked a seven-game winning streak, catapulted Bledsoe's career, and got the defense rolling, as they held each of their final seven regular-season opponents to 17 points or fewer and entered the playoffs with a 10–6 record, their best mark and first postseason appearance since 1986.

It came to an end at Cleveland Municipal Stadium, though. The Browns claimed a 20–13 victory in a winter slugfest, and Belichick beat his mentor in a game that offered a dose of foreshadowing for the future of the Patriots' franchise at the turn of the millennium.

"I remember, 'Shit, we're in the playoffs.' You're happy to be there," Zolak said. "I remember what a rinky-dink stadium Cleveland had, and it was snowing and cold. The game was competitive. Cleveland was a tough team, hardnosed. I don't know if we really believed that we could win games like that, and Parcells probably understood that was part of the process, just getting there, and then the next year you want to go a step further."

That step didn't materialize in 1995. They got some revenge against the Browns with a 17–14 victory in the opener but dropped their next five games, failing to score a touchdown in three of them. They were a disappointing 6–10 in 1995.

Super Run, and an End

The unmet expectations in 1995 didn't dispirit the 1996 Patriots. Again, they were confident in their toughness at every position on the roster, and their immensely talented group of youngsters was emerging. Ty Law, Willie McGinest, and Ted Johnson grew to become leaders on defense, and rookie Lawyer Milloy had a cocky style that added a fresh dynamic to the mix. Terry Glenn might not have been Bill Parcells' favorite draft pick in history, but he blew up in his first year with 90 catches for 1,132 yards and six touchdowns. Tight end Ben Coates was Drew Bledsoe's comfort blanket and red-zone weapon with nine touchdowns, and Curtis Martin had 1,485 yards from scrimmage and 17 offensive touchdowns.

As for their level of nastiness, they reveled in it during a December film session after they beat the San Diego Chargers 45–7 to improve to 9–4. Chargers linebacker Junior Seau was as respected as any defensive player in the league at that point, so

Patriots offensive coordinator Ray Perkins replayed highlight after highlight of fullbacks Sam Gash and Kevin Turner winning their battles against Seau to drive home the effect that their physicality had on opponents.

"We used to call Junior Seau 'the pile jumper,'" Zolak said. "We'd sit there and watch Kevin Turner and Sam Gash hit him, and they both had neck rolls, and you would see Seau's head snap back and snap back. And Ray Perkins would rewind it and play it and rewind it, 'Boom, boom, boom, watch his head snap.' I remember thinking our fullbacks are tougher than them, but it sucks to think it created permanent damage later in life. But we played a collision sport; [we] snapped on our helmets and we were pretty much crash-test dummies with every hit out there. We knew our team was tough. We were drafting and acquiring tough, hardnosed guys. You'd sit there and watch Bill Parcells' old Giants tapes, Harry Carson, Lawrence Taylor, all those guys. Our defense was big and tough the way they were, and you could see why Parcells built it that way."

Even with the necessary tools for success, the Patriots were held back by a dose of realism. The Denver Broncos were easily the best team in the AFC in 1996, and they smoked the Patriots 34–8 at Foxboro Stadium in Week 12. The Pats tried everything in that game, including a fake punt that would have worked if Tedy Bruschi didn't drop Tom Tupa's pass. If they encountered the Broncos again, they recognized the likely outcome.

But the Jacksonville Jaguars blew the doors off reality in the divisional round, and the Patriots' eyes lit up as they watched the game from Zolak's basement. The Broncos and Patriots each had byes in the first round of the playoffs, and the Patriots were set to open the divisional round Sunday against the Pittsburgh Steelers. So Zolak had everyone over to the house to watch the Broncos host the Jaguars for the Saturday afternoon game. The Broncos, who were 12.5-point favorites, jumped out to a 12–0 lead, but the Jags fired off 20 consecutive points. Quarterback Mark Brunell later hit wide receiver Jimmy Smith for a 16-yard touchdown to give the Jaguars a 30–20 lead with less than four minutes remaining in the fourth quarter, which stunned the viewing audience, including the Patriots. The Jags held on for a 30–27 win, opening the doors for the Patriots to host the AFC Championship Game if they could get past the Steelers the next day.

"Everything fell our way that year. Denver seemed like the world beater," Zolak said. "I had the first finished basement of the crew, so I had a nice pool table, a big screen, a couple couches, so we'd all go down there and watch games. I remember when Jacksonville popped Denver, the whole room lit up like, 'Holy shit, we actually have a chance here.' The world beater Denver was down. I don't think we ever thought we could beat Denver. Too many things had to go our way to beat Denver. But the second Denver was eliminated, it seemed these lightbulbs went off in everybody's heads."

The Patriots were especially confident against the Steelers, and they worked on their first offensive play of the game all week. They recognized cornerback Rod Woodson, an eventual Pro Football Hall of Famer, had the tendency to jump routes early in games, and the Pats knew Woodson would play man coverage outside against wide receiver Terry Glenn. So the Pats were going to open with a sluggo route—a slant and go—to bait Woodson with a double move. Woodson had never lined up against Glenn, so he couldn't appreciate Glenn's raw speed or an amazing ability to cripple a corner with a double move.

There was a slight issue, though. The teams were greeted by stifling humidity Sunday morning when they got to the stadium, and an eerie fog blanketed the area. The Patriots could barely see the Steelers from one sideline to the other, and they had no visuals of the top of the bleachers. It created a raucous home-field advantage, but it upped the difficulty level of Glenn's sluggo route, particularly with the heat that Bledsoe could get on the ball. Still, they practiced it far too frequently to bag the play, so after the defense forced the Steelers to go three-and-out, it was time to test Woodson.

"I've never seen somebody break somebody's legs the way Terry could on a double move," Zolak said. "Every day in practice that week, we'd practice that slant-go, slant-go, slant-go. Every once in a while, Drew would overshoot him or the defense knew it was coming. When you practice a play like that, it never looks perfect in practice. We get the ball, and the first play of the game, Drew does the pump fake and Woodson sucks up on it. I don't know how Terry Glenn saw the ball. To this day, Terry says he lost that ball in flight. Terry would never catch it with his hands. He would catch it into his pads and cradle his hands around it. Terry said he saw the ball in the last two feet of flight and it comes down and hits him in the pads. He catches it and we go up on Pittsburgh. And boom, we're going."

Glenn gained 53 yards on the catch, and Martin scored a two-yard touchdown on the ensuing play. It was the first of his three scores, and the Patriots rolled the Steelers 28–3. The Jaguars weren't much more competitive in the AFC title game, and the

Pats stormed to Super Bowl XXXI with a 20–6 win, which was highlighted by three things: the Foxboro Stadium power outage, the wind chill that dropped the temperature to 9 degrees, and Otis Smith's 47-yard fumble return for a touchdown in the fourth quarter.

To an extent, the Patriots were just happy to be at the Super Bowl in New Orleans, and the significance of the moment wasn't lost on a New England region that was spelled by a chasm of mediocrity among its four professional sports teams in the 1990s. And not that the Patriots knew it at the time, but they had some integral pieces for future Super Bowl champions on that roster, so they were more talented than they had gotten credit for, even if they were young. The trip validated the organization as a potential winner and not a laughingstock, so it was a fruitful journey despite its ultimate shortcoming.

Adding to that, the Pats were set to encounter the Green Bay Packers, who were 13–3 in the regular season. Quarterback Brett Favre had also won back-to-back MVP awards in 1995 and 1996, so this was viewed as their Super Bowl to lose.

The Patriots prepared well—with Parcells, how could they not?—but they had their chances to second-guess themselves. They enjoyed their week in New Orleans, no doubt. The Pats were staying at the Marriott on the corner of Bourbon Street near the White Castle, so the guys essentially used their per diem on one of two things (or maybe a combination of both). They either ate dollar burgers at the fast-food joint, or they went around the corner to Rick's Cabaret.

"The problem was Bourbon Street was right there," Zolak said. "Bill did a good job, 'Hey fellas, you've got to concentrate this week. It's a business trip.' Some guys had too good of a time, and I think maybe we would have approached the week a little bit differently if you really knew what was in store. But I think you have to get there first to win the whole thing. The game becomes too big for you."

The game was intense. After the Packers grabbed an early 10–0 lead, Bledsoe threw a pair of touchdown passes in less than four minutes to give the Pats a 14–10 advantage in the first quarter. He first called I-right tip zip, Rod 136 Z-pop to find Byars on a play-fake for a one-yard score in the back of the end zone. And then he pelted Coates with a four-yard touchdown.

Two plays defined the 35–21 loss. The safeties sucked up when Favre hit Antonio Freeman for an 81-yard touchdown that gave the Packers a 17–14 lead at the start of the second quarter, and Hason Graham missed his crease when Desmond Howard returned a third-quarter kickoff for a 99-yard touchdown on the game's final score, which negated Martin's 18-yard score a play earlier. For some reason, Graham dressed over Brown. The Pats also had no answer for Hall of Famer Reggie White, who had three sacks.

They understood why they lost. It was obvious. And it had nothing to do with the outside distraction of Parcells skipping the flight home to jump ship to the New York Jets. The players were actually blindsided by the news and had no clue something was awry throughout the week. In hindsight, they recognized some tension between Parcells and Patriots owner Robert Kraft, who was more hands-on at the start of his tenure. Parcells drove that point home when he uncorked his famous jab at Kraft while referencing the Glenn draft pick, saying if he's going to cook the dinner, he should at least be allowed to shop for the groceries. Parcells wanted more control and a new challenge, and the Pats knew that was his part of his reputation.

"The whole story was Parcells going to the Jets," Zolak said. "I think that stuff is overrated for players, especially when Parcells was with us in the Super Bowl in 1997, and he was going to the Jets. When you're in it and you're living it every day, you really don't care about that. It really doesn't concern you because you're so worried about doing your thing. Not one period during that week did anybody talk about it or have an inkling. I don't think anybody realized it until you look and realize that he wasn't on the plane going back with the team. But, okay, it's not a big deal. Once it was announced that he was gone, I don't think guys felt hurt. I think you kind of know what that guy is. You understand why he wanted to leave."

Parcells' four-year reign unquestionably revived the Patriots' organization, even if his controversial departure strained relationships for years. And Kraft has been open about that being an on-the-job learning experience that made him a better owner in the years to come. Parcells proved the Patriots could compete at an NFL level again, introduced Belichick to New England as an assistant in 1996, and reeled in cornerstone pieces to future Super Bowl rosters, including three-time champions such as Troy Brown, Tedy Bruschi, Ted Johnson, Ty Law, Willie McGinest, and Adam Vinatieri.

And by drafting Drew Bledsoe over Rick Mirer in 1993, Parcells ensured the Patriots would have a credible weapon at quarterback for nearly a decade.

CHAPTER 3

JUST HOW
THEY DREW IT UP

Afighter striking gold with the big-time hiring of head coach Bill Parcells, the New England Patriots had to address the most important position on the field in the 1993 NFL draft. They were armed with the first overall pick and had been in desperate search of a franchise quarterback since injuries took their toll on Steve Grogan in the late 1980s. Fortunately for the Pats, Drew Bledsoe and Rick Mirer each portrayed the appearance of a franchise-saving quarterback, but the decision to choose the right guy was a dilemma.

Bledsoe and Mirer were both small-town kids and the sons of coaches who stayed local to play college ball and were three-year starters for their respective programs. Bledsoe, of Walla Walla, Washington, starred at Washington State and claimed the top job over two upperclassmen by the end of his freshman year. Mirer was from Indiana and became a local legend, for better or worse in some cases, at Notre Dame, where he left as a record-setting passer.

Bledsoe had the big arm and was viewed as the quarterback with the higher long-term ceiling if his drafting team could withstand some growing pains. He ran a pro-style offense with the Cougars and threw the ball all over the field during his career. His scruffy image wasn't as polished, but he was undeniably relatable. Mirer was more athletic, ready to start right away, and used to the exposure after essentially growing up in front of the country due to Notre Dame's national television deal with NBC. He was clean-cut, looked the part, and was marketable. But Mirer was also inconsistent, prone to mistakes, and heavily criticized by the Fighting Irish fan base. For months, the debate in the NFL and certainly in New England was Bledsoe or Mirer, Bledsoe or Mirer, Bledsoe or Mirer. Prior to the draft, there didn't appear to be a wrong choice, but Bledsoe eventually became the consensus No. 1 pick. Ultimately, it would become the second time since the 1970 NFL-AFL merger that quarterbacks would be taken with the first two picks of the draft, and the Patriots got it right on both occasions, first taking Jim Plunkett in 1971 and leaving Archie Manning for the New Orleans Saints.

Patriots quarterback Scott Zolak was surely sold on Bledsoe before the draft. Though Zolak never met Mirer, he instantly hit it off with Bledsoe when the prospect visited Foxboro Stadium. Bledsoe was wearing the new Michael Jordan tear-away jumpsuit, had the long, grunge-rock hair like a typical guy from the Pacific Northwest, and was wearing a pair of Gargoyle sunglasses. Bledsoe's father, Mac Bledsoe, arrived alongside him with a huge belt buckle, skintight Wrangler jeans, and a cowboy hat that endeared him to Zolak but would have made him look like a foreigner to nearly everyone around Boston.

Bledsoe was the size of a prototypical quarterback. He was known to stand at 6'6" but always requested to be listed at 6'5", and he weighed 238 pounds. Bledsoe also had these long fingers that instantly stuck out to anyone who met him, and there's no doubt that helped him spin the ball with a bit more zip.

"Drew was the quintessential pocket passer," Zolak said. "The kid had a cannon. I remember the first time playing catch with Bledsoe, and we're warming up and the ball is just humming, almost cutting your fingers. I'm like, 'Whoa, okay, this guy can throw.'"

The Patriots made the right choice with Bledsoe, and it's not even up for debate. Parcells legitimized football in New England, and Bledsoe greatly aided the buzz factor as a quarterback who could be the face of the franchise and throw the ball up and down the field, often going toe-to-toe with AFC East stalwarts like Jim Kelly of the Buffalo Bills and Dan Marino of the Miami Dolphins.

As the prognosticators believed, Mirer showed a nice amount of promise as a first-year starter, but his career arc flattened out. He went 20–31 as a four-year starter for the Seahawks, and he had a losing record in three of his four seasons. The exception came in 1995, when he went 7–6 as the starter but threw more interceptions (20) than touchdowns (13). He didn't even make it to the final season of his rookie contract, as the Seahawks traded him to the Chicago Bears in 1997, and he played out his career with the Green Bay Packers (1998), New York Jets (1999), San Francisco 49ers (2000–01), Oakland Raiders (2002–03), and Detroit Lions (2004) before retiring with a 24–44 record as a starter, 11,969 passing yards, 50 touchdowns, 76 interceptions, and no playoff experience. The Seahawks never had a winning record with Mirer, and they didn't make the playoffs again until 1999, detailing just how costly it was to miss on a quarterback at that point in the draft.

Bledsoe's career was superior to Mirer's in every way. He had a 63–60 record while starting for the Patriots from 1993 to 2001, led the Patriots to the playoffs four times in his first six seasons, and completed 56.3 percent of his passes for 29,657 yards, 166 touchdowns, and 138 interceptions during his nine seasons with the franchise. Bledsoe was enshrined in the Patriots Hall of Fame in 2011.

Though Bledsoe's tenure as the starter came to an unceremonious conclusion in 2001 when Jets linebacker Mo Lewis delivered a jolting blow that resulted in a torn blood vessel and a nearly catastrophic level of internal bleeding, the quarterback still played a key role during the Patriots' run to Super Bowl XXXVI. Lewis' hit ultimately launched Tom Brady's career, but Brady succumbed to an ankle injury in the second quarter of the AFC Championship Game against the Pittsburgh Steelers. Bledsoe took over with the Patriots leading by a 7–3 score, and completed 10 of 21 passes for 102 yards and a touchdown. The Patriots won 24–17.

The Patriots traded Bledsoe to the Bills for a first-round draft pick that offseason, just a year after he signed a 10-year, $103 million contract extension. He spent three seasons with the Bills and another two with the Dallas Cowboys. When Bledsoe retired in

2006, he ranked seventh all-time with 44,611 passing yards and 13th with 251 touchdowns.

Brotherly Love

Scott Zolak led the Patriots to their only two victories in 1992 when he got his first opportunity to start at quarterback before succumbing to a season-ending high-ankle sprain. So he would have been within his rights to feel confident about the quarterback competition in the 1993 offseason if someone like Drew Bledsoe wasn't the headliner of the draft class.

But Zolak understood the process. If the Patriots selected Bledsoe or even Rick Mirer with the No. 1 overall pick, that quarterback would be the face of the franchise, and Zolak had to accept a more permanent responsibility as the backup. Plus, Zolak had become an instant hit with new head coach Bill Parcells, so he didn't want to do anything that could jeopardize his job security, especially while Parcells had a proven affinity for shuttling off anyone for any reason. So Zolak made it a point of pride to become the best backup imaginable, and he was willing to compete against any other quarterback Parcells would sign or draft to battle for that position on the depth chart.

"I had a full understanding of what the No. 1 draft pick was going to be," Zolak said. "He was the franchise. You were never going to beat him out, and you better quickly accept what your role was going to be and you better find a way to get along with that guy, be supportive, and get ready to go when your time is called.

"I was also still young and dumb. New coach, new situation, and you're pretty much in survival mode because your head is on a swivel because you see so many guys that Parcells is just [telling],

'Get the hell out of here.' The fact that he thought I was intriguing and wanted me to be around, wanted me to work with Bledsoe and talked about us working together. I kind of knew, 'Okay, I'm his handpicked backup.' He always made that Phil Simms–Jeff Hostetler comparison, and he had that in the playoffs and you've always got to be ready because you never know when your time is going to come. You never know when your time is going to come for someone to beat you out. He goes, 'I'm going to bring in guys every year.' I kept telling him, 'You do that. Bring in your Jay Walkers, your Jay Barkers, and I'll beat them out all the time.'"

Each quarterback harnessed his role, with Zolak seizing control of the backup responsibilities for several years and Bledsoe wearing the face of the franchise. From the start, the attention boomed around the Patriots, who had practically become irrelevant before Parcells and Bledsoe arrived. The team's head of security, Frank Mendes, used to coast through the Patriots' training camps at Bryant University in Rhode Island, but he might've given himself ulcers as the lone man in charge of the operation upon the integration of Parcells and Bledsoe. Everyone got a kick out of watching Mendes run up and down the ropes like a madman to keep the fans in check. (As an aside, that's comical by today's standards. The Gillette Stadium security command center looks like NASA, and Tom Brady can't sneeze without a team of security guards peering over in his direction. Apparently, Brady's Super Bowl jerseys haven't been afforded the same protection.)

The entire culture changed within the confines of the team, but the buzz from the fan base further enhanced the energy. The players loved that, but it added an element of pressure that obviously already existed for Bledsoe as the No. 1 overall pick in the draft. Plus, Parcells was an overbearing coach who forced every person in the building—players, coaches, whoever—to walk on eggshells all day long.

Zolak and Bledsoe quickly became friends, and Zolak took it upon himself to keep Bledsoe sane amid the chaos. They were locker mates, worked out together every day, listened to the same music, and hung out all the time outside of the facility. Bledsoe didn't like to go out all that much, so they'd usually hang out at one another's house. Bledsoe pulled some strings with a distributor in Bridgewater to regularly ship in Henry Weinhard's, his favorite beer from the West Coast, so they had plenty of that at the ready.

The quarterback pair was usually joined by Max Lane, Todd Rucci, and John Burke, and the group would hang out by the pool during the day and run the pool table at night. Bledsoe had a sweet setup with a room over his three-car garage that was a perfect lounge spot with the pool table. Bledsoe and Zolak also rushed to Lechmere to equip their houses with brand-new Sony projection televisions. Zolak got the 60-inch screen, but Bledsoe always had to one-up everyone and bought the 65- and 70-inch models. And they watched everything on those big screens, from the O.J. Simpson murder trial to boxing on Saturday nights to *Cliffhanger* with Sylvester Stallone. Bledsoe, naturally, had to be the first guy on the team with a LaserDisc player, and they marveled at the quality of the picture on Bledsoe's TV. That's a big reason why they always hung out at Bledsoe's house, whether it was a perfect day to jump in the pool or there was a big sporting event to watch at night.

They felt like they struck gold when they could transform their game film to VHS tapes because they could then take a stack back to Bledsoe's house, study their opponents, and drink a case of beer.

It was a heck of a lot better than being stuck at the outdated facility at Foxboro Stadium, that's for sure. There was a time when they were sitting in the audio-video room and literally splicing together 8-millimeter reels with Scotch tape. They'd go through first-down reels, second-down reels, third-down reels, and the like, so it was a time-consuming process that they felt incredibly fortunate to streamline with the VHS tapes.

"We'd go in to watch film at Bledsoe's like, 'Ohhhhhhh,'" Zolak said. "We had a couple 30-packs of beer and sitting around like, 'Hey this is awesome. We're watching tape at home.' But that's the way the game has changed."

The only impediment to the process was Bledsoe's yellow Lab, Billy. It also didn't help the cause that Bledsoe wasn't exactly the cleanest guy in the room, and they recalled a time when Bledsoe left a milkshake on his table after they all passed out. Billy knocked it off the table and onto the floor, eating through the carpet and onto the wood. Bledsoe had to store the dog in the garage while he cleaned up the mess, and Billy intensified his efforts, scratching up and mangling Bledsoe's prized midnight blue Porsche, which had been painted in a three-color tone. Bledsoe had to send Billy back to his parents' ranch in Montana before he digested the rest of the house.

During the workday, Zolak tried to keep Bledsoe as loose as possible to relieve some of the weight from a mentally taxing coach like Parcells. Zolak didn't view himself as a mentor or a coach or anything, just a friend and supportive teammate. The state of the facilities didn't help, either, so they had to have fun with the situation, especially during the daily 12-minute drive from Foxboro Stadium to the Wrentham State Hospital for practice.

Imagine that sight, as the locals watched a convoy of cars that snaked down the backroads of Foxboro and Wrentham. And the Patriots were decked out in full pads, sometimes even wearing their helmets to draw a laugh, because there was no room to practice at their stadium or any space to change at the open practice field. The rookies also had to drive their cars because the players and equipment stunk so badly that the veterans didn't want to mess up their nice cars.

Really, for Bledsoe or Zolak or anyone employed to play professional football in the 1990s, the inconvenience of having to drive to practice was wholly annoying, somewhat embarrassing, and borderline depressing. They had to find a way to make it as fun as possible to avoid going crazy, especially during the grind of a season as injuries piled up and Parcells alienated players who spent too much time in the trainers' room. They had to suck it up and go.

"I've never seen anything like it. So we're in full pads and going to practice," Zolak said. "There was a racetrack and those mobile homes back there, so there was like half a field that we'd practice on. The rookies had to drive because none of the veterans wanted to ruin their cars with the smell of ass sweat. It was gross. It was actually disgusting. So you're thinking as we drive down, 'We're an NFL team. We've got to drive to practice?'"

The Patriots got a catered lunch from Popeye's on Fridays, but there was another reminder of the penny-pinching. The players had to race out of practice, fly past the Foxboro Police Department, and try like crazy to be first in line to get the red beans and rice. If you were, say, the 20th guy in line, the good food was already gone. The racing might have lightened the mood at the end of the week, but there was still a degree of annoyance for the losers.

The ride was more of an event when Bledsoe showed up with his white Suburban. With all due respect to Hugh Millen and Tommy Hodson, no one really gave a damn to see those quarterbacks driving down the street, but Bledsoe's Suburban stuck out due to his rockstar status. They'd draw waves when they were stuck at the red light next to McDonald's on Route 1, and then the Bledsoe and Zolak group would usually stop at Dairy Queen before practice to grab an Ultimate Burger, a once-coveted sandwich that no longer exists with the exception of the Bellingham location that specially makes one for Zolak on Mondays after Patriots home games.

But Bledsoe, Zolak, Chad Eaton, and maybe another guy or two would grab some burgers and then head to practice, and they'd crank Bledsoe's stereo before practice, usually choosing Tool, Weezer, Everclear, Presidents of the United States of America, or some Seattle grunge. They'd keep it as light as possible, sometimes wailing away at "Peaches" until Parcells pulled up in his Cadillac, and they'd turn down the music and say, "Shit, we've got to get out of the car. Let's go."

Sometimes, these guys had to get creative to get the fun going, but that was easy with the Patriots' youth movement in the mid-1990s. They competed in everything, whether it was as simple as a basketball game or as expensive as a competition with their trucks. Shoot, they'd even make a random bet to see whose car was cleaner or they'd judge who had the best Mercedes. Bledsoe and Rucci were always trying to one-up each other with their trucks, either with a lift kit or with bigger wheels or adding a half dozen PIAA lights to the roof that could practically spot a deer through 10 acres of redwoods. So when Rucci got the biggest truck, it was time for

Bledsoe to install the loudest stereo. Rucci was a prankster, too, at one point unscrewing someone's wheel caps in a joke-gone-wrong because the tires rattled so much that the rims bent and the wheels nearly fell off.

When they'd go golfing, they knew to bring $500 in cash and bet on the craziest scenarios imaginable. This wasn't your average match or skins game by any stretch. The group would throw money down on which player could bank a ball off a tree and get it closest to the hole. Or they'd pinpoint the longest hole on the course and see who could get the best score with just a 7-iron, including as their putter. They'd find ways to make themselves think and compete. It'd happen in the weight room at the facility, too, because strength and conditioning coordinator Johnny Parker had a great way of motivating everyone to work out that much harder.

And Bledsoe used to get so pissed off at Tom Tupa, their punter and emergency quarterback whom Parcells nicknamed "Brooks Brothers" because he was always dressed in button-down shirts and khakis like he was on his way to take a high school yearbook photo. Tupa was great at everything—golf, basketball, skiing, pretty much everything Bledsoe liked to do outside of football. And Tupa would monopolize their competitions without breaking a sweat.

Without the best truck, Bledsoe turned his attention to the water, where he loaded up with a MasterCraft boat and some Sea-Doos. Typical, one guy found a faster one, so another had to buy the newer model that allowed you to stand up while riding. Their back-and-forths were relentless. They'd take their Sea-Doos to the lakes, usually in Webster or Hopkinton, because the water was comparatively safer than the ocean or rivers.

But they had an unforgettable day on Lake Webster (Lake Chaubunagungamaug, as it's more officially known to the locals). These guys would just screw around, flying across the lake at full throttle without really knowing the water as well as they should, maybe even hitting speeds of 90 mph. They were often friendly, waving back and forth at the other boaters who probably recognized they were sharing the lake with the Patriots. So one day, a group of boaters were waving a bit more aggressively at the players, who assumed they were simply excited to see Bledsoe. Eventually, the boaters were able to approach the players to loudly warn them, "Hey, assholes, there are boulders the size of Volkswagens just below you!" They quickly realized they were lucky they didn't hit one and cause the Sea-Doos to explode, or worse.

"We did some stupid shit," Zolak said.

Bledsoe, a helicopter skier in the winter, was a showman on the water, and he'd get a little cocky at times. He had a bit of a brain fart one day when he was attempting to do a backflip off his Sea-Doo while riding at full speed. The problem was that Bledsoe forgot about the safety measure with the accelerator, so the Sea-Doo came to a halt as soon as he took his finger off the throttle, and Bledsoe slammed his forehead into the back of the Jet Ski. At the time, the guys with Bledsoe were shocked he was still conscious due to the sound of the thud. It also occurred during a day off from training camp, so Bledsoe had to do his best to hide the stitches on his head from the coaching staff for a couple weeks.

This actually wasn't the only time Bledsoe dealt with an unfortunate, albeit hilarious, forehead incident. They used to go paintballing on the South Shore on Tuesdays during the regular season. They actually found the place because it was right near the Charlie

Horse, which was a favorite local watering hole. They had a big group one day with Bledsoe, Zolak, Rucci, Lane, Burke, Vincent Brisby, and Shawn Jefferson, among others. Under normal paintballing conditions, you're out when you get shot once, but the idea was downright laughable that professional football players would heed the one-and-done rule. They'd go hunting, pelt the ever-living daylights out of each other, and leave with welts all over their chest and legs. At some point, someone somehow rifled a shot that worked its way through Bledsoe's mask, hitting him right between his eyes and above his nose. It left a golf ball-sized egg on his forehead and actually got pretty nasty looking. Before practice the next day, Zolak used a scalpel to carve out an interior portion of Bledsoe's helmet so it would fit on his head around the wound. Bledsoe wore it like that for another couple weeks, laughing it off privately and doing everything possible to ensure Parcells didn't have a reason to ream him out. The coaches knew, but Bledsoe toughed it out so nobody really cared.

Franchise Quarterback

Drew Bledsoe validated his worth as the No. 1 overall pick in the 1993 NFL draft, which is an accomplishment in and of itself due to the catastrophic effects that such a miss can have on a franchise. The buzz factor lifted his teammates, an intangible factor they desperately needed due to the combination of losing seasons and poor facilities. But actually, Foxboro Stadium worked in the Patriots' favor when they were winning because it offered nostalgic memories of simpler times. It also embodied the rugged, blue-collar fan base that supported the Patriots in the 1990s, and the crowds got rowdy for big games. The metal bleachers caused the sound to reverberate throughout the stadium, especially when the 60,000 paying patrons were stomping on the cold tin benches beneath them.

Bledsoe restored that type of environment. He shared a similar type of build with Dan Marino, Jim Kelly, and John Elway and was a pure thrower like Jeff George and Jim Everett. Bledsoe could just sit on that back right foot and sling it, and the Patriots instantly recognized he delivered the ball with a different type of zip. His teammates grew excited, and the coaches clearly knew they had a difference-maker at quarterback after Hugh Millen and Tommy Hodson failed at the position before 1993. Bledsoe was self-aware, too, so he understood the magnitude of his status within the franchise and did a solid job to carry himself as a leader from a young age. He was a different type of guy, but his teammates dug it. They especially liked to hear Bledsoe tell the story of how he and his father got to training camp, as they spent a few days riding their motorcycles from Washington to New England with their tents and backpacks on their backs. The Patriots' No. 1 draft pick was anything but a prima donna.

Offensive coordinator Ray Perkins conducted long, intense meetings with the group, to the point where everyone returning from the 1992 team was actually impressed with the rededication to the craft. They also recognized the purpose. Bledsoe could absorb loads of information, so Perkins didn't see any need to baby the 21-year-old rookie by cutting the field in half and designing plays that were only intended for one side, or by giving him two quick reads to simplify the learning curve.

Bledsoe took on three- and four-step progressions, and a lot of his throws were orchestrated to go down the field because he had the arm and capability to make it happen. That's a stark difference from nowadays with rookies who have to rely on smoke and mirrors with the screen game. And because of the Patriots' desire to let Bledsoe run an offense that suited his strength, Perkins harped on the importance of sturdy work by the offensive line to give him time to make those throws. They didn't want Bledsoe to get his head caved in like Dallas Cowboys quarterback Troy Aikman during his rookie season in 1989.

Head coach Bill Parcells' practices were going to be intense regardless of the quarterback situation, but Bledsoe's ability to withstand the rigors of the workouts was another indication of future success. The Patriots would run live blitz periods, many of which were geared toward violently rattling the quarterback, and Bledsoe stood in there and took it. His toughness was evident from day one, and that's when those two-a-days were grueling on the minds and taxing on the bodies. Weaker rookies were immediately exposed.

Bledsoe had a marginal rookie season in 1993, winning five of his 12 starts while completing 49.9 percent of his passes for 2,494 yards, 15 touchdowns, and 15 interceptions. He made significant progress in 1994, leading the NFL with 400 completions, 691 attempts, 4,555 yards, and 27 interceptions, but he mixed in 25 touchdowns as the Patriots won 10 games and returned to the playoffs.

But two games stood out more than the others, starting with the regular season opener against the Miami Dolphins at Joe Robbie Stadium. It was a heavily billed showdown because the Patriots closed down the 1993 regular season with four consecutive victories, and Bledsoe delivered a 36-yard touchdown pass to wide receiver Michael Timpson to beat the Dolphins in overtime and keep them out of the playoffs on the final play of the season. Bledsoe completed 32 of 51 passes for 421 yards and two touchdowns, but the Patriots lost a 39–35 shootout against Marino, who threw the game-winning pass midway through the fourth quarter. Still, the performance validated Bledsoe's talent and ability to go pass for pass with one of the two future Hall of Fame quarterback opponents in the AFC East.

"We didn't even warm up for that game because it was a monsoon at Joe Robbie Stadium," Scott Zolak said. "It was still half baseball, half football. When that infield got soaked, man, it was just pure mud. Drew hit Ben Coates on two long ones down the middle. I remember Coates having those high-top cleats and they were coated with mud. I remember sitting on the sidelines with the offensive line coach and he was saying, 'All we have to do is just get in front of guys. We don't have to push them. We don't have to block it up. These guys are on skates.' It was a mud bath out there, so we put Bledsoe in the gun, and all they did was wall things off in front of him and let him pick Miami apart. Marino did the same thing going the other way. Neither pass rush could get after either quarterback, so it was one of those games like the Patriots handle it nowadays with Tom Brady. Let him pick people apart."

One of Bledsoe's greatest memories occurred in Week 11 against the Minnesota Vikings in Foxboro. The Patriots had fallen to 3–6 on the year due to a four-game losing streak and trailed 20–0 in the second quarter before the Pats ripped off 26 straight points for an overtime victory. Matt Bahr forced sudden death with a 23-yard field goal with 14 seconds to play in the fourth quarter, and Bledsoe completed all six of his overtime passes for 56 yards and added a chain-moving quarterback sneak on third-and-1. On the next play, he hit fullback Kevin Turner in the back of the end zone for a 14-yard touchdown.

Bledsoe hadn't ever been superstitious prior to that day, but he credited the turned tide to a change of cleats at halftime. Zolak saw it differently and laughs that Bledsoe still refuses to give him a tip of the cap for a major halftime adjustment with the play calling.

"The all-time favorite was the one against Minnesota when he hit Kevin Turner in overtime for the win," Zolak said. "We were just getting our asses kicked. Anything Ray Perkins did at that time, nothing was working, so we were going back and forth, 'Drew, do you like this and that?' I remember being in there at halftime down three scores, and I'm like, 'Hey, the kid is obviously comfortable when you put him in the gun in two-minute. Let him go two-minute the rest of the damn game and see what the hell happens.'

"Parcells looks at Ray and Ray looks at Bill. I never got credit for that, first of all. Drew to this day still won't give me credit for that. But they're like, 'All right, we're going two-minute. Let's go.' From that point on, he called everything. It was curl, curl, slants, digs, comebacks, everything he liked to throw. When you're a 6'5", 245-pound, quintessential drop-back passer, you like to throw the deep-out stuff, all that. Typical old-time Oakland Raiders football. Al Davis pushed the ball down the field. It's not the dink and dunk, get everything out of your hands as quickly as you can. This was good downfield football."

Zolak Interlude

More than ever, Drew Bledsoe showcased his admirable toughness toward the end of the 1998 season, but he ultimately had no choice but to finish on the shelf. It was a difficult way for him to shut down the season, especially since the Patriots were heading to the playoffs for the fourth time in a five-year stretch. Bledsoe complemented a stifling defense to get the Patriots to Super Bowl XXXI, and they won another playoff game in 1997 before a disappointing 7–6 loss to the Pittsburgh Steelers in the divisional round.

Bledsoe broke the index finger on his throwing hand by knocking it off the helmet of a Miami Dolphins pass rusher in Week 12 on *Monday Night Football*. Bledsoe instantly knew he broke the digit, but he stayed on the field and delivered a 25-yard, game-winning touchdown pass to wide receiver Shawn Jefferson with 34 seconds remaining. The 26–23 victory improved their record to 6–5 and halted a stretch in which the Pats had fallen four times in five weeks.

Bledsoe opted against surgery and could barely practice, and yet he still played the following two games. The first full game with the broken finger was a classic 25–21 comeback win against the Buffalo Bills in Foxboro. The miraculous, game-winning drive intensified over the final three plays, as Bledsoe hit Shawn Jefferson on fourth-and-9 for a 10-yard gain with six seconds remaining to get the ball to the Bills' 26-yard line. Bledsoe next fired a strike to receiver Terry Glenn in the end zone, but safety Henry Jones tackled Glenn and was flagged for pass interference as time expired. With an untimed down from the 1-yard line, Bledsoe hit tight end Ben Coates for the game-winner.

The Pats got some revenge against the Steelers the following week in Pittsburgh with a 23–9 triumph, but Bledsoe's finger wasn't holding up. They opted for surgery to insert a pin to stabilize the broken bone, and Bledsoe returned to practice Friday and played Sunday against the St. Louis Rams, a 32–18 loss. The pin dislodged during the game and was noticeably sticking out of the tip of his finger as he tried to gut it out. The details of that week were brutal, as Bledsoe endured an excruciating level of pain, both internally and externally, in order to get himself ready and then remain on the field.

"The best thing he showed through that was the toughness," Zolak said. "I knew he was tough prior to that, but I remember at practice and sitting in meetings at the time and they came in with the doctors. Drew and I were always tight, and you're sitting there hearing them talk about, 'Well, we think if we numb this thing up and stabilize it with the brace, maybe you can still throw.' He still wanted to play. Most guys today wouldn't play. If you stick a pin in the tip of their index finger in their throwing hand, that's the last thing that leads the ball. When Drew was throwing, the pin was actually the last thing leaving the ball.

"I remember them in the training room, three doctors holding down the arm so they could shoot up the joints. To shoot up the joints of the finger, you've got to get the needle in there and move it around until you see the twitch to hit that nerve, and that's when they release the medicine. You just hear him screaming. Once it got numb and he got through that, they taped it up and we go out to practice and he starts throwing, I'm like, 'Holy shit, he's got velocity on this thing, and it's spinning.' The ball might have even spun more because he was able to dig into the ball with that pin. We did that Friday and he didn't practice all week so I took all the reps. Then the walkthrough Saturday, and they shot him up Sunday with the same thing. I just had to leave the room. I couldn't even see it, getting your fingers shot up because your fingers are so sensitive. It's the toughest thing I've ever seen anybody do. I've seen guys shoot up knees and ankles. But you're shooting up your finger, that's pretty much everything to you. It's like an artist.

"He started that Rams game, got knocked around pretty good and got the pin dislodged. They went in to take an X-ray of it and could see it floating around again. That's when they decided to shut him down: 'If we do this anymore, you're going to callous this thing and you won't have the flexibility that you once had in it.' The smart thing was to shut him down and give him the opportunity to play a couple games."

Zolak always respected Bledsoe's rigor and durability, but the backup was also like any red-blooded human being who wanted to play. That's the most mentally taxing aspect of the quarterback position—only one guy gets the glory. Bledsoe and the medical staff made the smart call to keep him out, too. To this day, he still plays around with the tip of that right index finger, squeezing it out of habit as a memory of a wound that he suffered two decades earlier.

So Zolak felt awful for his close friend, and at the same time he cherished the chance to make his first start since 1995. That initial start was special, too, because the Patriots clinched a playoff berth when they toppled quarterback Steve Young's San Francisco 49ers 24–21 by scoring 10 consecutive points in the fourth quarter. Zolak completed 14 of 30 attempts for 205 yards, two touchdowns, and two interceptions, and he uncorked a 61-yard scoring toss to Jefferson that still makes him proud.

There was a stretch in the first half when Jefferson ran about a half dozen curl routes in a row against 49ers cornerback R.W. McQuarters, who was aggressive enough to sit on the route and physical enough to beat up Jefferson during his breaks. So at this point, less than three minutes after Young and wide receiver Jerry Rice connected for a 75-yard touchdown that tied the game 7–7, Jefferson got back to the huddle, heard Zolak relay the play, and quickly rebutted the idea of running another curl. It was third-and-6, and Jefferson took over.

As Zolak recalled, "Shawn goes, 'Nah-uh, I'm going right fucking by this guy. Just don't overthrow me. I'm going to give him a little shake. We'll give him the look like I'm going to give him the curl, and then I'm going to take off.' I'm looking at the sideline like, 'Should I do this or not?' But come on, I had a lot of faith in Shawn because he could fly. That kid was fast. He set him up, a little double move, got five yards behind, and I let the thing go. I threw it in the old ramp area where we used to come out of the tunnel and just got him in the fingertips, and he pulls it in for a 61-yard touchdown. That was probably my favorite moment from that year."

As a twisted form of foreshadowing, the New York Jets shellacked the Patriots 31–10 in the regular-season finale. Jets coach Bill Parcells, who beat the Patriots in four of six meetings from 1997 to '99, benefited from a classic game plan from defensive coordinator Bill Belichick. The Jets had some creative blitz packages with Belichick, so the Patriots prepped for every possibility during each period of practice during the week. That's all it was—blitz, blitz,

blitz—because they assumed Belichick would ruthlessly attack Zolak in his seventh career start. Instead, Belichick did the complete opposite, refusing to blitz and sitting back in cover-2 all day. "Typical Belichick," Zolak laughed. "That was funny because we're looking at all this film and going over blitzes. They sat in cover-2, beat us up at the line, and just frustrated us."

Zolak ultimately started the final three games of the 1998 season, including the 25–10 playoff loss on the road against the Jacksonville Jaguars. Other than 1992, it was the only time he made multiple starts in his eight seasons with the Patriots, and his tenure culminated with his starting debut in the postseason.

The Patriots might have been a little rattled after they were humbled by the Jets, and the Jaguars and their fans were maniacal over their first home playoff game in franchise history. The stadium was buzzing, and the Patriots didn't help themselves. On the first play of the game, the offense came out in the wrong formation, and it was loud enough already because they were backed up on their own 14-yard line. The atmosphere was dialed up even more when the Pats were flagged for an illegal formation penalty, leading to a three-and-out and a tone-setting moment for a flat first half, as the Jaguars built a 12–0 lead. The Patriots established some second-half momentum with running back Robert Edwards' 1-yard score, but tight end Lovett Purnell dropped an easy touchdown pass on the second play of the fourth quarter, yielding Adam Vinatieri's 27-yard field goal that made it 12–10. Quarterback Mark Brunell found wide receiver Jimmy Smith for a 37-yard touchdown six plays later to crush the hopes of a comeback.

The End Is the Beginning

Seventy-six years after Lou Gehrig replaced Wally Pipp, Drew Bledsoe lost his job to Tom Brady in a fashion that was nearly as innocuous. Pipp, a power-hitting first baseman for the New York Yankees, apparently asked out of the lineup in June 1925 because of a headache, and he was replaced by Gehrig in the first of a record-breaking 2,130 consecutive games.

Fast forward three quarters of a century, Drew Bledsoe signed a 10-year, $103 million contract extension with the Patriots in March 2001, signifying the strong belief that he'd play his entire career with just one team. During the fourth quarter of a 10–3 loss to the New York Jets in Week 2, the 13th defeat in Bill Belichick's first 18 games as the head coach of the Patriots, Bledsoe succumbed to a wicked shot from linebacker Mo Lewis that caused a torn blood vessel and internal bleeding. Tom Brady took over from there and launched the most successful career in the history of the sport.

There are varying viewpoints over the way the 2001 season transpired between Bledsoe and Brady. Some believe Brady was the better quarterback in training camp, while others dismiss such a notion. Some say Bledsoe was the perfect mentor to Brady during a professionally trying season for both, while others argue Bledsoe should have done more to help the sixth-round pick of the 2000 draft. Like most comparable arguments, the truth was almost certainly somewhere in between. Present day, the fact remains Brady and Bledsoe are friends, and the pair often spend time together when Bledsoe returns to the Boston area.

The most painful sting occurred in Week 12 when Belichick declared Brady had earned the right to finish the season as the fulltime starter, even though Bledsoe had finally been medically cleared to compete for his job. Bledsoe believed he'd have that opportunity to at least go snap for snap with Brady at practice, but Brady had won six of his first eight starts at that point and was even turning the veterans who were in Bledsoe's corner. As a competitor, no one should blame Bledsoe for wanting to fight for his job. Remember, Bledsoe was about nine months removed from a historic contract extension, so his helpless feeling of *I can't believe this is happening* can be excused. By comparison, does anyone think Brady planned to make it easy for Jimmy Garoppolo a decade and a half later?

Bledsoe internalized most of his frustration, and he unleashed his emotion in the AFC Championship Game against the Pittsburgh Steelers when he took over for an injured Brady and played a vital role in the Patriots' 24–17 win. It also did wonders for Bledsoe's career when he withstood a hit on the sideline in that game that was similarly devastating as Lewis' blow. The whole chain of events, most notably including a pristine 11-yard touchdown pass to wide receiver David Patten, led to Bledsoe tearfully hugging the Lamar Hunt Trophy when the Pats secured their trip to New Orleans for Super Bowl XXXVI.

Even that week, there was one final dose of drama. Brady was recovering from a high ankle sprain before the Super Bowl, which was being played without a bye week due to 9/11. But Bledsoe never got that last shot, and the confetti-soaked, on-field bath was as bittersweet as it could get. The franchise quarterback helped the 2001 Patriots' trek to the Super Bowl, but he knew he had relinquished his job to Brady in a passing of the baton that reshaped both the Patriots and the entire NFL landscape.

Bledsoe has received a hero's welcome from Patriots fans during every return trip to Gillette Stadium since the team traded him to the Bills in 2002. For that, he has been humbled each and every time. He was also elected into the Patriots Hall of Fame in 2011, his first year of eligibility. For that, he has felt honored. But that iconic nod wasn't symbolic. It had been earned. And for that, the Patriots are eternally grateful.

CHAPTER 4
CALIFORNIA PETE

As time has passed, the memories of the Pete Carroll era have been somewhat obscured. Now, there's a fair explanation for that. Carroll was the head coach of the New England Patriots from 1997 to '99, sandwiched between Bill Parcells and Big Tuna disciple Bill Belichick. Parcells revitalized a franchise that had been in a wretched funk during a four-year run that culminated with a trip to Super Bowl XXXI, and Belichick launched perhaps the greatest dynasty in football history. Parcells and Belichick led with similar styles and achieved results that had been, on a relative scale, unfathomably successful.

So that has left Carroll as the forgotten man, maybe even the placeholder. He was quirky during his three-year stint and never broke character in following stops with the University of Southern California or the Seattle Seahawks. His personality was the antithesis of the two Bills, and because it didn't draw championship-level results, it has since been mocked in New England. But to an extent Carroll was a winner, leading the Patriots to a 27–21 record over the course of three regular seasons: 10–6 in 1997, 9–7 in 1998, and 8–8 in 1999. They won a playoff game against the Miami Dolphins in 1997, although they had a disappointing exit the following week by a 7–6 count against the Pittsburgh Steelers. And with quarterback Drew Bledsoe on the shelf with a broken index finger on his throwing hand in 1998, the Patriots were one-and-done in the postseason. They failed to qualify for the playoffs in 1999 before Patriots owner Robert Kraft fired Carroll, partly due to a marginal downward slide and mostly because he finally recognized an opportunity to steal Belichick from the New York Jets.

Carroll was also a victim of the organizational structure at the time. Like Parcells, who vehemently complained about it upon his departure, Carroll didn't have final say over personnel decisions, so there was a divide between football operations and the front office, which had been led by general manager Bobby Grier. The symbol of that has been the notorious staircase at Foxboro Stadium that led to Grier's office. A group of veterans wore out that staircase to complain to Grier when they thought practice was too hard or they weren't getting enough playing time or they felt the need to complain about anything else that should conceivably be beneath a grown man and professional football player. So it was essentially an impossible working environment for Carroll, a tremendous defensive coordinator at previous stops with the Jets and San Francisco 49ers but a relative newbie as a head coach.

Carroll has admitted as much, at least with hindsight as his ally. There's no doubt he has benefited by corralling absolute power over the roster with the Seahawks, which he learned was necessary as the USC czar from 2001 to '09. But that option never would have been on the table with the Patriots in the 1990s because monopolized powers weren't as common with NFL teams at that point in time. Plus, Carroll wasn't in position to lobby for that type of authority with a singular head coaching season (his Jets went 6–10 in 1994) on his résumé. Nor did he recognize the necessity of having final say over the roster.

"I didn't have the job description to do what I wanted to do [with the Patriots]," said Carroll, who acquired 49 players on the Seahawks' 53-man roster that was victorious in Super Bowl XLVIII. "I wasn't sure then how important it was. I know that now because we have our style. We have our philosophy and a whole approach that we stand for, and when you're mixing styles and philosophies with other people that were in charge, it's difficult.

It was difficult for me. I realized that when I got to SC and I had total control. And I realize that now when we went to Seattle and had total control that it was necessary."

Carl Smith has been in Carroll's corner virtually every step of the way and can vouch for the way Carroll has progressed with his ability to run a program over the course of a couple decades. Smith served as assistant head coach, quarterbacks coach, and tight ends coach with Carroll's Patriots, made a quick stop over at USC as the quarterbacks coach in 2004, and rejoined Carroll's Seahawks as the quarterbacks coach in 2011. Smith hasn't seen Carroll change as a person or as a coach, but much more so as an administrator.

"He just didn't have as good of a job as he has now," Smith said in 2014 before Super Bowl XLVIII. "He was a hired hand [with the Patriots]. He was a plumber. He just had one job, and he did a great job coaching the team. The defense listened to him. Our roster wasn't quite what we have now. He's in control of the roster. He's in control of all of the coaching hires. He's in control of the intellect and understanding of football. That's why we're here at the Super Bowl, because of Pete's decisions. To me, that's why the Patriots have done so well [with Belichick]. They have a guy who really understands football who is making all of the critical decisions on game plans, on staff, on style, and he understands the game. It's not all personality. We can't all see those things. Those decisions are important, and Pete has made terrific decisions on all aspects and that's why we're here. Pete is thinking of stuff every day to make that day a good day, a good practice day, a good meeting to start the day. He's got 500 things going on."

For Pete's Sake

Bill Parcells demanded respect, accountability and excellence 24 hours a day. The Patriots who understood his motives were able to stick around and thoroughly appreciated the opportunity to play for him, but the workweek was anything but enjoyable. Parcells was hired to change Dick MacPherson's laid-back culture, and it's obvious Parcells conquered that challenge, among others.

Pete Carroll changed the culture again, though not nearly as intentionally or dramatically. The players knew Carroll's reputation as a great defensive coach, but they also remembered him from flashing the choke sign at Dolphins quarterback Dan Marino in 1994, just before Marino faked a spike and threw a game-winning touchdown pass that sparked a five-game tailspin and Carroll's firing. At any rate, the Patriots understood Carroll added a fun, rambunctious personality to the facility, and they reveled in that idea.

Rather than tip-toeing around Foxboro Stadium with Parcells, whose office was located right next to the door where the players entered, it was a party with Carroll. Parcells demanded perfection on and off the field. Sluggish practice? It didn't matter if they were two hours into the workout; Parcells would walk 80 yards in the other direction, spin his whistle around his finger, stare like a madman at his employees, and then tell them to start the whole thing over from the stretch. Bad game? Parcells would literally walk by players in a hallway wide enough for two people with his head down like they didn't even exist. It was a miserable work environment because Parcells made it that way. Go out the night before? Be prepared for a morning greeting from Parcells, who'd grip a coffee in a Styrofoam cup and chirp, "You have fun last night, honey? I know who you were with. I knew where you went." And then he'd peer in another player's direction and snap, "And I know where she went, too."

That wasn't Carroll's style, though. He was "California Pete," and he wanted his guys to have fun while winning. They'd crack up every morning when they'd walk past Carroll's office and hear him blasting that hilarious terrible one-hit wonder "Barbie Girl" by Aqua. My goodness, what an atrocious crime against a human's ears, but Carroll made it work because he was that type of guy. He was also a big fan of The Doors and a more appreciative generation of rock, so he'd be singing away at the crack of dawn while players were still trying to dislodge the sand from their eyes.

"Pete's energy was fantastic," Scott Zolak said. "You know how people say Rob Gronkowski never had a bad day? I don't think Pete ever had a bad day. Great energy. It made you feel young. He had a young vibe to him."

Carroll recognized a dip in energy a few weeks into training camp during his first season in 1997, so he concocted a plan to pick up his players. They all arrived in a team meeting room after a lackadaisical practice, probably aware of their lousy workout and somewhat tepid after being trained by Parcells' ruthless ways. Completely unaware of Carroll's scheme, the players were reserved as they watched Carroll bark at defensive coordinator Steve Sidwell over his group's inability to make a key stop during the workout. So Sidwell then turned his attention to offensive coordinator Larry Kennan, blaming the offense for giving them bad looks throughout practice. Kennan screamed back at Sidwell, and the two began grappling in front of the whole team, to the point where the players and coaches had to pull them apart.

As Zolak remembers it, Carroll then screamed, "'What the hell is going on here?' This is a team meeting. It's the doldrums of camp, three weeks into it. Pete goes, 'Whoa, whoa, whoa, stop this shit right now. I don't want to see this anymore. Here's what we're going to do. Everybody, get up. I want you to go outside. There's five buses out there. We've got beer on the bus and we're going bowling!'"

The room erupted. Sure enough, Carroll equipped the buses with kegs, and they had a team party. That was his thing. They had three-point shooting contests or trick-shot contests at the basketball court in the bubble in the morning before practice, and Carroll mixed it up with the players, commonly winning the battles. It was a valuable way to start each day with a dose of his energy, and the players loved it. He has carried those tendencies to the present-day Seahawks as well with the daily basketball games and competitions. Carroll likes to keep his guys on their toes, and he has a running joke with their newly signed players, who will be asked to introduce themselves and share their life story in the front of a meeting room. Carroll will then interject by yelling, "Shut up! No one wants to hear your sad story! Go sit down!" And the veterans will burst out in laughter every time.

Carroll turned the joke on his vets in 2012 by conspiring with legendary wide receiver Terrell Owens after his signing. Owens was sharing a story about his grandmother, and the players in the room got a bit anxious because they were aware of the receiver's volatile personality, fearing he'd snap on Carroll after his usual interruption. Of course, Carroll did his thing, and Owens played along with the prank by snapping right back at the head coach. They then cracked up in front of the room to the relief of the team, which appreciated being on the receiving end of the prank.

These antics work for Carroll because he is genuinely that type of guy. His players respect him because he is a good coach who is true to himself, but the dynamic was a bit off during his three-year run with the Patriots. He inherited a team that was molded by Parcells' overly demanding disciplinary measures, so the players felt like they could relax to an extent with Carroll.

"Pete was a players' coach," Zolak said. "It worked for Pete. It works for him in Seattle. Pete took the USC college model and made it work in the pros, and nobody ever thought anybody could do it. The problem was you had so many guys that were…not worn down by Parcells but trained by Parcells. Pete gave you luxury and space and trust to go do your thing. 'You guys go take care of yourself.' And I think guys were abusing it like the inmates running the asylum. It was a much more laid-back environment, and it was fun. We had a lot more fun at practices with Pete because Parcells, it was like game day every practice."

Parcells granted Carroll with a turnkey roster that was young, talented, full of potential, and coming off a Super Bowl appearance, and Carroll was a strong enough defensive mind who could guide the Patriots to continued success. Cornerback Ty Law and safety Lawyer Milloy particularly thrived with Carroll as two of the cocky, budding leaders on that side of the ball. The Patriots screamed out of the gates with a 4–0 start in 1997 and won four of their final five regular-season games to reach the playoffs. But their postseason efforts were thwarted with a maddening 7–6 loss to the Pittsburgh Steelers, as quarterback Kordell Stewart's 40-yard touchdown run held up against Drew Bledsoe's two interceptions and two lost fumbles.

That season was also sidetracked by a stage-diving incident during an Everclear concert in Boston, yielding a lawsuit from a woman who was injured at the show. (She had surgery, and Bledsoe and offensive lineman Max Lane settled out of court.) The players usually ventured into Boston during their nights off, and they were amped to see one of the most popular bands of the 1990s as one of their usual nights on the town.

"Drew's band was Everclear," Zolak said. "Of course, who didn't like Everclear? We all liked them. They came in and were playing at the Paradise one night. None of us had ever even been to the Paradise. Our night of going out was either going to Daisy's or Dad's Beantown on a Monday or Tuesday. Tuesday was the off day. Sunday, we'd go to Dad's. We would go out Thursday, Friday, Sunday, Monday for the single guys on a home-game weekend. We'd go right to Newbury and Boylston Street. Dad's was on the corner there by Whiskey's. We'd go to Dad's first and then go to Daisy's. Daisy's is actually where I met my wife. It's crazy.

"Such a small bar, but that's what made it feel like it was our bar. All the athletes were there, and it was great because you could go in there and get a drink and nobody would bug you. And at that time, you knew where all the girls were going to be on a Sunday or Monday night. So we heard Everclear was coming, and it was a Thursday night. We go in, took a limo. We always had a driver. None of us got busted for drinking and driving. We'd be pretty heavy into it those nights, so we'd always get a guy to drive us and took a limo. They saved a table for us out back.

"I just remember being in the mosh pit, and they started playing 'Santa Monica.' That's when we all snapped, all the shirts were off. The next thing I knew, Max Lane comes running out, sees me in the mosh pit and dives out. For a guy that size, 6'6", 320 pounds, to clear about six feet of air off the stage and into the mosh pit, man, we grabbed him and I was giving him a noogie. I think that's when Drew jumped on top of him. The next thing you know, the lights went on and supposedly somebody got hurt. We kind of got whisked out of there.

"I just remember being in a 9 o'clock quarterback meeting the next morning, and this is prior to cell phones. We hear the knock, knock, knock on the door, and Pete comes in. 'What happened last night?' Typical Pete Carroll. 'Did something happen? We've got people calling. The police?' We're like, 'Oh, god.'"

The Pats leaked a bit more in 1998, and Bledsoe missed the final three games, including the playoff loss to the Jacksonville Jaguars, with a broken finger. They started 6–2 in 1999 but lost six of their final eight games and missed the playoffs before Carroll was fired. Their talent was ultimately overmatched by California Pete's vacation-style leadership, at least in comparison to the Parcells era. Carroll wasn't yet ready to be a successful head coach at that point in his career, and his style didn't help maximize the potential of the roster over the long haul.

There was a perception problem within the confines of the locker room, too. A handful of veterans, including tackle Bruce Armstrong and some of the older running backs, used to march up a back staircase to complain to general manager Bobby Grier about Carroll's practices and such. Sometimes, a player would want to take a practice or a week off because he was tired. The requests were usually unbecoming of a good teammate and undermined Carroll. Even though the other players would roll their eyes, the jaunts up the staircase yielded the thought of, "Who is actually running this team?" It's also something Parcells would never tolerate or forgive.

Grier's office was located near the club on top of Foxboro Stadium, and that's also where the players would eat lunch. So it was almost comical the displeased veterans thought they were sneaking around by heading up that staircase under the guise of finding a meal, considering the team had eaten several hours earlier. There wasn't exactly a personal rift between Carroll and Grier, but the symbol of the staircase complaints didn't exactly breed the most well-structured working environment. It also didn't help that they didn't have great captains, notably Armstrong, who has been labeled an asshole by his former teammates. It's difficult to dispute that, considering Armstrong didn't give a hoot about his image as he'd sometimes refuse to even join the huddle on the field. It got to the point where Carroll reopened the captain vote prior to the 1998 playoffs, and Armstrong was stripped of his title.

"I don't know how good the captains were or weren't, or the communication," Zolak said. "There wasn't really any structure. You don't have the captain meetings like you do now with Belichick. I think it's safe to say we knew which veterans were running up there to bitch if the practices were too tough, or saying, 'This guy is doing this wrong, and that guy is doing that wrong. This guy is playing and shouldn't be playing.' You could tell the change. You knew something was off."

Split Decision

Scott Zolak played out his contract, which expired following the 1998 season, and his final game in a Patriots uniform doubled as his lone postseason start. Pete Carroll and the Patriots had decided to go in another direction behind starting quarterback Drew Bledsoe. They signed veteran John Friesz and drafted electric Kansas State quarterback Michael Bishop in the seventh round.

Meanwhile, Zolak was ready to play until the phone stopped ringing, and Bill Parcells obliged with a surprising phone call to Zolak as he was sitting with his wife, Amy, at Jimmy Johnson's bar in Miami Beach. Amy answered the phone and had a hilariously unexpected back-and-forth with the coach, who once again fulfilled his prophecy of always knowing where his players are located and what they're doing.

"This is Bill Parcells," the voice on the line said.

"This isn't Bill Parcells," Amy replied, causing Zolak's ears to perk up. He wondered, first, how the hell Parcells knew where to find him while they were on vacation and, second, why he'd be calling him.

"Put Zolak on the phone."

"If this is Bill Parcells, what are the names of our two dogs?"

"Boomer and Molly. Now, put him on the phone."

Amy looked at Zolak like, *Holy shit, it's him.*

Parcells asked how quickly Zolak could get on a plane while explaining that he wanted Zolak to compete with Ray Lucas to back up Vinny Testaverde for the 1999 season. Zolak jumped at the shot, and it was an exciting opportunity to reunite with Parcells while also joining one of the hottest teams in the AFC. Unfortunately for Zolak, Green Bay Packers general manager Ron Wolf publicly shopped quarterback Rick Mirer at the start of training camp, and Parcells was still drawn to the No. 2 overall pick in the 1993 NFL draft, even though he passed him over for Bledsoe.

So Parcells traded for Mirer and cut Zolak two days later. Mirer's nine lives had yet to expire. The transaction stung even more in Week 1 when Testaverde blew out his Achilles against the Patriots because Lucas and Mirer weren't able to replace Testaverde and fulfill the Jets' lofty expectations, as they finished 8–8 and missed the playoffs.

Instead, Zolak coincidentally got a call from Miami Dolphins coach Jimmy Johnson. The Dolphins wanted Zolak to back up Damon Huard when starting quarterback Dan Marino was dragging with neck, arm, and leg injuries. Zolak, Marino, and Johnson all closed down their careers together with the 1999 Dolphins.

"I was fortunate enough to have a background with Jimmy because he recruited me to go to the University of Miami," Zolak said. "He knew me, and we had an offensive line coach, Paul Boudreau, who was down at Miami. This was when Marino's shoulder started to deteriorate, and they picked me up about midseason. I wound up my last year there with Danny, and it was kind of cool to be around Marino because he was always one of my guys I looked up to growing up in Pittsburgh. I became great friends with Damon Huard, had some good relationships down there. Danny and Jimmy never really saw eye to eye either, and that was kind of the beginning of the end there for Marino. So Marino retires and Jimmy walks away."

Make no mistake, Zolak was among the herd of Patriots who loved playing for Carroll, but the quarterback's brief stint with the Jets served as a reminder of his admiration for Parcells' program. The stint also opened Zolak's eyes to the insane level of detail from Jets defensive coordinator Bill Belichick. Zolak got his first look at Belichick when he served Parcells in the same capacity with the

Patriots in 1996, and he was intrigued by his first conversation with Belichick when they were allies again in 1999.

"The first day I'm in the weight room, Belichick comes over with a pencil behind his ear holding a notepad," Zolak said. "We sat on a weight bench in the Jets weight room, and he had the entire Patriots roster. We went over strengths and weaknesses of each individual guy in detail. It's not because he knows he's going to become the coach there or anything like that but, 'All right, here's a player in our program, so let's find out as much as we can about our opponent.' Even though he was there in '96, the Patriots had some new guys and it had been a few years. 'What do you think of this guy, strengths and weaknesses? Can this guy turn his hips? Can he play the ball? Third-and-6, who are you going to?' Taking notes and writing it all down. I was amazed by it. We sat there for probably an hour and a half. So later in life down the road there, you see why it works for Belichick as opposed to maybe other coaches who don't put in the time. It's a constant grind. It's amazing."

Every coach finds success or failure for their own reasons. Just like it didn't work for Belichick and the Cleveland Browns in the 1990s, Carroll's operation with the Patriots never materialized. Sometimes, the circumstances just don't align the way the coach hopes or needs, and periods of reflection can help them change that tide at a future stop. Carroll was wildly successful at the University of Southern California, although he was burned by the reaper in the form of NCAA sanctions. And Carroll became the third coach in history (after Johnson and Barry Switzer) to win a college football national championship and a Super Bowl when he guided the Seattle Seahawks to the title in the 2013 season.

Carroll's style ran thin in New England but flourished as he reached the pinnacle of the sport in Seattle. He revitalized a franchise that was spelled by two miserable seasons, including one-and-done head coach Jim Mora.

"When he went to Seattle, he had an opportunity to bring in guys that fit what he was trying to do, so it was easier for them to buy into it, versus going to a veteran team already stuck in their ways," Patriots Hall of Famer Willie McGinest said. "There were all Parcells-type of guys. His way is totally opposite of Parcells, so it's kind of hard for certain guys to make that transition."

Carl Smith spoke for the Seahawks coaching staff and players when he added, "This is ball-playing the way people want it. Let's have fun. Let's enjoy it. It's work, but all these guys love to play ball. That's what Pete is about, and he puts it in every day."

In a roundabout way, Carroll's tenure was a victory for all involved. No, the Patriots couldn't back up their Super Bowl XXXI appearance during his three-year stay, but that era reaffirmed the type of culture that owner Robert Kraft preferred to spread throughout his organization, thus leading to the hiring of Belichick in 2000. Carroll also learned more about himself and the elements that he'd need to find success before returning to the college game for nine years.

Ultimately, as it specifically relates to the Patriots, Carroll's three-year reign laid the groundwork for the most fruitful and perhaps controversial coaching hire in the history of professional sports.

CHAPTER 5
KRAFT'S RISK
WORTH TAKING

Robert Kraft's vision is extraordinary, and the results have followed suit. He was strongly advised against completing the two greatest purchases of his life, as members of his inner circle cited financial recklessness prior to each transaction. Kraft followed his instincts each time, first with the procurement of a paper mill and then with the acquisition of the New England Patriots, and he has become one of the world's most successful businessmen as a result.

His late wife, Myra, questioned his sanity when he made an aggressive play to buy the Patriots in 1994, and a banking friend wouldn't even loan him the money to complete the sale. But Kraft had built up to that point for a decade and wouldn't assume he'd ever get a second chance.

By that point, Kraft was already used to others who pushed back against his instincts. A couple decades earlier, he made an equally brash move to purchase a paper mill in Newfoundland that ultimately sparked his credibility as a powerful businessman on an international level. When Kraft follows his nose and believes in the process, he may very well be undefeated.

The Patriots, like his paper and packaging company, have become the model operation in their field. He turned the worst team in the NFL into a dynasty that may reach unparalleled levels in a third decade, and consider the growth: as a longtime Patriots season-ticketholder, he never witnessed a home playoff victory. He now has the highest winning percentage in history of any owner with at least 200 victories. The Super Bowl LI win against the Atlanta Falcons doubled as Kraft's 28th postseason triumph, which is the most among any singular owner in league history. (The Rooney family has 36 playoff wins since 1933, and

Packers shareholders can claim 34 playoff wins since 1919.) Their eight Super Bowl appearances under Kraft doubled his next closest competitor.

What's more, the Patriots were an NFL-worst 19–61 in their five seasons before Kraft's purchase. And since that point, they've set the bar in every category that measures team success (wins, division titles, Super Bowls). Kraft also takes a great deal of pride in the fact that the Patriots are the only team in history to win five Super Bowls with the union of the same owner, head coach, and quarterback.

In June 2017, Forbes listed Kraft's net worth at $5.2 billion and set the Patriots' value at $3.4 billion. To think, Kraft bought the Pats in 1994 for $172 million, a price tag that significantly exceeded their value and was at the time the most money ever spent to buy a sports franchise on the planet.

Kraft wasn't rolling the dice, and he wasn't crazy, either. He simply had an amazingly detailed plan that he was devoted to fulfilling.

Paper Stacks

Kraft was a local kid who grew up in Brookline, Massachusetts, and got his Master's degree at Harvard Business School. He credited his true rise to a risky maneuver to purchase a Canadian paper mill that he believed would aid the explosion of his Worcester, Massachusetts–based company, the Rand-Whitney Group, which converted paper into packaging for various industries.

The global economy was suffering in 1972, and there had been an issue of potential corruption with a government-owned mill in Newfoundland that popped up for sale. At that point, Kraft had already recognized that he needed a mill because about 60 percent of his company's sales prices were devoted to raw materials, so mill owners were greatly benefiting from his business. The paper industry was also dominated by bigger companies in the United States, Canada, and Europe, so he viewed this as a perfect opportunity to take over the Canadian mill.

Kraft had to take on a major risk to complete the sale because he was competing for the mill with major companies in Canada. So he differentiated his pitch with an aggressive guarantee for the Canadian government that was selling the mill. Kraft knew the mill could produce 350,000 tons of paper per year, so he offered a take-or-pay contract. If he didn't sell 200,000 tons a year, he'd pay the difference to ensure the government wouldn't lose money on the sale.

The problem? "I didn't have the net worth, probably, to do it," Kraft said. He wasn't sure that he could financially support a significant short in sales, but he didn't think it would ever come to that.

Kraft also had legitimacy with his representation. His attorney, Ted Sorensen, helped President John F. Kennedy run the White House. Sorensen's reputation and Kraft's commitment to ensure a positive cash flow helped him beat out the major corporations to win the sale of the paper mill and launch International Forest Products. Kraft then caught a major break when President Richard Nixon added a regulation to the international market which helped spur Kraft's paper companies to drastically expand, and they're now doing business in 95 countries.

"None of the other big paper companies would make the big commitment that I would make because they owned the other mills," Kraft said. "If the market got weak, they'd take down-time. They'd shut down the mills to keep the prices up. So to run 200,000 tons and they're making $4 to $5 million, and you take the market down $50 of the 4 million tons, that would be $200 million. I realized that was my niche. I didn't know what the heck I'd do if I had to buy it, but I made the commitment and was able to sell them on the idea. That's the reason they should go with me, and they bought in. The general world economy was a little weak at the time, so none of these big mills would make the commitment. This was in the end of 1972.

"What happened, shortly thereafter, President Nixon put on price freezes that didn't allow the U.S. to export paper at different prices than they were selling in the U.S. That tightened the market. All of a sudden, I had the only new supply anywhere in the world, and I had people in Korea, China, England, Africa coming to me. The market changed. I used that to build. That was the basis of my international company."

Kraft also learned some valuable lessons in the mid-1970s when he bought the Boston Lobsters of World Team Tennis. He recognized how to run a team in several capacities. On the court, Kraft found the importance of having a great coach when the Lobsters replaced Ion Tiriac with Roy Emerson, who was adept at relating to all of his players, which was important in a league that employed players of both sexes. Kraft also wanted a star player, so he paid an exorbitant $50,000 fee to acquire the rights of Martina Navratilova. Kraft especially reaped the rewards when she returned from a Wimbledon championship to play in a packed Cape Cod Coliseum for a special summertime match.

On the business side, the Lobsters' home was Walter Brown Arena. Kraft's revenue was strictly generated by ticket sales (hence the Navratilova trade), while Boston University raked in money from the parking, concessions, and sponsorships. That was a major lesson for Kraft, a Patriots season-ticketholder since 1971 who already dreamed of buying the team, because he recognized the significance of owning a franchise and all of its properties.

Trust the Process

As a business owner, it was second nature for Robert Kraft to study the way the Patriots were operated. (It was probably also easy for the mind to wander for several Sundays a season when the team wasn't winning.) Kraft also became friends with Billy Sullivan, the Patriots' original owner, and even told Sullivan to keep him in mind if he ever decided to sell.

Kraft began to put together a plan in the early 1980s to buy the Patriots, and he learned a group of a dozen people owned the 300 acres around Sullivan Stadium (Foxboro Stadium's name from 1983 to '89). That land included a racetrack, stables, and a trailer park along with the football stadium. So with the long term in mind, Kraft approached those 12 land owners in 1985 with a purchase plan that was ultimately approved. He proposed a 10-year option in which he'd lease the land for $1 million per year and have the choice to buy the land for $17 million at the conclusion of the lease. So for $27 million over the course of the decade, Kraft put his stake in the land surrounding Sullivan Stadium.

Kraft earned back about $600,000 to $700,000 annually in parking revenue for games and concerts, but it was a strategic play, like his Lobsters experience in reverse. Kraft later made a move to buy the stadium after Billy Sullivan's son, Chuck, made a catastrophic mistake to bankroll and promote the Michael Jackson family Victory Tour in 1984. After a few years of trying to stay afloat, the Sullivan family had no choice but to unload the team and stadium. The short of the story is Chuck Sullivan guaranteed the Jacksons and Don King $40 million for the rights to promote the concert tour, and he used Sullivan Stadium as collateral. Through a variety of reasons, the tour was a financial disaster for the Sullivans. To relieve their financial debt, they sold the Patriots to Victor Kiam for $84 million.

All the while, Kraft and Kiam got into a bidding war in the bankruptcy court over Sullivan Stadium, which was valued at $50 million. Kraft won with an offer of $25 million to Kiam's $17 million. But Kraft had a friend in the banking industry who wouldn't loan him the money for the sale because it had been widely assumed at the time that the Patriots were going to relocate. Kraft in turn used a private bank to fund the transaction.

Kiam wasn't the most financially stable owner either. He was in significant debt to St. Louis businessman James Orthwein of the Busch family that owned Budweiser, and Orthwein took over the Patriots in 1992 as a result. Orthwein's goal was essentially to move the Patriots to a publicly funded stadium (Edward Jones Dome) that was already being built in St. Louis, and those efforts were intensified when he couldn't get the public backing for a new stadium in New England. When he tried to move the Patriots to the south, Kraft flexed his muscle, and his years of effort and planning for that very moment were validated.

In a key twist, the bankruptcy judge who sold the stadium to Kraft included an operating covenant that guaranteed the Patriots had to remain in New England through the balance of their lease in the 2001 season. Orthwein legally couldn't move the Patriots to St. Louis— or anywhere—without Kraft's permission, so Orthwein offered Kraft $75 million to get out of the lease. Myra Kraft wanted her husband to take the deal and triple the money that he spent on the stadium six years earlier. Kraft didn't want the region to lose the Patriots.

"My sweet wife said, 'You'll take it. You'll still own the stadium. You'll get another team,'" Kraft said. "I remembered what happened with the Boston Braves when they moved to Milwaukee. I knew what that meant to the fans. Even though the Patriots hadn't done that well, there was a very loyal following, of which I was one, so I refused."

Kraft's power play with the lease led to the next step. Orthwein had a finite window to move the team to his hometown of St. Louis, so this wasn't a process that he could afford to drag out for years or even months. The NFL was in the midst of an expansion with the Jacksonville Jaguars and Carolina Panthers, and the league was also trying to get a team into the Edward Jones Dome in time for the 1995 season. That ultimately yielded the Los Angeles Rams' relocation.

So, to Kraft's delight, Orthwein decided to sell the Patriots, and Kraft went to St. Louis for the pivotal meeting. Kraft believed the right number to buy the Patriots was $115 million, and he told Myra that he'd go as high as $122 million if necessary. Orthwein said he wouldn't take less than $172 million, so Kraft left for an hour to talk it over with his son, Jonathan, and another advisor before agreeing to meet Orthwein's price.

"In life, you don't get second chances sometimes," Kraft said. "When you believe in something—and I believed in the value of the franchise and thought it was undermanaged—I agreed to pay the price, which was not my normal way of doing things. We wound up paying the highest price for any sports franchise for anywhere in the world. And it happened to be the worst team in the NFL. My wife really thought I had gone insane."

Kraft's expenses grew from the $172 million price tag because he inherited the Patriots' debts from the seemingly countless lawsuits against them. It's funny now, but Kraft couldn't find a local lawyer to help him at the time because so many attorneys had clients who were already suing him. Myra had a point when she questioned her husband's sanity, but Robert Kraft had a plan to rescue his favorite team.

All in the Family

Robert Kraft instilled a family atmosphere that the organization had desperately lacked. There were smaller details like a babysitting program for the players, and linebacker Marty Moore's wife started a wives club to get the families involved with the games and community endeavors. Kraft also threw parties for the team and their families at the Cape, and his guests remain impressed with his genuine generosity at those gatherings.

Look, the ownership's culture matters, probably even more so for a team with a lousy facility and very little history of winning. Just keeping the team in Foxboro was a victory for his reputation with the players who didn't want to sell their houses and move to St. Louis. Kraft also injected passion through his admirable confidence when he bought the Patriots in 1994.

For instance, Scott Zolak recalled his first meeting with Kraft in 1992 when he was in the practice bubble getting ready for his first career start when Patriots CEO Sam Jankovich brought Kraft over for an introduction. Kraft told Zolak that he'd been a longtime fan and season-ticketholder, and he proclaimed that he'd own the team someday. It was a brash prediction, but in hindsight, it's almost identical to the story of Kraft's first encounter with Tom Brady in 2000 when Brady walked down the Foxboro Stadium stairs with a box of pizza and told Kraft he was the best decision the organization had ever made. The greats have a way of distinguishing their "it" factor.

Spin it forward to 1994, and Kraft stunned the players on his new team. He walked into the locker room one day and showed them his plans for a new stadium, a Hall of Fame, and an adjacent mall. Imagine the players' faces, as they're sitting in a glorified high school stadium with showers that were short on hot water, and Kraft already had visions of Patriot Place.

It was a complete reversal from Victor Kiam and James Orthwein. Kiam's Christmas celebrations were an embarrassment.

"At Christmas, he would come in with this shiny red tie," Zolak said. "There was an old partition in the back of the meeting room, and they would lay out a folding table and they would lay out probably about 100 ties—ugly ass ties that you'd never wear. And Victor would come in and say, 'I want all the eldest veterans, the 10-year veterans to stand up, and they can have the first pick in ties.' So it was like, 'Okay, here's an NFL owner telling us to pick ties.' He thought it was the biggest thing ever to give his players ties as a Christmas gift. That's how shitty things were then. And here's Mr. Kraft doing what he does now. That's real ownership."

Orthwein was a ghost during his short ownership tenure, so Kraft's presence was a welcomed breath of fresh air. Kraft was a presence at the facility and practice, and he'd invite players over to dinner, becoming particularly close with Curtis Martin. Kraft was always so easy to get along with because he was approachable and willing to relate to everyone. At the end of a team party, Zolak wanted to bring Kraft to the players' after-party, and it wasn't a hard sell.

"I get in the limo, and Bob Kratch, our guard, was in the limo with us," Zolak said. "It was me, my fiancée, Bob and his wife, a couple other players. I'm like, 'You know what? I like this guy. I'm going to grab the owner.' Bob says, 'You don't have the balls to go ask him.' I guaranteed I'd get him into the limo with us for the party, so I go into his office and I'm like, 'Hey, guys like hanging out with you. Come to the party.' It blew him away like, 'Are you serious?' I'm like, 'Yeah, damn right I'm serious.' He says, 'Hang on, let me call and ask permission.' Myra says yeah, and he opens up this drawer with the Johnny Walker good stuff, the expensive one. I remember opening the door and seeing Bob Kratch's face, and he looked like he was going to piss his pants because I had Robert with me. We went to the party and had a good time."

Zolak had another great story that detailed his relationship with Kraft. Bill Parcells had been giving Zolak a hard time over the final year of his contract, but Zolak and Kraft orchestrated a new deal at Drew Bledsoe's wedding in May 1996 in Portland, Oregon.

"We're having a good time," Zolak said. "My final year was coming up on my contract, and I was slated to make $850,000. I remember the way that year ended, Parcells was like, 'Honey, you better find another position where you can contribute because I can't pay you $850,000 to be the backup.' I didn't want to redo my deal, and he was already bringing in other guys like Jay Walker and Jay Barker, and I kept beating them out. We'd go back and forth like that, but it was fun. He was always like. 'That's good, that's good, but don't ever get comfortable.'

"So I'm out there at Drew's wedding, and Robert is there and Robert is like, 'Look, he is pushing me to bring in another guy. You're obviously at this number. Obviously, we all understand we need to get it done.' We're at the bar. Robert is eating peanuts out of a jar. Robert takes a cocktail napkin and says, 'Okay, you've got one year left at this number. Here are three more years at these numbers. I'm going to put an X here and a line there. You sign that. I initial it. You got the extension done.' Boom, I did it right there. I actually had a couple drinks and probably should have negotiated for a little bit more. So Robert and I got the deal done at Drew's wedding at the bar at the reception. I just remember seeing Parcells' face when we got back home like, 'You son of a bitch. Okay, glad we took care of it, though. Let's get going.' That was a cool moment."

On a far greater scope, Kraft has handled more recent negotiations. He has a strong rapport with Brady, and the two breezed through a two-year, $41 million extension through the 2019 season. It basically happened in one casual conversation early in the 2016 offseason, as they figured out the numbers and then shuffled the deal over to the lawyers. In 2015, Devin McCourty was hours away from becoming a free agent and had offers from a few teams, including one that was ready to make him the highest-paid safety in NFL history. Kraft called McCourty to increase the Patriots' offer and express his desire to keep him in town, and McCourty agreed to the terms.

Over the years, Kraft did have to learn on the job, and his most famous firsthand lesson came with Parcells, who had been hired in 1993 by Orthwein. The powerful head coach drew a throng of attention to their spat by saying Kraft wanted him to cook the dinner without shopping for the groceries, and Parcells' departure for the New York Jets was the ultimate betrayal. From Kraft's perspective, it was frustrating that Parcells had a five-year contract but told him that he'd decide his own future after each season. So it was difficult for Kraft to want to give Parcells complete authority over the roster. Because if and when Parcells left, the roster and its financial implications would be someone else's problem.

"Look, I had all this debt. I owed all this money," Kraft said. "And I thought I had a coach with a five-year contract, which I did, but he coached year to year. He told me he'd decide at the end of the year. After the year, the New York Jets hired him away when he was still under contract to us. It was hard for me to let a man make strategic decisions. The salary cap came in 1994, and a guy like Parcells could just get people they wanted under the old system, no free agency, could spend whatever they wanted.

"He had freedom, but if he was going to leave, had signed some people who were maybe his favorites but their best years of their career were beyond. I realized I needed a better check and balance. It was great having Parcells. He brought such credibility, and he was a fun guy to be around. But I also learned what division from within an organization, how it could be dysfunctional. I probably went overboard with Pete Carroll with checks and balances in a way that hurt him. I think I understood I needed a guy that I could connect with, that I had respect for their intellect financially, as well as football-wise."

Kraft was drawn to Bill Belichick in 1996 when he was an assistant coach with the Patriots, so Belichick was easily Kraft's preferred target after firing Carroll. Kraft was strongly advised against hiring Belichick by NFL and network executives who went so far as to send tapes of the coach's lifeless news conferences during his five-year stint with the Cleveland Browns. Like Kraft's instincts to follow his gut with the paper mill in Newfoundland and the extra $50 million splurge to buy the Patriots, Kraft wanted Belichick and wasn't deterred by others' objections.

"I felt a connection with him, and I watched what he did at the Jets," Belichick said. "I knew Parcells and I knew him, so I knew they were pretty good. If I've made any good decisions in life, they're my instinct and what my nose tells me. I still felt it was right for me and I could work with him."

Kraft's impact has been felt league-wide as well. He recently helped Raiders owner Mark Davis with their relocation to Las Vegas and played a key role in the decision to bring Super Bowl 50 to New York/New Jersey. Kraft has also served as the chair of the broadcast committee for more than 15 years, and that has helped the league generate 60 percent of its revenue.

At the height of Kraft's accomplishments on a league scale, he has taken pride in resolving the lockout in 2011 because Myra wanted him to make it happen. Myra was in intensive care in her last days with ovarian cancer when Kraft was called back to the negotiating table with the NFLPA and the league. NFLPA representative and Indianapolis Colts center Jeff Saturday credited Kraft shortly thereafter as "the man who helped us save football."

With his on-field product, Kraft's legacy is secure, and it came with a plan. The Patriots launched their dynasty with remarkable stability at head coach and quarterback. They obviously lucked into Brady, the 199th pick of the 2000 draft, but there's never been any semblance of a contract dispute between Brady and the front office. The extensions have a history of getting done with about two years remaining on the term, and that's hardly always the case for big-money quarterbacks in the modern era. It harkens back to memories of the Boston Lobsters, who experienced more success after Kraft hired the right coach and acquired a star.

"How blessed am I to have a guy like that as the face of the franchise?" Kraft said of Brady. "I tell people this all the time, he's a physically handsome guy. But as handsome as he is, he's more special in terms of being a genuine person who is nice and caring. Otherwise, how would he have the respect in the locker room, the huddle, the community? When I've been through tough periods of my life, especially the time of my wife's passing, he was just tremendous. I'm going, 'How lucky am I to have this guy who is like a fifth son?' He's the first quarterback to win five Super Bowls. And in the salary cap era.

"And he's just an awesome person, and he happens to live down the street from me. I've watched him grow, when he was that beanpole skinny kid coming down the steps of the old stadium introducing himself to winning the first Super Bowl after 9/11 to becoming a super celebrity, but still remaining a wonderful, humble, caring person, and someone I have great affection and love for, really, separate from what he does on the football field.

"In life, picking good people and continuity, sort of like a marriage—marriage is tough but you try to get through the tough times and build on it. Think about having the same head coach. This is his 18th season. I'm in my 24th season. I've hired two head coaches and had two quarterbacks start the season. If you go in our division and look at how many coaches and starting quarterbacks, that doesn't happen by accident. It's work, and tough things happen. And you have to quietly work to try to make it happen. Winning football games and championships is my dream and passion. It's not going to happen by remote control. You've got to work and do things."

Kraft has put in a lifetime of that work, and he earned the right to make the series of bold decisions that crafted his empire. He not only saved a franchise that was a signature away from moving to St. Louis. He then took the Patriots and helped guide them to a historical level of dominance.

CHAPTER 6
BILL BELICHICK: UNDER THE HOOD

New England Patriots owner Robert Kraft allowed Bill Belichick to leave once. But after firing Pete Carroll following the 1999 season, Kraft had no intention of repeating his mistake with Belichick. Kraft weathered a Category 5 hurricane to reel in Belichick because the owner firmly believed he'd be the right coach to take the franchise back to the Super Bowl.

Belichick had only spent one season with the Patriots prior to his hiring in 2000. He was Bill Parcells' assistant head coach and secondary coach for the 1996 team, and Belichick left a slew of positive impressions with so many people in the building. But when Parcells controversially burned Kraft and the organization by quitting after Super Bowl XXXI, skipping the team flight home to Foxboro and agreeing to take over for the New York Jets, Kraft understandably decided to wash his hands of all Parcells-related employees. Parcells even recommended that Kraft hire Belichick as his replacement in 1997, and the Patriots' defensive backfield universally praised Belichick during routine exit interviews after the Super Bowl defeat. It all reinforced Kraft's feelings toward Belichick, but the Parcells exit would had been too fresh, too close in the near future and Belichick's presence would act as a reminder of Parcells' stunning fallout. So Kraft hired Carroll as an about-face in both system and culture.

"I thought very seriously in '96 when [Parcells] left to hire [Belichick]," Kraft said. "But it had been such a strange experience with Parcells that I just didn't want anyone who had ties to him. I hired Pete, and Pete was good, a completely different style. I just decided I wanted to make a change."

Kraft was ready to make it right in 2000, but it took a serious amount of effort and perseverance. The process began south down I-95 where Belichick was tabbed as Parcells' successor with the Jets, but Belichick notoriously resigned "as HC of the NYJ" with a quick script on a sheet of paper. Belichick always took a measured approach while scanning for head coaching jobs, even turning down opportunities that weren't the right fit in the late 1980s when he was with the New York Giants, and he recognized his second gig might also be his last. The Jets were dealing with an impending sale in 2000, several months after the death of Leon Hess, and Belichick's tenure with the Cleveland Browns was sabotaged five years earlier because owner Art Modell relocated to Baltimore and hung Belichick out to dry during an impossible coaching situation.

So with Belichick there for the taking, Kraft tried to pounce. It just wasn't going to be a straightforward hiring process, because the Jets didn't want to release Belichick from his contract to become the coach of a division rival, especially three years after the Patriots demanded compensation from the Jets for Parcells under similar circumstances. But after a three-week back-and-forth between the Patriots and Jets, whose pushback was led by Parcells, the rivals reached an agreement and NFL commissioner Paul Tagliabue greenlighted the hiring. Kraft got his man, and the Patriots yielded their first-round pick to the Jets in the 2000 draft.

"I was patient and waited for him," Kraft said.

Kraft didn't just go to battle with the Jets, though. He dealt with critics from the NFL office and media outlets that tried to dissuade Kraft from bringing Belichick to New England. The league wanted the Boston market to boom, and it said Belichick didn't have the personality to make it happen. The television stations said Belichick was a "disaster" of an interview and provided tapes of his Cleveland news conferences as examples. But Belichick's dryness wasn't off-putting to Kraft, who cared far more about Belichick's mind as a football coach and front-office leader, which was of growing importance in the salary cap era.

Kraft was smart enough to recognize the attention would come along with a winning football program. Some coaches like Mike Ditka and Jimmy Johnson brought the spotlight with them regardless of the results, but no one would ignore the Patriots if they were consistently victorious, regardless of the man in charge on the sidelines. It turned out to be excellent foresight on Kraft's part. Heck, when the Patriots went 5–11 during Belichick's first season in 2000, Belichick's staunchest critics continued to hound Kraft about their belief in his mistaken hiring.

"Very prominent people at the league office advised me against [hiring Belichick] because they wanted this market to come around and be strong," Kraft said. "Thank goodness I listened to my own instincts. Most things I do in life, I try to do my homework and make sure it's right for me and then have long-term continuity. I look for stability, and I think you need to give someone two years, if not three years, if you believe in them. For me, it was always a two- or three-year window. You look at what goes on in the NFL, and people are changing constantly."

Kraft's patience and faith in Belichick, through multiple episodes, has had historic implications. Belichick became the first head coach to win five Super Bowls when the Patriots defeated the Atlanta Falcons at the conclusion of the 2016 season, and he has compiled an exhaustive list of records that will eventually be documented beside his name at the Pro Football Hall of Fame in Canton, Ohio. Also, through the 2016 season, Belichick had the fourth-most wins in history with a 263–125 record, including his playoff successes.

There's little doubt he'd quickly surpass Tom Landry's 270 wins for third all-time, and Belichick's ability to climb further up the list will essentially be determined by his health and desire to remain in the business. The Patriots averaged an astounding 13.8 victories per season, including the playoffs, from 2001 to '16. If they continued to average 13 wins per year, Belichick would surpass Halas in 2021 and Shula in 2023, when Belichick would be 71 years old.

But to understand Belichick's achievements, you've got to understand how he got to this point, how he learned something new at every point of a coaching career that has spanned more than four decades and how there are traces from his style and decisions from every step along the way. There are characteristics from the 1970s that still ring true with his principles today and elements of his game plans from the 1980s that helped jumpstart the Patriots' dynasty under his guidance.

Belichick is a fascinating individual. While it can be argued that he has forgotten more football than anyone else has ever known, there's a counterpoint that he's never forgotten anything at all.

Billy's Breakthrough

Bill Belichick wasn't always Bill Belichick, by reputation or even name. To those who knew him decades earlier, such as Ted Marchibroda, he was more simply "Billy."

Marchibroda's five-year run as the head coach of the Baltimore Colts began in 1975, and he told general manager Joe Thomas that he needed an assistant who could break down film of opposing offenses. Belichick's first job basically resulted out of a favorable coincidence, but he has also never shied away from the importance of using connections as an advantage in any walk of life. Thomas planned to hire his cousin, who ultimately backed out of the job, so Colts special teams coach George Boutselis chipped in with an idea to bring in Belichick for an interview. Boutselis knew Belichick through his father, Steve Belichick, whose name was well-known in the Baltimore area because he was a coach and scout for the Naval Academy. Marchibroda was so smitten with Belichick's interview that he hired the 22-year-old on the spot.

"I decided to hire him because of the fact that I felt like, 'Well, if he runs into any trouble, we have his father as a backup,'" Marchibroda cracked before his death in 2016. "It worked out real well, and I could see and felt when I interviewed him that he was one of those guys that once you gave him an assignment, you didn't see him until he was through. And he pretty much has turned out that way."

It's downright laughable today, but the Colts could only offer Belichick $25 per week. Obviously, Belichick didn't care about his salary. He strictly wanted to break into the NFL after cutting his teeth while working with his father on scouting trips for virtually the entirety of his life. This was Belichick's chance, and he wasn't going to pass it up.

Marchibroda found other ways to compensate Belichick, who was worth spoiling due to his unrelenting work ethic. Although, considering Belichick's meager paychecks, the extra perks were important. Steve Belichick once told Marchibroda that he was still claiming his son as a dependent on his tax returns because Bill Belichick wasn't earning enough in his salary. Marchibroda's friend was a manager at the local Howard Johnson hotel, so he got free rooms in exchange for Colts parking passes. Belichick took advantage of the lodging and drove Marchibroda, Boutselis, and offensive line coach Whitey Dovell to and from practice every day, and it wasn't uncommon for Marchibroda to duke Belichick some extra cash during these rides as a thank-you for the effort. Marchibroda also bought Belichick plenty of his meals, and the younger assistant liked to eat breakfast with the staff, partly because the price was right but mostly as a way to listen to them talk and soak in as much information as possible.

Belichick has famously installed the "do your job" mantra with the Patriots, and he was a living example of that philosophy early in his career. He mastered the film breakdowns, organizing Colts opponents' plays on cards by down, distance, formation, direction, play type, and any other key points that were influential for their game-week preparation. Belichick treated each assignment like it was the most important thing in his life at that moment, as he'd disappear into a room and wouldn't reappear until he was done.

The staff admired Belichick, and the players respected him. If a defensive player's positional coach wasn't around, they'd ask Belichick for pointers. As the 1975 season progressed, Marchibroda gave Belichick more of a role on special teams. Belichick also served as the vaunted turk who had to relay the bad news to players who were about to get cut.

The Colts won two games in 1974, but Marchibroda turned them into a 10–4 squad that ended a three-year playoff drought in 1975. After the season, Belichick asked for a $4,000 salary, and Marchibroda was downtrodden that Thomas inexplicably wouldn't give it to him. So Belichick hopped onboard with the Detroit Lions, who were led by former Navy assistant Rick Forzano. And as a cherry on top, the Lions gave Belichick a $10,000 salary.

"I don't think there's ever been a coach that got $25 a week, but this was what the Colts would pay him," Marchibroda said. "I'm very happy for him and very proud of the guy. To me, a guy like Billy deserves it. He has worked for it and has earned every bit of it."

Laying the Groundwork

Belichick has always reflected fondly on his ability to coach the offense as a Lions assistant because it was his lone chance to immerse himself on a different side of the ball and analyze how the other half views play construction, strategy, and things of the like.

But the two-year tenure wasn't successful from a team perspective, as Forzano resigned after a 1–3 start in 1976. Tommy Hudspeth shuffled Belichick to tight ends coach in 1977, but the entire staff was fired after that season. Belichick then hooked on with head coach Red Miller's Denver Broncos in 1978.

This was another pivotal stepping stone for Belichick, who worked as an assistant on defense and special teams. The eye-opening element was the opportunity to learn under defensive coordinator Joe Collier, the architect of the Orange Crush defense. Collier deployed a 3–4 system, which was a rarity at the time, and although it didn't come close to resembling Belichick's 3–4 models, it at least afforded Belichick a chance to study a new philosophy. As a reference point, Collier's 3–4 system yielded a revolving door of defensive fronts and they rarely changed their coverage patterns. But with few exceptions over the years, Belichick's fronts remained standard while he mixed up coverages seemingly on a play-by-play basis.

"I think he at least picked up a lot of good ideas from the 3–4 techniques that the linemen and linebackers have to use," Collier said. "It was a good beginning for him, and I think probably some of it stuck with him."

But again, Belichick was onboard with the Broncos to break down film of their opponents' offenses. Collier could frequently see the wheels spinning in Belichick's head when the coaches mapped out each game plan, but Belichick didn't have a say in those matters so he kept his mouth shut. Belichick's bosses recognized that he could probably chip in with some thoughts, but they respected his appreciation for his job description and the hierarchy in the room.

"He was a grinder, and that's what you have to be, particularly in your early years as far as coaching," Collier said. "You've got to be a grinder and you've got to listen to other people and talk to coaches from other teams and that type of stuff. It takes you a number of years before you feel confident in doing your own thing.

"He didn't contribute a hell of a lot because he had only been in the league a couple years at that time. I was impressed with him as a young guy who was interested in learning as much as he could, and he learned it pretty fast. He was a sponge. Just about everything we were doing at that time, he soaked up pretty good."

While on the field at practice, Belichick's primary responsibilities were to assist with the defensive backs, and he also had a voice during special teams drills. More than anything, Belichick was there to learn, and he happily worked long days with the rest of the staff. Miller never had to worry about Belichick's commitment because he was so obviously the son of a coach whose entire life revolved around his job. First in, last out, enjoyed the work and all that stuff.

Plus, as the technology in the game evolved in the 2000s, Belichick could still hang on to that old-school immersion into the exhaustive nature of logging film breakdowns. Those systems have all become computerized to the point where they are so absurdly easy to use, especially with the detailed filters. And Belichick finally gave into the technology in the mid-2000s after hiring a literal rocket scientist in Matt Patricia as a low-level, computer-savvy assistant coach. But before Belichick caught up to the digital age, he put in the work that helped him appreciate certain elements of these breakdowns. (And if Patricia's engineering background wasn't enough to impress Belichick, his ability to update the clock in Belichick's car due to Daylight Saving Time surely did.) Collier preferred his staff to log film together, and Belichick was responsible for tracking it in those meetings.

"I always felt doing the individual breakdown of film was the best way for a coach to prepare for the game planning because you see all that stuff and you're not just reading it off a computer or off a list," Collier said. "So breaking down film yourself as a coach is much better than having somebody else do it. Him doing that film breakdown, he was not only learning schemes from us, but he was learning schemes from other teams that he was watching, too, at the same time. If you see something good that another team is using, it automatically clicks in and you say, 'Hey, that looks like a pretty good idea.' It's a learning process and getting yourself ready to do game plans.

"You've got to write stuff down in those days. You had to say, all right, it's first-and-10 on the 20-yard line, and this is the formation on this hash mark and the score. You write that stuff down and note off to the side, 'This play is going to be a play that we better practice against.' As you go through it, that to me is the value of breaking down the film yourself as a coach."

And maybe not to the extent of Ted Marchibroda with the Baltimore Colts, but Collier and the Broncos' staff tried to take care of Belichick from a financial perspective as much as possible. Sure, Belichick was probably thrilled to be making a five-figure salary just a few years after his father was still claiming him on his tax returns, but coaches can't exactly pay for meals with defensive flip cards. Collier's group would go out for dinner from time to time, and the defensive coaches would take turns paying for the table. Belichick usually looked a little queasy when he figured it was his turn to take care of the bill.

"When it came around to his turn, I could just see him cringing when it came time to pay the tab," Collier said with a laugh. "I think we all pitched in for that dinner because he wasn't making a very good salary. He was probably just scraping by. I remember when we were at dinner, I could just see him worried, and I don't think he enjoyed that dinner when he thought about paying for it."

Giant Step

The historic unification between Bill Belichick and Bill Parcells was actually sparked by a chance encounter in the early 1970s. Parcells went way back with Belichick's father, Steve, because the two worked for rival service academies, with Steve Belichick at Navy and Parcells working for Army in the late 1960s. In that era, it was standard for the service academies to split up their scouting responsibilities by sharing game film of their opponents. So that's where Parcells and the elder Belichick initially crossed paths.

Parcells later joined Vanderbilt as the linebackers coach from 1973 to '74, and the Commodores had Army on the schedule. Coincidentally, Steve Belichick was recruiting the game and, like so many times before, had brought Bill with him, which led to the introduction. Parcells and Bill Belichick launched their professional relationship together in 1979 when Ray Perkins was hired to take over the New York Giants. He landed Belichick as a special teams coach and defensive assistant and Parcells as his defensive coordinator, if only for a short time before Parcells' surprising resignation.

In a way, Parcells' departure had an instrumental impact on the pair's coaching style. He temporarily left the NFL for a business venture that ultimately drove him crazy and led to his return to the league in 1980 when he became the linebackers coach for the New England Patriots. Head coach Ron Erhardt's defensive coordinator was Fritz Shurmur, and Parcells was drawn to his system. He brought it to the Giants during his return as defensive coordinator in 1981.

Belichick spent his first half dozen seasons in the NFL cultivating his identity, emulating his father's work ethic while picking out some of his favorite ideas from coaches like Marchibroda and Collier and even opponents who provided unique challenges. Belichick's confidence was growing, and that momentum sprung in 1976 when his Lions were getting set to host a loaded Patriots team. The previous season, Belichick recognized the Patriots defense struggled with a two-tight end package, so Belichick pitched an idea to Tommy Hudspeth's offensive staff to unveil a formation they hadn't ever used. It worked in dominating fashion, as the Lions won 30–10, tight ends David Hill and Charlie Sanders combined for three touchdown receptions, and running backs Horace King and Dexter Bussey totaled 187 yards and a score on the ground behind the heavy formations. Quarterback Greg Landry's 83.3 completion percentage was the highest of his career in a wire-to-wire start, and his 140.0 passer rating was the second-best mark of his 17-year career. For a Lions team that lost its head coach a week earlier and finished 6–8, that level of offensive success was comical, and Belichick realized that day he could make it as a coach in this league.

Belichick grew more confident with his ability under Parcells, who asked Perkins to give his understudy more defensive responsibilities over time. Parcells appreciated Belichick's special teams work as much as anyone, but he knew Belichick would be an asset on defense.

"That's how he really started with the defense," Parcells said. "He had been around some good defensive coaches in Denver with Joe Collier, so he had his identity. Being the son of a coach, of course, that's a very, very good pedigree. He's lived the life. He's seen it. He's seen the ups and downs, those kinds of things. He's bright. We just went from there. He just went on and did a great job for me all the time he was with me."

Parcells took over as the Giants head coach in 1983, but interestingly, he left the defensive coordinator title vacant until he promoted Belichick in 1985. That's a similar tactic Belichick has used with the Patriots at both coordinator spots. Offensive coordinator Charlie Weis departed New England for Notre Dame following the 2004 season, and Josh McDaniels had play-calling responsibilities in 2005 before his promotion in 2006. McDaniels was hired as the head coach of the Broncos in 2009, and Bill O'Brien was the play caller in 2009 and 2010 until his own promotion to offensive coordinator in 2011.

And when the Patriots split with Dean Pees following the 2009 season, Belichick was the de facto defensive coordinator for two seasons before Matt Patricia earned the bump in pay in 2012. That was the most notable example of the three, because Patricia was viewed by outsiders as the defensive coordinator in 2011, but the players recognized Belichick to be the boss that season. Regardless, with McDaniels, O'Brien, and Patricia, the delayed promotions were part of the learning curve, as well as a way to dangle a carrot in front of them to earn it, and it can be traced back to Belichick's stint with Parcells' Giants.

"Parcells was demanding on everybody, all the coaches, and I think that's the thing that he treated everybody basically the same as far as the coaching went," said Romeo Crennel, who was the Giants special teams coach under Parcells and later won three Super Bowls with the Patriots from 2001 to '04. "He put pressure on you to perform and get your guys to perform, and I think we all learned from that. But as Parcells gave Bill more responsibility, he saw that Bill was able to handle that responsibility. So as a result, the relationship grew, and the defense grew and got better. I think sometimes in the NFL, when you're the head coach, giving responsibility to a young coach gets to be difficult. But like Parcells said, he was able to give him the opportunity to be in front of the defense even though he didn't have the title. But then he saw that he could handle that responsibility. He could run the defense. Then he gave him the title, and he was able to take it and build on it."

Belichick's meticulous notetaking transcended the chalk on the field, too. Giants assistant coaches shared an office, and Crennel was amazed by the way Belichick scoured the league's transaction wire. Belichick tracked every personnel move in a notebook, including draft picks and veteran movement. Of course, that was a practical practice for scouting purposes, but Belichick's peers also recognized his long-term view. He was in a way preparing to lead an organization down the line.

"He was concerned about his job, but he was also concerned about the league and what was going on in the NFL, how other teams were conducting business, evaluating talent and acquiring talent," Crennel said. "He was keeping up with every team in the league at that time, even at a young age. He had his book on every team, who they added to their team, who they were removing from their team. He had an overall view of the whole league. That was one of the things I noticed about him that bode well for him over the years."

Belichick was also respected for his willingness to teach and delegate. He shared special teams responsibilities with Crennel from 1981 to '84, but Belichick was clearly the boss in the kicking game. He wasn't the type to monopolize the duties or information, though, and that helped his fellow assistants stay involved, even while Parcells continued to increase his responsibilities. Decades later, Crennel could still recall a time when he called a punt rush that wasn't supposed to be in the game plan for that particular situation. Belichick questioned Crennel's decision by asking Crennel to unveil his intended strategy, and then Belichick closed the conversation by relaying the importance to follow the game plan. Crennel has always appreciated the way Belichick has refused to blow up on his coaches on the sidelines, and that professional dialogue has been reciprocated in the process.

Belichick cultivated his reputation on defense, though. During his six seasons as the defensive coordinator, the Giants surrendered the third-fewest points in the NFL (16.8 points per game, about a half point more than the league-leading Bears). The Giants ranked fifth in points allowed in 1985, second in 1986 when they won Super Bowl XXI, 13th in 1987, ninth in 1988, second in 1989, and first in 1990 when they won Super Bowl XXV.

Parcells undoubtedly had a hand in the defensive system, but it was Belichick's group.

"I tried to let my coaches coach," Parcells said. "Now the basic philosophy that we used on defense there was my defense that I had brought from the time I was an assistant at New England and had learned from Fritz Shurmur and Ron Erhardt when I was an assistant there. But Bill put his own ideas in it and refined it, and we kind of modernized some of the coverages a little bit as we went. As anything cyclical is in football, there are always little tweaks and additions every year, but we always had the basis of conversation because the fundamental structure of the defense never changed. We always were able to, and this is much to his credit, just go forward with what we thought was necessary at the time, and he did a great job with it."

Belichick took a calculated approach to his future in the NFL, and he was ahead of his time in that regard, too. Nowadays, coaches jump at the first opportunity to become a head coach, and their short-sightedness typically results in their demise. Belichick was courted by teams in the late 1980s, but those openings didn't present the right fit and Belichick had other business to tend to before venturing away from the Giants.

During his first four years as defensive coordinator, Belichick still had an emphasis on leading the linebackers, which made sense considering the Giants had superstars like Lawrence Taylor and Carl Banks. In 1989, though, Belichick asked Parcells if he could switch his focus to the secondary. First, it gave Belichick a chance to spend additional time with a new position group. Second, and more importantly, a defensive coordinator's greatest concern is the performance of his defensive backfield, so Belichick wanted to harness additional control over the back end of the defense. Belichick could try out some new coverages at the same time to test out how specific disguises aligned, for better or worse, with the Giants' variations of the 3–4 and 4–3 fronts.

"Just as he's done with everything else, he became the best secondary coach I've ever been around," Al Groh said.

Groh viewed himself as the chief beneficiary of Belichick's slide to the defensive backfield. As a result, Parcells hired his long-time friend to coach the linebackers. Groh was a football junkie, so he was doing cartwheels over the big break to take over a positional group that had previously been led by a pair of football geniuses. Groh said he was going to football school, and he was ready to get a Master's degree.

"I wanted to find out everything I could about the reads, the techniques, the personalities," said Groh, whose transition was also aided by his time with Taylor at the University of North Carolina. "But in front of both of us, as far as the linebackers coach, had been Parcells. So here was Parcells who had been the linebacker coach and passed all that on to Bill Belichick, who was then passing it on to me. Let's say I was in a pretty fortunate position to be able to get a significant amount of input from those two guys."

Belichick was developing his reputation as a coach with an assembly line of defensive packages, as he believed it was vital to be game-plan oriented on a weekly basis. He knew within the basic structure of their philosophy, the Giants needed to be able to play the type of game that was necessary to beat each particular opponent. Every offense presents different challenges based on talent disparity or particular strengths at certain positions, and Belichick relished the chess matches. He wouldn't have the same game plan for a run-heavy team a week after lining up against a big-time aerial assault. Remember, that was during a time when most offenses fielded two receivers, one tight end, a running back, and a fullback, so defensive coaches often stubbornly kept their base units on the field from start to finish. The idea? They'd do what they do and go down with their guys.

But Belichick didn't see the point in the regimented paint-by-numbers approach, and there was no greater example than his final three-game masterpiece with the Giants.

"At the heart of it all was Bill Belichick," Groh said.

Three Games to Glory

The 1990 New York Giants won 13 games and were the NFC's second seed in the playoffs, and they faced a treacherous path to Super Bowl XXV. Bill Belichick's defense generally deployed a 3–4 front and used zone coverages on the back end, but Belichick turned Big Blue into a chameleon during their postseason march.

They hosted the Chicago Bears in the divisional round, and the visitors led the league in rushing attempts and had to roll with backup quarterback Mike Tomczak due to starter Jim Harbaugh's shoulder injury. Pretty straightforward from there, as the Giants uncorked an eight-man box that included some six-man fronts that still utilized 3–4 techniques. The Giants dominated by a 31–3 count, and the Bears were stuck in the mud with 27 rushing yards.

The Giants visited the top-seeded San Francisco 49ers next in the NFC Championship Game, and quarterback Joe Montana and wide receiver Jerry Rice led a brilliant West Coast offensive passing attack. Belichick got a read on them during a 7–3 loss in Week 13, but it was still going to take an incredible effort. So the Giants implemented a nickel package with a defensive back replacing a linebacker, and Belichick called an uptick in man coverages to take away the short, easy completions as much as possible. The Giants squeaked out a 15–13 victory.

Belichick orchestrated the implementation of these wrinkled game plans, but he also solicited the input of every coach in the room. His trust in their ideas aided the excitement level to deploy the new strategies, and that was important. Comparably, it's like trying to learn a new language when the teacher hands out a different textbook every week. And these two victories merely set the stage for a victorious game plan against the Buffalo Bills that resides in the Pro Football Hall of Fame.

"We played an entirely different defensive scheme in each one of those games because of the different circumstances that they presented us," Al Groh said. "It all was Bill Belichick thinking about it and bringing it to the table and saying to the rest of the defensive coaches, 'What do you guys think?' From that might come an idea or two that would enhance it, but he was the father of the idea to do those three different schemes. We had good defensive games. I know we couldn't have beaten San Francisco with the Chicago plan, and I know we couldn't have beaten Buffalo with the San Francisco plan.

"Extraordinarily thorough, extremely well-thought out, he had a plan for everything. Bill knew a whole lot more about the defense than I certainly did and probably anybody else who was in that room, and most likely could have done the whole thing by himself. He knew what he wanted to get done, but he was always very willing to sit there and solicit any input from anybody else or patiently listen to what anybody else might have to offer even though he might have already had his plan in mind. That was one of the things that I learned as a coach from Bill. It wasn't just about strategy and tactics. The value was of being a very good listener."

The greatest trick the mad scientist ever pulled was convincing the Bills that his type of game plan could never exist. Quarterback Jim Kelly operated the K-Gun offense that scored the most points in the league (26.8 per game) and spread out three receivers with a fair amount of frequency, and this was about a decade and a half before the rest of the league almost universally adopted three-receiver sets. They were fast. They didn't like to huddle. And they had a running back in Thurman Thomas who complemented the passing assault.

If the Bills prepared for the Super Bowl by studying the Giants' previous playoff games, they wasted their time. And like the 49ers a week before, Belichick had a chance to draw upon an experience from earlier in the season, as the Bills topped them 17–13 in Week 15.

The Giants' game plan was a masterpiece, especially considering it had to be installed without the traditional bye week before the Super Bowl. They used a 3–2–6 scheme (three defensive linemen, two linebackers, and six defensive backs) and constantly mixed up their zone coverages to force Kelly to think as much as possible before and after the snap. Linebacker Lawrence Taylor became the right defensive end with his hand in the dirt, and Carl Banks and Pepper Johnson remained in the second level as inside linebackers. They were flanked by a pair of safeties who acted as outside linebackers to increase their speed in coverage and mitigate the matchup disadvantages.

It also enticed the Bills to call more runs for Thomas, which the Giants hoped would slow down the game. Thomas was actually outstanding with 15 carries for 135 yards and a touchdown to go along with five catches for 15 yards, but that in a way played into the Giants' hands because Kelly wasn't chucking it all over Tampa Stadium.

"We played the game we needed to play, and that can be uncomfortable for coaches and players who would just like to walk into the first meeting of the week every week and just say, 'Oh sure let's just do what we did last week,'" Groh said. "It challenges everybody mentally to really bear down. We had multiple ways we were going to play them, but our core look was an odd-man front. We wanted to get speed on the field, but they were a very good running team with Thurman Thomas. But their big point production was coming out of the passing game, one of those big players being Andre Reed at wide receiver. The more yards they ran for, the better for us.

"You have to play strategy. There's an excitement about it because you know you're on the right track. You think you had the best solution, the best plan in order to get the best results against this team because it's not a carbon copy defense every week, pulling out the plan from last week. Until coaching and player-wise you've got it all down to your satisfaction, sure, there's a little bit of stress involved in it until you get it down. But once you get it down, I think there is a comfort level of, 'This is a little more challenging to get this put together, but this is the right way to go after these guys, and now we've got the best chance.'"

Bill Parcells also preached the importance of complementary football, as the 6.5-point underdogs absolutely must control the clock to give the defense a chance. Running back Ottis Anderson ran 21 times for 102 yards and a touchdown, and the Giants had the ball for an absurd 40 minutes and 33 seconds during the 20–19 shocker, which was famously capped by kicker Scott Norwood's 47-yard miss to the right in the final seconds.

"Just managed to pull it out," Parcells said. "It was just a perfect example of complementary football. "That was our way of trying to limit Buffalo's offense. It was two aspects to it. I think we had a good defensive plan that was a little different, but it was tested because that was a close game and they didn't have nearly as many opportunities as we had.

"I'm a big complementary guy. I think the whole team has to know how we're going to try to play the game. So I don't think it's, 'Okay, well this is the defensive plan and this is the offensive plan.' That's not how I would basically look at my opponent. I would look at my opponent and go, 'Okay, what appears to be their weaknesses, and how can we exploit those? And how can the two units, offense and defense, complement each other in such a way that it's effective for both?'"

If that sounds similar to the way Belichick's Patriots unraveled the St. Louis Rams in Super Bowl XXXVI, well, it should. But at this point, in the aftermath of the Giants' Super Bowl XXV victory, Belichick was still a decade shy of launching his dynasty. And he needed to learn some hard lessons in Cleveland before he'd reach that point in his career.

Dawg Pounding

The results of Bill Belichick's five-year tenure with the Cleveland Browns can be argued in a neverending circular fashion. He took over a locker room that spiraled out of control under head coach Bud Carson, who was fired midway through his second season in 1990 when the Browns finished 3–13. And Belichick led the Browns to six wins in 1991, seven wins in both 1992 and 1993, and then an 11–5 march in 1994 that yielded the franchise's first playoff victory in five years. The Browns restored a blue-collar toughness that made their roster relatable to the fan base, boasted the NFL's top-ranked scoring defense (12.8 points per game), and possessed enough young blood to really launch something special.

The Browns opened with a 3–1 record in 1995 before players started to question the direction of the franchise due to a smattering of whispers, and they were 4–4 when owner Art Modell officially announced they'd relocate to Baltimore for the 1996 season. It was an unprecedented move with an owner hanging a franchise and its fan base out to dry like that in the middle of a season, and the Browns went in the tank. They lost seven of their final eight games to close down the season with a 5–11 record, as the players felt betrayed and mailed it in for the rest of the season.

Modell essentially turned Belichick into the scapegoat by firing him, but Belichick's locker room wasn't willing to throw him under the bus. Look, Belichick wasn't perfect in Cleveland by any stretch of the imagination, but he dealt with an impossible situation due to the move.

"I don't think he got, I know—K-N-O-W—that he got the appreciation of the job that he had to do when the move was announced," said Ozzie Newsome, who has been with the Browns and Ravens since 1978 as a player and executive. "To be able to get that team to finish that season, never in the history of sports, because he and I looked for something to [compare to it] during the season. To be able to get that team to be able to compete and play for the remainder of the season, I don't think you can put a measure on how tough that was."

Belichick even accidentally bestowed a parting gift to the franchise that, ironically, voyaged to his homeland of Baltimore without him. Belichick traded the 10th overall pick of the 1995 draft to the San Francisco 49ers, who so desperately wanted wide receiver

J.J. Stokes that they included a first-round pick in 1996 as part of the four-pick package that went to Cleveland. The following year, the Ravens used that selection on linebacker Ray Lewis, who joined fellow first-round pick and left tackle Jonathan Ogden as one of the great one-two combinations in draft history.

(So here's a bizarre coincidence. In the 1990s, it was argued Belichick wouldn't have drafted Lewis because he was too small to fit his system as a prototypical inside linebacker. Lewis was 6'1" and 245 pounds. Then, during the 2007 draft, Belichick made a comparable trade with the 49ers, who wanted the Patriots' 28th overall pick to select tackle Joe Staley. The Patriots landed a first-rounder in the 2008 draft, which they used as ammunition to trade down three spots to select inside linebacker Jerod Mayo, who was 6'2" and 230 pounds. So the Lewis-was-too-small argument wasn't just ultimately disproven, but it was done so in spookily ironic fashion.)

Belichick's first opportunity as a head coach opened his eyes to the challenges that it's essentially impossible to prepare to face as an assistant. Belichick knew how to command the room, so that wasn't a problem at the start of his tenure, especially considering he was coming off a Herculean defensive effort in the Super Bowl. He had the players' attention because he had a unique ability to relate to them despite not being a player himself.

Newsome had a keen vantage point. The Hall of Fame tight end wrapped up his playing career after the 1990 season. Modell's efforts to talk Newsome out of retirement had fallen flat, but the two worked out an agreement to keep Newsome in the front office. A couple days after Belichick was hired in 1991, he too sat down with Newsome to see if he'd reconsider his decision to step away from the gridiron, and offensive assistant Ernie Adams followed suit with the same effort. Newsome was indeed done, but he appreciated Belichick's pitch and respected his football acumen, partly from the way Belichick schemed up ways to defend him and also because of Belichick's connection to the program at the University of Alabama, where Newsome starred for head coach Bear Bryant in the 1970s. Belichick was most directly connected through Ray Perkins, who hired Belichick with the New York Giants in 1979 and succeeded Bryant in 1983.

Anyway, Newsome was an outstanding player, a no-nonsense guy and a locker-room leader. Even though he stopped playing upon Belichick's arrival, Newsome remained close with the players on the roster. Newsome liked Belichick, so that filtered through the system. Belichick was still demanding of Newsome, though, as the former tight end continued to work out at the Browns' facility before he was scheduled to begin his executive duties in March.

"I thought you were coming to work," Belichick would say throughout February.

At first, Newsome would just volley a puzzled glance in Belichick's direction.

"No, we need to start working," Belichick would continue.

Not before long, it became their running joke. "Hey, when are you coming to work?" They'd say it over and again.

Belichick instantly implemented the structure that had essentially evaporated under Carson, who didn't have the same effect on the room as his predecessor, Marty Schottenheimer. Belichick outlined the practice and workout schedules, preached team over individual, and created an atmosphere that bred accountability. As Newsome found out earlier in the winter, the Browns were there to work, and the players were excited to reciprocate Belichick's eagerness.

"Things got out of hand a bit," Newsome said of the Carson years. "[Belichick] was very demanding on, 'This is the way it is going to be. I'm coming off a Super Bowl. This is what it takes to win Super Bowls.' Nobody had won a Super Bowl in Cleveland.

"Players really loved to play for him because he could explain to them why they were doing what they were doing. And if they made a mistake, he could help them correct it. Everything was black and white. He took the gray out of it, and that's what a player wants to know. They don't want any gray. They want it black and white. He had a working knowledge of former players. He would talk about [former Vikings linebacker] Matt Blair and people like that, that he had a working knowledge of, and it showed he had an appreciation for tradition and the men that have played the game.

"He's very thorough. He is a great listener. He is willing to take a chance. He's not afraid. Those were the things at the outset. And his football IQ is off the charts."

Belichick had credibility, and like his time with Giants assistant coaches, he encouraged a back-and-forth with his players. They liked the fact that their coach was demanding but also accountable in his own right, and there weren't any barriers between the boss and his employees. That sentiment was also relayed back to Newsome.

Belichick adapted well, too. He put his players in positions of strength and didn't try to fit a square game plan into a circular roster, for lack of a better metaphor. Harken back to Alabama, as Bear Bryant used to have quarterbacks Joe Namath and Kenny Stabler throw it all over the yard, but he switched to the wishbone offense later to suit his players' best assets. Miami Dolphins coach Don Shula had a run-heavy offense with backs like Larry Csonka and Jim Kiick, but they aired it out when quarterback Dan Marino arrived.

Fast forward to the 2000s with quarterback Tom Brady, who was responsible with the ball at the start of his career before he transformed into one of the greatest passers in history. To use one example from Belichick's first head coaching gig, he took over the Browns in 1991 when quarterback Bernie Kosar was coming off a 15-interception, three-win season, and the offensive skill pieces around him were largely unspectacular. The Browns didn't do a lot of things well offensively during that 6–10 season, but they had the fewest turnovers and second-fewest interceptions in the NFL. And as a result, the Browns were competitive, as they lost six games by a total of 17 points (all by four points or fewer).

Newsome has since become one of the league's most accomplished general managers, and he learned a ton about roster building from studying Belichick, even during the coach's infant years at the head of a program. First and foremost, the team must draft from the inside out, knowing the roster from within before branching out. That's how Belichick thinks.

"You have to know your team," Newsome said. "You have to know the players, their practice habits. You've got to have more information on your players than anything else, and then you go from that to knowing the league. If you don't really know your team, for me, it's hard to be able to make decisions because you've got to know your players. The other part of it is you having a thorough understanding of what your team is trying to do from a schematic standpoint, offensively, defensively, and special teams, that really helps you to be able to go out and assess talent that you think can be on your ball club.

"If you don't have a thorough understanding of what the defensive linemen are expected to do and the safeties are expected to do and the type of offense you're going to run and what kind of offensive linemen you want, if you don't have a thorough understanding of that, and why, then it makes it doubly difficult to go out there and say, 'I like this player.' But does he fit?"

Belichick's philosophy set the table for the most controversial decision of his five-year tenure, and it alienated him from a good chunk of the fan base. Belichick signed quarterback Vinny Testaverde in 1993 to replace Kosar, who ultimately reclaimed some playing time due to Testaverde's injury woes. Belichick then cut the immensely popular Kosar after the season, and there was no way for anyone in the organization to debate the move. It was definitive. Belichick made the call, and it was time to move on.

A year later, after the Browns won a playoff game, Belichick decided to part ways with defensive lineman Michael Dean Perry, a five-time Pro Bowler and 1989 AFC Defensive Player of the Year who also ingratiated himself with Cleveland sports fans. But Perry wanted to be paid for what he had already done, as opposed to what Belichick thought was in store for his future production. Perry made another Pro Bowl with the Denver Broncos in 1996, but he only played three more seasons.

With Kosar and Perry, Belichick proved he could differentiate personal feelings from business matters. And once those splits were finalized, he had to learn how to deal with a confused locker room. There's no way to replace that type of on-the-job training, and Belichick put it to use a number of times with the

Patriots. Belichick still catches up with Newsome nowadays, and they'll freely discuss the Cleveland days, the good and the bad and how Belichick has put those experiences to use, particularly if he believed he could have handled a transaction a bit differently.

"I think Bill, like most great leaders, learned from his mistakes," Newsome said.

Second Helpings

Bill Belichick was dearly humbled in 1996 when he was fired, leading to his greatest deal of adversity in two decades in the NFL. But Belichick had prepared for the big time since he was watching film with his father while other kids in the neighborhood were infatuated with sandboxes. There was a plan in place, and there's no shame in adjusting the blueprint as long as there's something to be learned along the way.

Bill Parcells brought Belichick back onboard his staff, this time with the New England Patriots as the assistant head coach and defensive backs coach. After his half decade in Cleveland, Belichick's closest peers were impressed with the newfound scope on the game upon their reacquaintance.

"He had a much greater perspective on things," Parcells said. "Once you're a head coach, it's different than being an assistant coach or a position coach or a coordinator. You have a much greater understanding of how things work. I think experience improves us all. You learn some things that were successful for you, and you continue to implement those, and then you correct things that weren't successful for you. We all go through that."

Belichick endured an interesting dynamic. He wasn't the defensive coordinator because that role was occupied by Al Groh, but Belichick had the universal respect of the coaching staff. If Belichick needed to grab someone's ear for a teaching moment, he had the right to do it. Belichick's reputation with these familiar faces provided a lot of leeway. And again, aside from Belichick's intrepid football knowledge, his macro approach in 1996 added a new layer to his teachings.

"The first time somebody becomes the head coach, there's a degree of baptism by fire," Groh said. "Once you prepare yourself for it and have the skills for it, there are a lot of different issues that come across the head coach's desk that have never crossed an assistant coach's desk before, and you learn from those circumstances. But Bill always had a plan. Bill was always in control. Whether it was as the defensive coordinator or as the head coach, it was always a very rewarding time and a very stimulating time because we always seemed to be on the same wavelength the way we saw the game. If Bill brought up an idea, I was either learning from that idea or saying, yeah, that's exactly the way I would see it, too."

Belichick had changed for the better, but he knew he needed to continue to evolve. Even if he got dealt a bad hand in Cleveland, Belichick was self-aware enough to realize he needed to improve. He pulled certain tendencies from each stop, laying them on top of the foundation that was built by his father, and the truest way to become successful with a second head coaching gig would be to learn from the shortcomings of the first.

That was an ongoing process, something that could only come with experience and application. Watch Parcells, interact with players through every circumstance, build up life lessons. And of course, try to forecast what is to come. Belichick's knowledge of the intricacies of the game—how to attack formations and realign philosophies to suit the strength of the players—and evaluation of talent was second to none, and no one could take those qualities away from him. But becoming a head coach and making all the right decisions? That's an impossible task, though the most successful leading figures can find a way to get as close to perfect as possible. Every single coach encounters those hurdles, but they can't appreciate the challenges until it's their ass on the line.

"He experienced what a head coach has to experience because there's no book on being the head coach," Crennel said. "Things happen when you're sitting at that desk that many times change your overall perspective about the game and about a team. I think that's one of the things I noticed after Bill was at Cleveland, and he came back to us at New England. I think he had the big-picture view at that time about the game, about players. When you're an assistant coach, you have your job to do and your little niche, and you concentrate on your niche. But once you've been a head coach, you see the big picture and see how things are impacted by what your guys do and how it impacts the team."

Belichick's new outlook threw off backup quarterback Scott Zolak at one point during practice in 1996. Zolak had never before worked with Belichick, but the quarterback was obviously well-aware of his credentials due to some of the Patriots' run-ins with the Browns. Right away, players knew Belichick had the authority to refine certain elements of the defense, and Groh was more than willing to oblige.

One of Belichick's most notable lessons led to a dose of confusion, which is a bit more comical in hindsight. Zolak ran the scout team every day in practice because Drew Bledsoe was the starting signal caller, and Parcells didn't want anyone to get into any bad habits on the practice field. By definition, Parcells applauded Zolak for not throwing interceptions because those miscues could carry into a game if he were called upon.

But Belichick had a different idea of how the scout team should work. Belichick always held up the cards that detailed the offense's plays, which were there to mimic their upcoming opponent's playbook. But beyond that, Belichick studied the opposing offense's tendencies to gain a better understanding of their best and worst attributes. So the Patriots were preparing for a quarterback who had a track record of forcing the ball into his first read, even if the coverage was overly tight. During a practice period, Belichick ordered the defense to triple cover a scout-team receiver, so Zolak kept checking down to the open receiver on the backside of the field. Zolak's decisions to make the completions were perfectly logical, but at the same time, Belichick was a step ahead of everyone and they weren't even aware of it.

"I remember him getting so pissed off, specifically at me to where he'd pull me out of the huddle and put in Tom Tupa, our punter and third-string quarterback," Zolak said. Bill would scream, 'Throw the ball where I tell you to throw the ball!' And the coverage would be so scripted to where there'd be three guys around the guy where they want me to throw the ball. I wouldn't throw it there. I'd throw it to the open guy on the backside.

"I remember Parcells saying, 'That's it. Don't throw interceptions. Don't get into bad habits.' So I've got one guy in one ear yelling at me to not get into bad habits, and I've got Belichick yelling at me that, 'They're not going to throw the ball there.' Belichick knew what he was doing. It was the attention to detail. He wants the quarterback to read it the way the opponent is going to read it. 'You've got to understand you've got to throw the interception. It's going to help us as a defense.' You didn't understand it at the time as a player because I don't want to be throwing picks every day at practice. But that's the way Bill drew it up."

Belichick followed Parcells to the New York Jets from 1997 to '99, and the pair helped reconstruct a franchise that had fallen to abysmal levels. The Jets were 1–15 in 1996, which was their eighth consecutive season without a winning record, and had the second-worst scoring defense in the NFL. The Jets went 9–7 with the sixth-ranked scoring defense in 1997, 12–4 with the second-ranked scoring defense in 1998, and 8–8 with the ninth-ranked scoring defense in 1999.

Parcells decided to step away from the sidelines after the 1999 season to focus more on front-office responsibilities, and he had worked out a deal with upper management to name Belichick as his successor before one of the most shocking resignations in the history of the sport. Maybe Belichick didn't want to remain in Parcells' shadow. But he definitely didn't want to be stuck in an organization that was in the process of being sold, not after the debacle with the Browns. If circumstances sabotaged Belichick's second coaching gig, he knew there would be a minute chance of landing a third opportunity, so he had to be careful.

Look, the entire staff knew Belichick would be a head coach again. He spent four years working on his weaknesses and wasn't going to leave anything up to chance. Belichick quit his post at the Jets when he was a few months shy of his 48th birthday. Think about that. At that point, he had basically spent 40 years preparing for quite possibly the last big break of his career.

"Bill had a great deal of confidence in himself as a coach," Groh said. "But Bill has always been a guy, whatever level of success he had at various stages of his career, he's also been very focused on his own personal and career development and introspective of, 'What do I have to do to make my team better?' And he was always, 'What do I have to do for myself to make my coaching better?'

"While he was fully immersed with the Jets, he was always in his mind putting together his plan for when he got the next chance, how was he going to go about doing it. Whatever the results were in Cleveland, they were certainly results that were below what he had hoped for in the beginning. So he had assessed then, 'Okay, the next time I get my next chance, what are the things I'm going to change, how can I improve the structure of things, how can I improve myself in this particular role?' He made pretty good use of that time because he had a hell of a plan."

Patriots Dynasty

Weeks after the world survived Y2K, Patriots owner Robert Kraft made it out alive from his contentious negotiations with the New York Jets. Bill Belichick was freed from his contract and found comfort in Kraft's plan. Kraft had always been a likeable guy, so that wasn't a problem. But Belichick also was convinced that Kraft had become a great owner to work for, as he learned from prior mistakes during the Bill Parcells era. In the understatement of the new millennium, they've forged an historically fruitful partnership together.

The success didn't happen overnight, though it seemed to arise from out of nowhere. Belichick lost 13 of his first 18 regular-season games after he was hired as the Patriots head coach in 2000, at first solidifying the smiles of his detractors. The final loss of that stretch, which occurred in Week 2 of the 2001 season against the hated Jets, also cost the Patriots their quarterback, as Drew Bledsoe succumbed to a hit from linebacker Mo Lewis that resulted in a torn blood vessel and internal bleeding. But along came Tom Brady, and the defensive and special teams units provided paramount levels of complementary football.

That example was prevalent in Brady's first career start, in which he merely needed to complete 13 of 23 passes for 168 yards, no touchdowns or interceptions in a resounding 44–13 victory against quarterback Peyton Manning's Indianapolis Colts. (This turned into a pattern, as Brady routinely got the better of Manning and the Patriots usually whooped on the Colts.) But with a team effort, running backs Antowain Smith and Kevin Faulk combined for three rushing touchdowns, and cornerback Ty Law plucked one of the defense's three interceptions.

The following week was noteworthy because the Patriots were roughed up by the Miami Dolphins 30–10. There are so many memories that stick out from 2001, but this loss certainly wasn't one of them. However, it was as necessary to their success as just about any game on the schedule because Belichick created a masterful teaching moment when they fell to a 1–3 record.

The Patriots returned from the road trip and were set to hit the field Monday for conditioning work when Belichick gathered the group for a message. Their curiosity was piqued when they saw Belichick with a shovel, and they were fully invested when he began to dig a hole at the practice field. Belichick took a ball from the game, threw it in the hole, and buried it. His ensuing message was the loss to the Dolphins was in the past. They needed to forget about it and put all of their focus into that week's home game against the San Diego Chargers. It also spawned Belichick's first famous phrase, "One game at a time."

That rallying cry, as dry as it has become, engulfed the locker room and prioritized the concentration Belichick required to buy into the process. At that point, Belichick had a 6–14 record through the first month of his second season. The veterans, who adored Bledsoe, lost their franchise quarterback and locker-room leader for the foreseeable future. And if there was to be any hope, they had to concentrate on the details and not the greater picture.

"In the NFL, if you dwell on things that have happened in the past, you're not able to focus on the job at hand. That's what we were selling them" said Romeo Crennel, who was Belichick's defensive coordinator from 2001 to '04. "I think [burying the football] helped ease some of the tension that all the players have. When you screw up and have concern about your job and all those things, by him digging the hole and putting the ball in and covering it up, I think that eased some of the tension and allowed guys to focus on the next game. So now we could play the next game."

In a sign of things to come, Brady revived the Patriots from a 26–16 fourth-quarter deficit against the Chargers, who entered the game with a 3–1 record, by sparking a 10-point rally in the final four minutes. Adam Vinatieri kicked a 44-yard field goal in overtime for the 29–26 victory. The Patriots evened their record at 3–3 the next week when wide receiver David Patten contributed a touchdown reception, run, and pass on the road with a 38–17 win against the Colts. It was the first memorable example of the Patriots' willingness to have fun on offense due to coordinator

Charlie Weis' creative play designs. (Another occurred in Week 17 when running back Kevin Faulk threw a 23-yard pass to Brady against the Dolphins. It was the only catch of his career until a 36-yarder from slot receiver Danny Amendola in 2015.)

The Patriots boasted a 5–4 record and appeared to be midseason overachievers when they were preparing to host the St. Louis Rams in Week 10 on *Sunday Night Football.* The Rams entered the game with a 7–1 record, and they were embarrassing teams, having already won three games by at least 32 points and another by 20 points. They were a juggernaut two seasons after winning Super Bowl XXXIV, and they escaped Foxboro Stadium with a 24–17 triumph.

It was a moral victory for the Patriots, though. And with the benefit of hindsight, it resembled Belichick's season with the New York Giants in 1990 when they fell to the San Francisco 49ers and Buffalo Bills. All three teams had incredible offenses but scored less than their season averages against Belichick's defenses, and those games showed the players that they could compete with the cream of the crop. With some tweaks to the game plan and better execution, they believed they'd change the outcome in a postseason rematch.

"I don't know that you ever know in a situation like that that your team is going to be a Super Bowl team or Super Bowl champ," Crennel said. "The thing we felt like was after the Rams game that we played them in New England and had one approach to that game and they ended up beating us. After that game, our team started to gain some confidence. They started playing together better. We started getting on a roll and started winning, and winning builds more confidence. Then we started to get on this run that took us through the rest of the season.

"It's an attitude. It's a momentum thing. It's a confidence thing that we were able to develop because guys were buying into the system, and they were able to see the system work. That's one of the big things about dealing with players. If the system works, they buy into it a lot more. When we started winning those games, they really started buying into the system, and it took us to the Super Bowl."

There was some undeniable magic with the 2001 Patriots, and they closed down their championship run with a 20–17 upset of the Rams in Super Bowl XXXVI. The Rams were 14-point favorites, so the Patriots needed an effort that was nothing short of perfect, if not miraculous, to pull off an upset that no one would have predicted.

Look, there was an ever-present "why not?" element that followed the Patriots throughout that season. They got some breaks that helped them earn a first-round bye in the playoffs, which was unfathomable given the nature of a rebuilding process. And Vinatieri booted the Pats past the Oakland Raiders in the divisional round "Snow Bowl," otherwise known as the Tuck Rule game. Then, in the AFC Championship Game, the Pats breezed past the top-seeded Pittsburgh Steelers 24–17, thanks to a 55-yard punt return for a touchdown by Troy Brown, a Bledsoe touchdown pass to Patten, and Antwan Harris' 49-yard touchdown return after Brandon Mitchell's blocked field goal and Brown's heads-up lateral. The Patriots took it personally when the 10-point favorites spent the week discussing their Super Bowl travel arrangements.

But to beat the Rams? Everything had to go right. The credit is deservedly dispersed to dozens, and Belichick's game plan is part of that equation. They had to beat the ever-living hell out of the Rams' skill players, especially running back Marshall Faulk when he escaped the backfield in a passing pattern. There was also some advanced scouting involved, as Belichick factored Rams coach Mike Martz's stubbornness into the mix.

Remember in 1996 when Belichick ordered scout-team quarterback Scott Zolak to throw the ball into triple coverage at practice because that fit the opponent's tendency? Well, this was similar. Martz was infatuated with his creative passing attack, and he deserved to feel that way. But Belichick banked on Martz going overboard, so the Patriots sold out to stop the pass. Years after the Super Bowl XXXVI victory, one Patriots defensive starter was asked how the game would have played out if the Rams just ran the ball with Faulk. "We would have lost by fucking 50," he replied.

Belichick sent his second game plan to the Pro Football Hall of Fame after the Patriots won their first Super Bowl in franchise history. And it's funny, because Belichick knew how to pick apart an opponent's weakness, either on paper or in their mind. He didn't just do it on the football field, either. Crennel likened Belichick's game plans to his prowess in racquetball, and that stemmed back to the 1987 strike year. Talk about success that didn't happen overnight, Belichick had to work at racquetball, too. His immediate boss with the Denver Broncos, defensive coordinator Joe Collier, used to beat Belichick pretty good at racquetball, so Belichick had to find a way to improve.

"The thing Bill was so effective at was exploiting your weakness," Crennel said. "We were playing singles in the racquetball court, and he picks out the weakness, and boom, shot after shot, he goes high to the backhand or low to the backhand. He knows that's a tough shot. When you apply it to game plans for those big games that we won, basically, look at the weakness, look at your strengths, and try to exploit their weakness with your strength. I think in both of those games [Super Bowls XXV and XXXVI], that's what we were able to do. We were able to win those as a result of that."

Even though Belichick had his first Super Bowl at the conclusion of his second season with the Patriots, he has admitted it took upwards of four years to get his system in place. It's unfathomable to him that there are head coaches around the league who get fired after a season or two because it's unrealistic to think those impulsive decisions are good for the organization, whether it's the owner or general manager who is making the call. Similar to the way Pete Carroll was eventually run over by Parcells' players, all head coaches have to bring in their types of players to fit their culture and scheme.

It's crazy because the Patriots got off to a 3–0 start in 2002, but they had some major flaws that were exposed during the 9–7 season. Most notably, they ranked 31st in run defense, and they missed the playoffs for the only time ever with Brady as a fulltime starter. But it all validated the weaknesses that had to be addressed. Belichick had to filter out some of Carroll's guys, and even though he won with some of Parcells' star draft picks, there was a bit of a recommitment to the price they had to pay to win. Belichick isn't an easy coach to play for, so he needs to know which players are onboard and which ones need to be shuttled off campus. It all takes time, and he described the process in 2015 while lamenting the Philadelphia Eagles' decision to fire Chip Kelly in 2015.

"The coach that comes in usually has a different philosophy than the coach that left, so you have to try to implement that philosophy," Belichick said. "That means you're going to turn over a high percentage of the roster because the players that the other coach had don't fit the new philosophy, so a lot of the players are going to have to change in part because of the philosophy and probably in part because of the scheme. Those role-type players, now that role is not needed in the new scheme and a different role is needed, so you get different players.

"And then just getting your team acclimated to doing things the way that the philosophy of the new program. You're going to have to go through a lot of tough situations, tough games, tough losses, tough stretches in the season, whatever it happens to be, to build that up over time. It doesn't happen in training camp.... I don't think there is any shortcut to it.

"We won in '01. In '02, we had a lot of issues. [In] '03, that was a good football team. [In] '04, that was a good football team. So I don't think there was any doubt '01 wasn't the best team, but that team played the best, so we won. But I think we saw in '02 more of probably overall where the '01 team was. Just the '01 team played great when they had to in critical situations in big games, and that's why they won. You can't take anything away from them. They deserved it because they were the best team. But it wasn't the case in '02."

The Patriots were dominant in a pair of 14–2 seasons in 2003 and 2004 when they won back-to-back Super Bowls and became the only team in the salary cap era to win three titles in four years. Yeah, the program was in place.

The Genius

Bill Belichick demanded accountability from the early moments of his first-ever team meeting in the spring of 2000. The meeting was a few minutes old when a former first-round draft pick walked in late into the tiny, packed room and sat down in front. Belichick immediately kicked him out to set the tone for his tenure.

Without exception, players are fined for being late to meetings, and defensive lineman Brandon Deaderick was even suspended for a week during the 2010 playoffs for being a habitual offender. Linebacker Brandon Spikes was lambasted in 2013 for not showing up at all during a postseason bye week because of a snowstorm. And in 2009, when Belichick couldn't get through to his locker room, he sent home wide receiver Randy Moss and linebackers Adalius Thomas, Gary Guyton, and Derrick Burgess for being late due to the snow. Thomas made headlines for criticizing Belichick's decision, claiming he didn't have a "Jetsons" car that could fly through the snow.

But hey, there are players who have actually practiced driving to Gillette Stadium because they want to know how long it takes, and they've done it during different times of the day and throughout various weather elements just to see how long they've got. They take it seriously because Belichick deserves that respect.

He'll discipline anyone, too. Running back Jonas Gray went from obscurity to *Sports Illustrated* cover boy in 2014 with his 201-yard, four-touchdown game against the Indianapolis Colts. Five days later, he was sent home from the stadium for being late because he was failed by his alarm clock. Gray never recovered, as he only managed to rush for 80 yards the rest of the season and 256 for his career before finding himself out of the league. It was an inexcusable mistake because it was just a month after cornerback Darrelle Revis woke up late and was told to stay home for the day when he called to inform the team that he was on his way to work.

Then in 2015, cornerback Malcolm Butler was months removed from being the hero of Super Bowl XLIX when he ran into his own issue. Butler returned home to Mississippi for the weekend during the voluntary offseason workout program, but storms across the south prevented him from flying back to New England on Sunday night. His punishment for arriving late Monday? He couldn't hit the practice field for two weeks. Unfair? Probably. But veterans in the locker room informed Butler that's why they've learned to return two days early if they travel out of state.

There are smaller examples. Players are often reprimanded and sometimes fined for saying too much to the media. Another believed he was benched for disclosing classified information. Amazingly, there are likely dozens of examples like this that never got out.

Belichick has earned that authority and even the benefit of the doubt because his players almost entirely believe Belichick is acting in their best interests. Heck, Spikes always butted heads with Belichick, but he gladly returned for three weeks in 2015 before he was ultimately cut because of a late-night hit-and-run citation.

Belichick demands his players' undivided attention because that's the requirement for success. They can't fulfill the obligations of a brutal game plan in February if they aren't focused on a relatively easier opponent in September. And they can't buy into the game plan in September if they haven't committed to the process in May.

Belichick exposed Rams head coach Mike Martz's stubbornness in Super Bowl XXXVI, but that's hardly the only time he's reached for the stars and actually touched one. In 2003, the Patriots trailed the Denver Broncos 24–23 with 2:51 remaining in the fourth quarter, and they faced a fourth down from their own 1-yard line. Punter Ken Walter didn't have the biggest leg, and it'd be a short snap to the back of the end zone that would be incrementally more difficult by the hostility of the Denver crowd. Rather than risking a blocked punt or a short kick that put the Broncos in field-goal position, Belichick decided to have long snapper Lonie Paxton fire the ball through the end zone for a safety and a 26–23 deficit. But after the free kick, the Broncos went three-and-out and had to punt due to the change in field position. Belichick was simply hoping for a field goal to force overtime, but Tom Brady trumped that idea with a game-winning, back-shoulder touchdown pass to wide receiver David Givens.

Belichick's ideas don't work with universal perfection, but the unconventional methods at least draw the universal trust of the team. The most spectacular failure has forever been known by a simple "fourth-and-2" in reference to Belichick's decision to go for it on their own 28-yard line with 2:08 remaining in the fourth quarter even though the Pats held a 34–28 lead against the Indianapolis Colts. Four plays later, quarterback Peyton Manning delivered the decisive touchdown pass to wide receiver Reggie

Wayne to improve the Colts' record to 9–0. Belichick's thinking? The way Manning was going that night in Indianapolis, he was going to score regardless of field position, so Belichick figured the Pats could get two yards for the win. Hard to find fault in that.

Belichick made another uncommon decision that was immediately second-guessed in 2015 when the Patriots won the overtime coin toss against the New York Jets at MetLife Stadium and opted to kick off. It completely blew up in Belichick's face when the Jets breezed down the field for a five-play touchdown drive, but there was some well-calculated reasoning behind the call. First and foremost, the Patriots defense had just forced three consecutive fourth-quarter punts and hadn't allowed a touchdown in the previous five series. Second, the Jets defense had dominated the Patriots offense that season, and the Pats' average starting field position that day was the 20-yard line when the Jets were kicking off. Consider the Patriots orchestrated a single 80-yard touchdown drive against the Jets in two games that season, and their only touchdown march in that game traversed 66 yards and required two fourth-down conversions. With all of that in mind, the Patriots had a better chance to win the game by kicking off, getting a stop and a field goal than they would have had by receiving the kickoff and mounting a touchdown drive. The logic backfired, but the players were comfortable with Belichick's idea after the game.

It's really all part of a comprehensive process. It'd be easy to just say the players should blindly trust Belichick because he has led the greatest dynasty of the salary cap era and will eventually be inducted into the Pro Football Hall of Fame. But Belichick puts in the work that challenges his players and forces them to think. They practice every scenario imaginable in practice, starting with the standard stuff like running out the clock in the four-minute drill to getting into scoring range in the two-minute drill. Sometimes, Belichick will even throw a curveball at the offense by letting them think they've got time to make an extra play to get into field-goal range before wiping out the clock and demanding a 40-yard Hail Mary. This tactic simulates a slow spot from the referee or a penalty that wipes off 10 seconds.

They'll also routinely work through exhaustive special teams situations like free kicks after safeties or snapping the ball to the punter in the end zone and seeing how long the punter can run around to waste clock at the end of a game. These strategical blueprints extend beyond the practice field, too. Belichick once put a kicker through an extensive pre-draft workout just to measure the height and distance of his onside kicks. The kicker would be a surefire NFL starter, and Belichick wanted to have a book on him in the event the Patriots ever had to recover one of his onside kicks.

Belichick's advanced scouting is legendary among his players. He once advised them before a playoff game that the opposing offensive tackle picked up his head just before the snap on passing plays, but the tackle kept his head down on runs. And safety Devin McCourty recalled a practice week in 2012 when Belichick taught the defense about the wind patterns in Buffalo, so the defensive backs were alerted to account for the wind if they had a chance at an interception. As it turned out, McCourty had two picks, and he adjusted to a high-arching ball accordingly for one of them before the wind even took over.

With examples like this, it's easy to understand why the Patriots believe they're the better-prepared team every time they hit the field. It's fascinating, though, because the players don't tune him out even when they can drown in the details. The ones who aren't fully committed don't last. Wide receiver Reggie Wayne, who built a potential Hall of Fame résumé with the Colts, landed a $450,000 signing bonus to join the Patriots during the 2015 pre-season, but he wanted preferential veteran treatment, thought he could sit out practice periods, and quickly realized the difference between the two programs. He was gone in two weeks.

Belichick runs a "football retreat," as Al Groh put it, for those who are willing to put everything aside for the sake of winning. Groh is one of a countless number of coaches who has descended upon Foxboro to watch how he runs his show. The victories are the reward for the players. If players simply want to get paid or hang on in the hope to be carried to a Super Bowl, they find out New England isn't a vacation destination. And that's why Belichick brings so much success so consistently.

Wide receiver Donte Stallworth played for six coaches and six teams over the course of his career from 2002 to '13, and he suited up for the Patriots in 2007 and 2012. So he was able to compare Belichick to others to detail why he's as successful as he's been.

"There are a lot of things that Bill says repetitively over and over in meetings or throughout practice, just different scenarios that he will harp on that might come up in a game once or might come up every four or five games," Stallworth said. "It's the little things that he harps on all the time that you have to be aware of. I just remember always thinking back to the session he would do when he would really dissect every team we played. He would tell us, 'This is what we need to do to win this game. This is what this team likes to do. This is who they are as a team. This is what they're capable of. This is what they've done.' He tries to scare the living shit out of you to let you know no matter what that team's record is, they can beat your ass on any given Sunday.

"You get caught up in the [hype from the] media, your family and friends, the fans are saying how good you are, so you may slack off in your film study or in the weight room just a little bit. And you may beat that team, and it becomes a pattern. Bill fights that, not every game, but he fights it in every meeting, every rep in practice. It's always about moving forward and getting better. He would always call this session, 'Gotta have it.' It's usually third downs, important parts of the game, end of the half, end of the game, fourth down, very important things. He would always dissect those plays and players and the scenarios, and he would show the whole team, 'When this team has got to have it, this is what they do. On third-and-8, they run this route, or they run this protection, and they like to do this and that.' He'll show on defense, 'This is the coverage they like to play. This is the blitz they like to bring or the zone blitz.' He'll show it over and over and over in different scenarios, so we're like, 'Okay, now we know what to expect.' Other coaches don't do that.

"I don't shy away from saying it, and I respect all the coaches in the NFL and the former coaches and greats. And I'm just speaking from what I know—he is the greatest coach ever. He has a laundry list of goals, accolades, and achievements. There is no other coach who just dissects teams the way he does and specifically tells you what you need to do to win games and, 'If you do this, you'll win, and if you don't, you'll lose.' It's not the simple, 'Hold on to the football and score more points.' That's generic. That's bullshit. He goes into depth, shows you plays, shows you coverages, dissects teams and shows you, 'This team has lived by getting turnovers. They score when they get turnovers, and that's how they get most of their points.' This was about playing the Redskins in 2007, and he broke them down and was like, 'If you don't think this player won't be in there, don't worry, he'll be there.' That was his thing. If a guy was on the injury list or didn't play the week before, he would always have this way of keeping guys on edge no matter who we were playing.

"No matter what was going on, we always had the fear of god that this team could beat your ass. He would always use that Dolphins game on Monday night in 2004 as an example. Obviously, he has much more to use now. There's no other coach that I've ever been around. [Ravens head coach] John Harbaugh was pretty close, but no other coach was so on point with scenarios of the game, the rules of the game. You'll never, ever have an unprepared New England team out on the field as long as they're coached by Bill Belichick. His attention to detail, he operates like a military would from a standpoint of don't worry about what's going on outside this building, focus on the job at hand, one day at a time, work hard, put your body through the motions in the most intense and frantic and serious situations as you can, so when you get to the real action, it's like second nature to you."

It's time for one more example. Seahawks head coach Pete Carroll has been widely and deservedly criticized for one of the most boneheaded play calls in history by failing to give the ball to Marshawn Lynch at the 1-yard line in the final minute of Super Bowl XLIX. But don't discredit Belichick's synchronized chess match. Lynch had a solid game, but there were two situations earlier against heavier defensive packages when he was stuffed for no gain on third-and-2 and third-and-1. Belichick changed his defensive personnel and let the clock wind after Lynch's four-yard carry that set up second-and-goal from the 1. All the while, Belichick predicted Carroll would call a passing play because of those two run stuffs on "gotta have it" plays.

And Malcolm Butler, who was the last cornerback on the 46-man roster that day, was only on the field because Kyle Arrington was getting torched by wide receiver Chris Matthews, who entered the game without a catch in his career. Arrington had the best season of his career in 2014 and Butler was an undrafted rookie who barely saw the field, so this was a virtually unpredictable circumstance. But Butler worked on that exact pick route as the Patriots closed down their Friday practice in the once-in-a-lifetime chance Butler would have to defend it against the Seahawks two days later.

The preparation was in place. The prediction was spot on. And Butler was there to make the greatest defensive play in Super Bowl history. If players ever wonder why they spend a few training camp practices working exclusively on unlikely situations, Belichick merely needs to turn on the tape.

Financial Plan

Bill Belichick ripped the collective heart out of the city of Cleveland in 1993 when he cut beloved quarterback Bernie Kosar. And remember how Belichick addressed it: he told the team he made a decision, it was final, and it was time to move forward.

Belichick has made some similarly unpopular calls while running the Patriots, but it's possible he never orchestrated a move that shook the defense as much as the shocking midseason trade of linebacker Jamie Collins in 2016. And guess how he addressed the team the following morning during their full-squad meeting.

"We made a transaction. I did what was best for the team," one observer relayed.

Belichick traded the Patriots' most athletically gifted defensive player to the then-winless Browns for a third-round draft pick. A few months later, the Browns gave Collins a four-year, $50 million contract that further validated his talent. But in New England, Belichick had reached the conclusion that he could no longer get through to Collins, and it was time to part ways while also delivering a strong message to the rest of the locker room. The Patriots were far too talented to let players go rogue, and Belichick was ultimately proven right when they won Super Bowl LI.

It was a wild situation, because the trade occurred during the bye week, and every crucial member of the defense, particularly captains Dont'a Hightower and Devin McCourty, admitted they didn't understand the purpose of the trade. Hightower was especially unnerved by the move, but he quickly put the defense on his back to get them looking ahead and not behind.

Like his on-field scouting work, Belichick had long since built up the cache to shake the locker room, to the point where it's become second nature to the players. One other point: Belichick is often mocked for unveiling little, if anything, to the media. But take the Collins trade. Belichick delivered the same message in front of the cameras as he did behind the scenes. Even if he was only speaking in generalities, he wasn't going to tell the public anything he wasn't going to say to his team. It also pressed the players to analyze what went wrong during Collins' tenure and what they'd need to do better to ensure they weren't on the wrong end of a one-way ticket out of town.

Indirectly, Belichick also concluded he wouldn't re-sign Collins, so the trade was a way to accelerate their draft compensation by a year when he walked in free agency. That's the other element at play with Belichick's masterful roster maneuvering, and that traced back more than a decade and a half. The NFL implemented its salary cap in 1994, the first year of Robert Kraft's ownership, and Kraft recognized the significance of hiring a coach who could build the roster while managing financial constraints.

"I thought that Bill had an understanding of economics and talent that was a manager I could be ready to work with," Kraft said.

When Belichick was interviewing for the job, he used linebacker Chris Slade as an example. Slade was another popular Patriot and a saintly human being, and the 1993 second-round draft pick had 51 sacks and a Pro Bowl appearance during his eight-year run with the Pats. Belichick unveiled a scouting report on Slade that went as far back as his days at Tabb High School in Virginia. Belichick detailed Slade would remain on the roster in 2000, but the linebacker wouldn't live up to his $2 million price tag when he turned 30 in 2001. The theme here: it wouldn't be popular to cut ties with Slade, but the on-field production had to sync up with the salary structure or the relationship wouldn't benefit the football team.

Belichick had a far more difficult time a week before the 2003 regular-season opener when he had to sell the release of safety Lawyer Milloy, a captain who had never missed a game in seven seasons. The Patriots coach called it the hardest decision of his career, but Milloy was on the books for a $5.25 million cap hit in 2003 and wouldn't budge on contract negotiations. Milloy was coming off the least productive season of his career, but he didn't want to take a pay cut. Milloy stood by his principles and believed agreements between men must be honored, but it led to a release that shocked the locker room so ruthlessly that they lost to Milloy's Buffalo Bills in Week 1 by a 31–0 score.

Belichick also cut cornerback Ty Law for cap reasons in February 2005, traded defensive lineman Richard Seymour a week before the 2009 season opener, wouldn't relent on contract negotiations with slot receiver Wes Welker in 2013, and traded captain Logan Mankins during training camp in 2014 because Mankins wouldn't take a pay reduction a la Milloy. The locker room was unsettled by each decision, even if some were easier to explain than others, and quarterback Tom Brady was friends with each of those players who got the boot. But Belichick was similar to legendary Celtics coach Red Auerbach in that he believed it was better to unload a player a year early than a year late.

"I always feel like Bill may be one year or two ahead of the league," Ravens general manager Ozzie Newsome said of his former boss.

Surely, there were ramifications. Without Seymour, an intimidating leader with a corner locker stall, the Patriots' locker room went haywire in 2009. And when Belichick wouldn't pay cornerback Asante Samuel after the 2007 season, the Patriots had major issues at cornerback until 2012 when they acquired Aqib Talib during a midseason trade with the Buccaneers. Then again, when Belichick is fearless to make enough of these moves, it's impossible to bat a thousand.

Like Collins, they won the Super Bowl without Milloy in 2004 and Mankins in 2015. After moving on from Welker, Julian Edelman and Danny Amendola picked up the slack. When

Belichick realized he'd be severely outbid by the New York Jets for cornerback Darrelle Revis in March 2015, Belichick actually coordinated a perception the Patriots were still attempting to keep him. The Jets actually bid against themselves in the 24 hours before Revis signed. All the while, Belichick knew he'd be promoting Malcolm Butler. Heck, rewind it a year and Belichick pulled a Revis rabbit out of his hat less than 24 hours after Talib bolted for the Denver Broncos.

And during the 2016 offseason, Belichick determined he wouldn't offer a contract extension to defensive end Chandler Jones, the team's best pure pass rusher since Willie McGinest, partly because of off-field concerns and also because of Jones' likely price tag. So Belichick traded Jones to the Arizona Cardinals for the draft collateral that netted guard Joe Thuney and wide receiver Malcolm Mitchell, who both played pivotal roles on the march to Super Bowl LI. That trade worked well for all involved, as Jones landed a five-year, $82.5 million contract from the Cardinals.

With Collins, the Patriots told his agent, Bus Cook, prior to the 2016 season that he was worth $11 million annually, though the Patriots never exchanged a formal proposal with that number. Still, it's proof that they believed in him. Collins was still productive during the season, but he had some issues with consistency. Collins sucked inside to miss a gap on the second play of the Patriots' Week 8 victory against the Buffalo Bills, but the miscue led to Mike Gillislee's 28-yard run. Gap control was a major focal point from the coaching staff that week, so Belichick reduced Collins' playing time the rest of the game. A day later, Collins was a Brown. Three months after that, Belichick led the Patriots to their fifth Super Bowl.

Steady Hand

There's always been this debate around New England: who is more responsible to the Patriots' success, Bill Belichick or Tom Brady? The Belichick corner will say he deserves a tick more credit because he constructs the roster and draws up the game plans. And the Pats went 11–5 without Brady in 2008 and opened the season with a 3–1 record with second- and third-string quarterbacks when Brady was suspended in 2016. The Brady corner will point toward his on-field magic, as his late-game heroics in the playoffs have been otherworldly and he led his 51st game-winning drive in the 51st Super Bowl. And when Belichick wasn't on top of his game from a personnel perspective, leading to a lack of depth on offense and defense from 2010 to '13, Brady almost single-handedly still made the Patriots one of the most feared teams in the NFL.

The fact is it's impossible to answer because each figure provides an irreplaceable value to the success of the organization. But here's what Belichick brings: a steady, unwavering attitude that filters through the locker room and prevents the players from getting jerked around on a season-long rollercoaster ride. That leadership has perhaps never been more necessary than in the fallout of Spygate in 2007, Aaron Hernandez's murder charge in 2013, and Deflategate in 2015 and 2016.

Belichick was at fault for Spygate, when the Patriots were caught videotaping the New York Jets' sideline signals in the 2007 regular-season opener. It caused plenty of Patriots detractors to line up and publicly criticize their tactics, and members of the 2001 St. Louis Rams and early-2000s Pittsburgh Steelers were especially salty, questioning the legitimacy of their first three

Super Bowl victories. Of course, those displeased voices were conveniently coming from players on teams that were on the wrong side of heavy upsets.

Regardless, Belichick spun it in the Patriots' favor. He hit it hard once, ensured the players harnessed their energy appropriately, told them to duck the topic in the media, and ultimately focus on themselves and their preparation. He motivated the players to validate their work and prove it was beyond reproach. Locker-room leaders like Tom Brady, Tedy Bruschi, and Mike Vrabel were particularly peeved over the criticism, and the Patriots did heed Belichick's advice and turn it into something good. Brady (50 touchdown passes) and Randy Moss (23 touchdown receptions) set NFL records, and the Patriots shattered the league mark with 589 points in the first 16–0 regular season in history. They won games by an average of 19.1 points along the way.

"I know the Spygate year, [Belichick] talked to us just once how they were saying we weren't good enough to win games, and everything in the past was due to us cheating," Donte Stallworth said. "I won't say we needed the extra motivation, but it definitely helped. I'll be honest. You hear guys say all the time for a big game, the Super Bowl, a playoff game, 'If you need any extra motivation to get up for this game then you shouldn't be playing.' And that's not true. It's just human nature. That's like if someone before the game starts and guys are walking out to shake hands or do the coin toss, and one player starts talking major trash to the other side, of course that's going to motivate them more."

The Patriots' lopsided victories took on a life of their own during the opening two months of the season. They beat their first eight opponents by an average score of 41–16. The Patriots were absurdly talented, but they were also vengeful. The blow-outs became contagious, and the players rolled their eyes at pundits who took offense to the criticism that professional athletes shouldn't dare run up the score against their opponents.

"You know what, we didn't mind it," Stallworth said. "If Bill wanted to go out there and put 100 points on whoever, we didn't care. We were looking forward to scoring as many points as we could. The funny part about it was our first three games, we scored 38 points. We scored 38 points against the Jets. We scored 38 points against the Chargers and 38 points against the Bills. We were happy scoring 38 points. That's a lot in the NFL. But then we started putting up those crazy, crazy numbers. We put up 48 points on Dallas when we were both undefeated. Those guys, the players, are going to want to embarrass people."

Count running back Kevin Faulk among the group of established veterans who was happy to stick it back to the league that had it out for them.

"We just run the play that is called in the huddle," Faulk said. "But at the same time, we are competitors. Yes, we did feel a certain way about the whole situation, so we wanted to go out there and prove to the world, 'Hey look, we don't need any of this to go win football games.' We have a good football team. We have a good nucleus, a good core group of guys that Bill brought in together, and that's what makes this organization successful."

Belichick used the same approach in 2015 when the Patriots returned to work to defend their Super Bowl XLIX victory against the Seattle Seahawks. Of course, Deflategate originated months earlier in the aftermath of their 45–7 victory against the Indianapolis Colts in the AFC Championship Game, and an absolutely livid group of Patriots prepared like hell in the ensuing two weeks for the Super Bowl. But the NFL's poorly orchestrated investigation, which was spearheaded by Ted Wells' subjectively slanted report, dominated the 2015 offseason. Brady was suspended four games, though it was delayed to 2016 because of the appeal process, and Belichick took it head on at the dawn of training camp.

The Patriots' "scorched earth" mentality rivaled that of the 2007 team, and they flew out of the gates with a 10–0 start before a crippling string of injuries led to their demise. But again, a lot of this was put in motion by Belichick's steadiness at the start of the season. Believe it, the players had Brady's back in a big way, and those feelings were incrementally enhanced upon his return in 2016, but the locker room shut down all Deflategate-related talk throughout 2015 by Belichick's order.

"It's one of those things where everyone is going to have an opinion," wide receiver Julian Edelman said. "The more time you take away by thinking about what other people are thinking about, that's just wasted time on your preparation and trying to improve. People want to keep on talking about that and bringing stuff up, they can go ahead. We're just going to continue to prepare and keep them hating us."

And there was the case of Hernandez, who was arrested in 2013 and charged with three murders. (He was eventually convicted of one and acquitted of two, and he killed himself in prison in 2017.) Belichick brought the spotlight upon himself on the first day of training camp in 2013. He addressed a group of more than 100 media members, opened with a seven-minute introductory statement, and then fielded 29 questions over the final 15 minutes. The Patriots also had their captains, including Brady, Devin

McCourty, and Jerod Mayo, take their turn with the Hernandez questions.

And as soon as they started practicing, the Patriots dismissed all questions, deferring to the ongoing legal proceedings and their leadership's comments at the start of camp. With one swift surge, the Patriots pushed Hernandez into the shadows, and he was never again a distraction.

Belichick found out the hard way in 1995 that a head coach truly has no way of preparing for the challenges that will hit his desk. He had to tackle an unprecedented relocation announcement with the Cleveland Browns, more unprecedented penalties with the Patriots in 2007 and 2015, and the fallout from rostering a charged and convicted murderer in 2013. Through it all, the Patriots reached the Super Bowl in 2007 and the AFC Championship Game in 2013 and 2015. It's unfathomable to think another team would have gotten that far under any of those circumstances.

Growing Legacy

Bill Belichick's coaching tree has ensured his methods will continue to develop long after he leaves the game, whenever that happens to be. He has assistants who have become NFL head coaches, including Josh McDaniels (Denver Broncos), Romeo Crennel (Cleveland Browns), Bill O'Brien (Houston Texans), Nick Saban (Miami Dolphins), Al Groh (New York Jets), Jim Schwartz (Detroit Lions), Eric Mangini (Jets), and Matt Patricia (Detroit Lions). Saban (Alabama, LSU, Michigan State), O'Brien (Penn State), and Groh (Virginia) also led college programs after working with Belichick.

Others to join the college ranks as head coaches include Charlie Weis (Notre Dame), Kirk Ferentz (Iowa), Pat Hill (Fresno State), and Pete Mangurian (Columbia). And notable front-office colleagues have taken prominent roles in NFL front offices, such as Scott Pioli (Kansas City Chiefs, Atlanta Falcons), Thomas Dimitroff (Falcons), Ozzie Newsome (Baltimore Ravens), Bob Quinn (Detroit Lions), Jon Robinson (Tennessee Titans), Jason Licht (Arizona Cardinals, Tampa Bay Buccaneers), and Phil Savage (Browns, Philadelphia Eagles).

That list will undoubtedly grow, as some of Belichick's former players have also become coaches. Mike Vrabel, Larry Izzo, and Wes Welker are among O'Brien's contingent in Houston, but it goes deeper than that. Belichick has hired Ray Ventrone, Sammy Morris, and Joe Andruzzi in various capacities with the Patriots, and other former players don't need the bright NFL spotlight to make their mark.

Kevin Faulk has worked as the offensive coordinator at his alma mater, Carencro High School in Louisiana, since retiring in 2012. Donte Stallworth took a coaching internship with the Baltimore Ravens in 2014 and also moonlighted as a trainer at Bommarito Performance Systems in 2010. And Rosevelt Colvin got into youth sports to spend more time with his family, leading his son's school basketball, launching a flag football program in Indiana, and helping out in a fill-in capacity with his daughter's track team. Colvin has even noticed himself sounding like Belichick while running his UPS store.

"Oh, I say, 'Do your job,' all the time," Colvin laughed.

Colvin appreciated Belichick's attention to details and situations, so he has harped on those things with his son's basketball team. For instance, if his son is inbounding the ball and he senses the five-second clock getting set to expire, it's time to throw the ball off an opponent's foot to preserve the possession. And because Belichick used to give his players the book on that week's officiating crew—they call too many holding penalties or keep the flags in their pockets with defensive holding, for example—Colvin takes pride in his early game adjustments when he notices the referees' tendencies. One game, they were calling ticky-tack fouls, so Colvin instructed his players to pump-fake to draw more whistles.

"Bill didn't teach me that because it's basketball, but it's paying attention to details, so many details, the finite details that help put yourself in a position where you can be competitive," Colvin said. "You can have the best team in America when you walk out on the court, but if you don't take care of the details, make lay-ups, make free throws and play defense, you can possibly get beat."

Faulk, who is one of the most decorated athletes to ever come from Louisiana, knew after high school that he wanted to get into coaching. He devoted himself a bit more to that idea in 2010 when he missed most of the season with a torn ACL. Belichick asked Faulk to stay close to the team because he knew the respected veteran could help the younger players on the roster. It gave Faulk a different perspective in that regard, and he observed Belichick more closely to see how he went about teaching certain lessons. Faulk looks back on those lessons while trying to relay a message to his high school team, especially since they're still at an age where they sometimes think a little too much about themselves and not as much about the team success.

Like Colvin, Faulk all too often catches himself sounding like Belichick.

"Oh definitely, hell yeah, there are a whole lot of times," Faulk said. "You hear yourself, and you catch it right away like, 'Dang, I heard, wow, did I just repeat that?' It's funny."

Faulk preaches the significance of the details, too. And when the players don't respond, well, sometimes he hears some of Belichick that he preferred not to repeat.

"It's censored," Faulk cracked. "A lot of it is censored."

Stallworth worked for renowned trainer Pete Bommarito in 2010, and he helped prepare an impressive group of prospects get ready for the draft, including Patriots tight end Rob Gronkowski and Pittsburgh Steelers wide receiver Antonio Brown. Then, in 2014, Stallworth was deciding what to do with his post-playing career, and he didn't want to regret not giving coaching a chance, however small of an opportunity he received. So he reached out to Ravens head coach John Harbaugh to hop onboard for an internship.

Stallworth enjoyed each stop, and he grew even more appreciation for the work that coaches like Belichick put in to be successful.

"Unless you're doing it, you don't know, man," Stallworth said. "There are no breaks for coaches. As a player, you have all the breaks in the world. The coaches are over there at 6 in the morning, sometimes 5, and they don't leave until after 10 PM at the earliest. It's a crazy schedule. I didn't mind putting in the work. That's something I always relished, putting in the work and getting good results. The thing to me was I couldn't personally be consumed 24 hours a day, seven days a week for damn near 365 days a year with football all over again for another 10 to 20 years of my life. As much as I loved it, I figured for me personally it'd be better to cover it as an analyst during the season and then politics in the offseason."

Stallworth couldn't help but think back to the days when he'd arrive at Gillette Stadium before the sun came up. There'd be one light on in the building, and it doesn't take much to figure out whose office could be spotted from the parking lot.

Gonna Need a Bigger Boat

Bill Belichick renamed his boat, again, after the Patriots beat the Atlanta Falcons 34–28 in Super Bowl LI. It was his fifth crown with the Pats and seventh overall, so VI Rings needed a facelift for the second time in three years: VII Rings.

At times over the past decade, pundits, coaches, and players have wondered whether the Lombardi Trophy might also need a new inscription, but that might just be a fairy tale for New Englanders.

"I don't think there's ever been anybody in the NFL, let's just say there have been a lot of great coaches," Al Groh said. "But I think we can say nobody has ever had a better grasp of the totality of the game, roster management, personnel selection, offense, defense, special teams, game planning, managing the game than Bill has had. And the record certainly supports that."

There's no official statistic for such things, but it's likely no other coach ever took a job for $25 per week and eventually entered his fifth decade in the NFL. It's also fair to wonder if an owner in any sport ever took as much heat from the league office and television executives as Robert Kraft did while hiring Belichick.

And still, Belichick's first boss sounded like Belichick himself when asked in 2014 if he ever foresaw this level of success. Ted Marchibroda actually scoffed at the question.

"To be honest with you, I didn't think about him in the future," Marchibroda said. "I was just concerned with the job he did with us, and he did an excellent job."

It's another example of how Belichick took something from every stop. Staying in the present was a Marchibroda staple, and it's been a classic philosophy of Belichick's.

There was no way to ignore Belichick's ambition, though. Joe Collier saw it with the Denver Broncos in the 1970s. He knew Belichick was in store for success, even if there was no way to predict his historic voyage with the Patriots.

Groh was prescient during a 2014 interview while discussing Belichick's upcoming season, which was his 40th in the NFL. At one point, Groh was surveyed for his opinion for Belichick's place among the all-time greats if he won one more Super Bowl to tie him with Pittsburgh Steelers legend Chuck Noll with four.

"Why put a limit of one more on it?" Groh immediately responded.

Groh was right. So was Bill Parcells, who brought Belichick along in the 1980s and took him back under his wing in the 1990s. And yeah, they battled during Belichick's split with the New York Jets in 2000, but that was partly because Parcells knew Belichick was capable of something special up north with the Patriots.

Not long thereafter, the two Bills mended fences. From the man who restored the Patriots' legitimacy to the man who transformed the Patriots into the class of professional sports, one thing is abundantly clear.

"The people in New England are lucky to have him," Parcells said.

CHAPTER 7

TOM BRADY: THE G.O.A.T.

Tom Brady had essentially reached superhero status with New Englanders even before the Patriots won Super Bowl XXXVI against the St. Louis Rams to cap one of the most unexpected championship runs in history. Of course, he solidified that reputation with the game-winning drive to knock off the 14-point favorites. What else could the 24-year-old accomplish? Apparently, he was ahead of the game off the field, too.

The Patriots were holding their annual rookie party after the 2001 season at Abe & Louie's in Boston. It's viewed as a rite of passage for the rookies with the biggest contracts to pay the dinner and bar tab for the veterans, and some of the elder statesmen find fun in going overboard. They've been known in the past to take home an extra steak or lobster (or both). There's another story of a group of players who ordered the most expensive bottle of wine and box of cigars, only to light the cigars and immediately extinguish them in the glasses of wine. But in February 2002, shortly after the Patriots' Super Bowl victory, the team was on the way toward racking up a tab of around $30,000, and they did it by ordering rounds of $375 shots of Hennessy Timeless. Hell, some of the players didn't even like the cognac, but it was the most expensive shot on the menu that night.

Brady recognized where the night was heading and got out in front of it. My father, Joe Howe, was the bar manager at Abe & Louie's for years, and he worked the bar for that party. Brady pulled my father aside with a special request: *When they order me a shot, please just give me a water. I'll pay for the shot if I have to. I just can't drink that stuff all night.*

So as the team was getting legless by the end of the night, Brady was the most sober guy in the room, and no one had any idea that he was drinking water. Linebacker Willie McGinest, who always treated my father great, saddled up on a barstool, had his head in his hands and lamented as he looked at a completely coherent Brady: *Joe, who is this guy? First, he takes over for Drew Bledsoe. Then, he wins us a Super Bowl. Now, he can outdrink all of us? What can't this guy do?*

In the Numbers

Tom Brady recorded the 51st game-winning drive of his prolific career in the 51st Super Bowl. Along the way, the Patriots quarterback has shattered every significant postseason record in league history: wins, touchdowns, passing yards, starts, everything.

Brady's legacy was initially launched in the playoffs, as the Patriots won three Super Bowls in his first four seasons as a starter and vaulted himself into the conversation for the greatest quarterback of all-time before he even entered the prime of his career. That debate essentially died when Brady won his fourth Super Bowl in 2014, and he undeniably closed the coffin with his fifth ring. The only argument Joe Montana supporters can make is his unblemished record in four Super Bowls, but they're whistling past the graveyard with that one. It ignores the fact that Montana went one-and-done in the playoffs in three consecutive seasons. Brady has done that twice in his career.

Brady has also been the greatest regular-season quarterback in history, and he might eventually go down as the best passer of all-time. Peyton Manning retired with 200 career victories, including the playoffs, and Brady surged past that mark in 2016. If Brady plays into his mid-40s, which he has proclaimed he'd do for the better part of the last decade, it's a near certainty that no one will break his wins record. It also seems like a long shot anyone will reach his Super Bowls perch.

Brady could easily take down Manning's passing records. If Brady continues to average 4,500 yards and 33 touchdowns per season—his averages during his seven full seasons from 2009 to '15—he'll eclipse Manning's records (71,940 yards, 539 touchdowns) midway through 2019. At that point, Brady will have monopolized the real estate for which quarterbacks are measured.

To echo Willie McGinest, what can't this guy do?

Diamond in the Rough

John Hughes could have screwed up everything. In fact, that was essentially his job description.

Tom Brady was on the fast track to baseball stardom as he progressed through Junipero Serra High School in San Mateo, California. The Montreal Expos selected the left-handed hitting catcher with their 18th-round draft pick in 1995, and they dispatched Hughes to Brady's hometown to sign him. The Expos knew it'd be a monumental task, though, because the long-running book on Brady was that he wanted to play college football and had already committed to the University of Michigan.

To sweeten the pot, the Expos had graded Brady as a third-round pick and were prepared to pay him like one. That was a fair measure of his talent, too. But again, the reason Brady fell to the 18th round was due to the widespread belief that he was unsignable for football reasons. Dan Duquette, who was the Boston Red Sox general manager at the time, didn't even include Brady on the draft board because he had no confidence in their ability to bring Brady from the gridiron to the diamond.

Hughes adored Brady and the entire family. He was a dimple-chinned teenager with an all-American smile and personality. He was popular, accountable, a leader, and dedicated. Behind the plate, Brady's presence reminded Hughes of Minnesota Twins All-Star catcher Joe Mauer. Brady called his own games, a rarity for high school catchers, and he had good footwork to make strong throws. He was a perfectionist, evidenced by a time when he blamed himself for failing to throw out a runner at second base even though the umpire blew the call.

So it was Hughes' job to sign Brady, but Hughes wanted him in the organization just as badly. It's crazy to think, had things unfolded differently, the Expos could have had a battery of Pedro Martinez and Brady every fifth day. Instead, the pair became two of the most iconic figures in Boston sports history.

"I could have ruined this guy's career," Hughes quipped.

Brady had a touch of power, too. He hit a pair of home runs to right field over the ivy-covered wall during a playoff game against Bellarmine, a rival from San Jose, and the second pounded off the roof of the team bus and woke up the driver.

"It scared the heck out of him," Pete Jensen laughed.

Jensen was Brady's coach when he converted from first base to catcher as a senior at Serra. He noted 10-15 scouts were attending a preseason game to watch Serra center fielder Greg Millichap, but the flock did an about face when Brady began throwing during infield practice. The scouts were initially confused because, first, they didn't know Brady switched positions and, second, they weren't sure if they should waste their time on the local football star.

But they surely couldn't ignore Brady. Jensen had a history at the Serra program with Barry Bonds and Gregg Jefferies, and guess who was the most impressive.

"I saw Barry Bonds play in high school. I saw Gregg Jefferies play in high school. And Tommy," Jensen said. "If I were to say [who was better] as a high school player, it would definitely be [Brady] over the other two, to be honest with you. That's probably not fair to Barry because of his genes, but as far as skill level or being a little further ahead as a baseball player, I would pick Tommy. Barry was immature, especially physically. He wasn't very strong. Gregg was kind of an overachiever. He was a great hitter, but he really had to work at what he did. Tommy was a natural. He had a great ability to throw and catch, and he was a left-handed hitter with some power."

Add that to Hughes' Mauer comparison, and what's not to like?

"He was very similar on the field in his presence to Joe Mauer," Hughes said. "Joe Mauer didn't have a lot to say. He wasn't real vocal. I don't remember Tom being extremely vocal, but just his presence on the field was captivating. He seemed to gain respect by the way that he went about his business. To this day, he is without a doubt the most impressive young man as a person as a high school player that I have ever been around. There was just something unique about him.

"Joe was more advanced than Tom was in his position. I think he was a little bit more refined, maybe a little bit more arm strength. When I say [they're similar], I'm clearly not saying that Tom was going to be Joe Mauer. That would be steep. But the similarities, they were both good athletes, both quarterbacks, similar frames, left-handed hitters. Mauer probably had a little bit more power than Tom did, but Tom had power. The way they carried themselves on the field was very similar, too. Joe's game was a little more refined, not that Tom was raw."

Brady was a can't-miss kid, and he was refreshing in comparison to many prized baseball recruits. Jensen raved about Brady's work in the community in high school—spending time talking to middle schoolers or with his Christian service endeavors—and how he always wore an approachable smile. He wasn't flashy in the beat-up car that he drove around town. Hughes recognized the roots of Brady's personality while spending time with the family, either at their house or talking sports with Tom Brady Sr. at a local pub near Bay Meadows Racetrack.

Hughes even recalled the quick-witted nature of the family during his first trip to their home when Brady Sr. cracked, "I just want to tell you that we really appreciate the fact that you drafted Tom, but he's not the best athlete in this house. These girls over here are better athletes than he is." Brady's three older sisters were well-known at the time to be the best athletes in the family.

Hughes attempted to intensify the recruiting pitch because the money wasn't cutting it. So he brought Brady to Candlestick Park when the Expos were in town to play the San Francisco Giants. Hughes set up Brady with an Expos uniform, a slot for batting practice with the team, and gave him full access to the clubhouse to mingle with the team. In a hilariously ironic turn of events, the plan completely backfired on Hughes when players like Rondell White and F.P. Santangelo couldn't figure out why Brady would ever want to live the minor-league life when he could rule the Big House.

"After a while, I come back and here's Tom sitting on a stool in front of a locker and there were seven or eight guys standing around him," Hughes mused. "He was holding court. He's got this presence about him. I heard one of the guys say to him, 'So let me get this right. You have a scholarship to play football where?' And he says the University of Michigan. They're like, 'Well, go to frigging school. Are you kidding me? You want to ride around in buses?' I went over to the G.M. and was like, 'I don't think these guys are giving us a heck of a lot of help over here.'"

Hughes strongly believed Brady would have been a major-league catcher within five years of turning pro, but he understood why it never happened. Brady had the whole package, a choice between football and baseball and the Bay Area boy who idolized Joe Montana had a chance to earn a college degree while pursuing his true passion. A few years later, Hughes even tried to talk the Expos into drafting Brady again just in case he fell out of love with football.

Brady's loyalty to the gridiron was ultimately tested, but there were periods of his development that offered a perfect analysis of the drive that has propelled him to unparalleled success in his preferred field.

Building a Legend

Tom Brady's photos have become laughable from his medical evaluation at the 2000 scouting combine, primarily because they hardly resemble the physique of an athlete who would later become the best to ever play his position. And really, that was years after Brady started to intensify his dedication to a regimented workout routine. But if Brady's career arc was even remotely predictable, he wouldn't have been the 199th pick of the draft. His internal drive, which couldn't be photographed or measured, has always been the root of his success.

Brady was a slow-footed, underdeveloped backup quarterback and outside linebacker for his freshman football team at Serra High, so he barely played. He showed progression as a sophomore quarterback for the junior varsity squad, so varsity coach Tom McKenzie pegged Brady as his starter for his junior and senior years. McKenzie sat down with Brady and his father during his sophomore year and said he'd probably have a chance to play in college.

But the quality of those opportunities would be dependent upon Brady's progression as an athlete. He began working with a personal trainer and jumping rope like a madman, to the point where it would have been comical if the rope-jumping workouts weren't so impressive. McKenzie said he usually struggled to get his baseball players into shape for football season, but he really respected Brady's routine because he arrived ready to go.

Serra deployed a run-heavy offense during Brady's junior season, and he only attempted six passes in his first start. But McKenzie redesigned the scheme to a three-receiver West Coast passing attack for his senior year, and Brady attempted 27 passes in that opener. Brady's talent was worth featuring as a senior, but Serra didn't have any capable running backs that season to further prioritize the passing focus. Brady's three starting receivers finished in the top four in the league in receptions.

The lack of running backs enhanced Brady's ability as a passer because defenses were blitzing frequently. They incorporated a short passing game, and McKenzie wanted Brady to get the ball out quickly and spread it around as much as possible. At one point, McKenzie thought Brady was getting too greedy and holding the ball longer than necessary to look for the deep stuff, so McKenzie made a threat: if Brady didn't follow the script, McKenzie would color-code the play calls with a red, white, and blue system to predetermine where Brady would throw the ball—red for the short option, white for the intermediate receiver and blue for the deep throw. Brady complied, and the offense soared.

"Teams gave up trying to blitz us because we would welcome it because the ball would be out already," McKenzie said.

It almost sounds like a mirror image of Brady's success with the Patriots. As defenses backed off Brady and tired throughout the game, he went to more five- and seven-step drops to open up the offense. Brady left Serra as the second-most-prolific passer in school history despite only getting one true season to show his capabilities.

McKenzie really trusted his quarterback because Brady had such an impressive confidence about himself. Brady, the master of the comeback at the NFL level, was always ingrained with the necessary swagger in those situations. When Serra trailed, McKenzie recalled Brady's philosophy during a conversation with the senior.

"Let's let it rip and see what we can do," McKenzie recalled. "If we worry about what we might do, we're going to lose anyway, so why not go for it? That's the attitude he has had. Let's try to make the comeback and make something special happen. He has great belief in himself and what every coach wants in every player, and that's a great competitive spirit. Of all the athletes I have ever coached, there is no one close to him in his competitive spirit."

Brady could have played college ball just about anywhere, and he was most heavily recruited by California, UCLA, Michigan, Illinois, and USC. He probably could have played both football and baseball at Cal and USC, and it was an absolute stunner when he chose Michigan. McKenzie even recalled getting a nasty phone call from someone at Cal after Brady's commitment to the Wolverines, a decision that even shocked his parents. But Brady was infatuated with Michigan's aura and the hard pitch from head coach Gary Moeller.

"They did one hell of a sales job," McKenzie said of Brady's visit to Ann Arbor.

Brady's five years at Michigan were imperfect, but he had a life-defining moment. It all started when Moeller lost his job in 1995 and was replaced by defensive coordinator Lloyd Carr. Brady redshirted and had a good offseason, and Carr remembered being impressed with the young quarterback's ability to keep his head upfield while under pressure. Scott Dreisbach won the quarterback competition in 1996 but injured his throwing hand five games into the season. Carr appointed Brian Griese as Dreisbach's replacement, which infuriated Brady.

Brady walked into Carr's office, sat down at a chair in front of his desk, and told him he was going to transfer. There was no doubt Brady would have been able to hook on elsewhere, as the University of California was among the schools that contacted McKenzie to see if they should reach out to Brady about a move. But the exchange with Carr and the ensuing 24 hours reshaped his attitude during his time at Michigan.

"[Brady] sat down in my office," Carr recalled, "and said, 'Coach, I think I'm going to transfer.' I said, 'Why?' He said, 'I just don't think I'm ever going to get a chance to play here. I don't think I'm getting a fair shot. I'm not getting the same reps.' I said, 'If you leave here, it will be the biggest mistake you'll ever make. You came here for the academics, and you came here to be a quarterback. You need to fight through this. You need to go out every day and just work as hard as you can, commit yourself to improvement every day. Have you made up your mind?' He said, 'I think so.' I said, 'Have you talked to your dad?' He said, 'Yup.'

"I said, 'Well, why don't you think about it tonight and come back tomorrow? If you want to leave, I'll give you your release, but I urge you not to leave.' So he came back the next day, sat down in the same chair right in front of my desk and leaned forward. He said, 'Coach, I've decided that I'm going to stay at Michigan, and I'm going to prove to you that I'm a great quarterback.' It was a powerful thing for a young kid. Really, from that day forward, there was nobody more committed to being the best he could be than Tom. He was fun to be around. He was such a great competitor. He brought his energy and his enthusiasm every day. He made us a better team simply because of the way he competed."

Brady finally won the starting job in 1998, but he still had to battle prodigal prospect Drew Henson for snaps in games. The pair rotated at times, even on a quarterly basis in 1999, but Brady was clearly the better of the two as the Wolverines closed the season with a five-game winning streak. In the final three games, Brady erased a 10-point, fourth-quarter deficit against Penn State, led a game-winning drive against Ohio State, and revived Michigan from a pair of 14-point holes against Alabama to win the Orange Bowl.

Brady still wasn't the most sought-after quarterback in the run-up to the 2000 draft, and a half dozen signal callers were selected before him. The Patriots did tip their hand with some interest, though. General manager Bobby Grier watched closely at Brady's pro day and called Carr again about Brady before the draft. Dick Rehbein, the Patriots quarterbacks coach from 2000-01 until his death, also expressed plenty of interest in Brady.

Shortly after the Patriots brought Brady to New England, the quarterback was the subject of another iconic moment. He walked down a flight of stairs at Foxboro Stadium, pizza box in hand, when he encountered owner Robert Kraft for the first time. Brady told Kraft he made the best decision of his life with the 199th pick of that draft.

Somehow, Brady might have undersold that point.

The Drive

Tom Brady bought a condo in Franklin, Massachusetts, from Ty Law, who previously acquired it from Scott Zolak. (Law wanted to give Zolak the full $263,000 in a check after he cashed his signing bonus, but Zolak advised Law to take out a loan and build up his credit. Just an example of how plenty of rookies have to grow up quickly when they get to the league.)

Brady was one of the only players from the 2000 draft class to own a place, so it became a natural hangout spot for some of the young guys. The place was equipped with a pool table and big-screen TV in the basement, and they racked up a lot of hours playing three-ball. Brady also hooked up an old-school Nintendo, and they'd gamble on games of Mario Kart and Tecmo Bowl, sometimes even setting up a tournament format.

Brady took it all so seriously, and he'd piss off his teammates to no end when he'd spike a controller and freeze up the whole system. He possessed an extreme competitive edge, and it was a window into his soul. With the understanding that success isn't universally derived from chucking a Nintendo controller, Brady's teammates at least recognized there was something different about him, even as a fourth-string rookie quarterback.

There were other clues over the years, too. Brady preyed his golfing companions with the ruthlessness of Michael Jordan. He'd grind away at their will, take their money, and walk off the course as best friends without fail. Brady is simply ingrained with an incessant need to beat everyone at everything.

Here's another one. Brady and his crew have been regulars at the Kentucky Derby for years. When word got out a couple years ago that Green Bay Packers quarterback Aaron Rodgers was going to bring some teammates to the Derby, Brady declared to his entourage that nobody would bring a bigger, livelier group than the Patriots contingent. So Brady made sure to get as many guys involved as possible, including Rob Gronkowski. As they were getting ready to leave, Brady caught wind that Gronk might be bailing on the trip, so Brady called Gronk about a half dozen times at the crack of dawn. For some context, the two don't talk a ton outside of the workplace due to their busy schedules and the fact that they're in different stages of their lives—Brady has three kids, and Gronk is a man child—so Gronk's eyes popped out of his head when he realized Brady was blowing up his phone. The pair finally connected, and Brady made damn well sure Gronk was getting on that plane with him because there's no way Rodgers could top a Gronk party. And a Julian Edelman party. And a Wes Welker party. And Larry Izzo. And Danny Amendola. And, you get the idea.

Brady is maniacal about it all, and he truly met his competitive counterpart in Darrelle Revis in 2014. They talked endless amounts of trash to each other all season, and there was one day when Bill Belichick decided to have some fun with it. Belichick closed down practice and split up the team for a soccer shootout, with one side of players working as shooters and the other side as goalies. As always, it came down to Brady against Revis. Who do you think won?

He wasn't always victorious. The quarterbacks set up an exercise called "the bucket drill" in the late 2000s, and Brady and his counterparts would simply try to throw a high-arching pass into a barrel from anywhere between 20 to 40 yards. It wasn't easy or common to sink a shot, so each successful throw yielded a handsome payment. Brian Hoyer drained more shots than Brady in 2011, and it infuriated Brady to hilariously preposterous levels. It was no coincidence the drill disappeared from practice until 2016.

Brady has been historically successful in the NFL for nearly two decades because he essentially dedicates his entire existence to his craft. Even during the occasions when Brady is attending an event or conducting one of his charitable endeavors, he'll chug a shake or bottle of juice at a pre-planned hour. His diet is well-documented and non-negotiable, and his workout regimen is comparable. There are tons of examples of Brady remaining after practice to work out with a resistance band around his waist and tethered to a trainer. After that, he'll run sprints, maybe lie on the grass for a few minutes, and then rip off a series of sit-ups and push-ups, sometimes 45 minutes after the entire team returned to the locker room.

The quarterback had another great sequence during training camp in 2016 when he controlled first-team reps despite his impending suspension. The Patriots split up into a blue-white scrimmage during the second week of camp, and Brady completed

188

all 25 of his pass attempts during a 17-9 victory against Jimmy Garoppolo's team. Beyond the ridiculous numbers, Brady's intensity shined when he called a timeout before a third-and-5 to discuss the ensuing play call with assistant coach Brian Daboll, which caused Belichick to roll his eyes and order his quarterback to return to the huddle. Brady then delivered a touchdown pass to Chris Hogan. The quarterback also lost his damn mind while firing up his team after a touchdown throw to Brandon Bolden and another time when James Develin made a diving grab. There was another stretch when Belichick blew back-to-back plays dead on would-be touchdowns, and Brady gave his coach a "you've got to be kidding me" look. On his last possession, Brady slowed down his unit into a four-minute drill to run out as much clock as possible, simulating a game situation amid the eighth practice of training camp. Afterward, Brady got close enough to Gronk's earhole to whisper some colorful trash talk to his losing opponent.

The Patriots had a rematch the next day, but there was a twist when Belichick made it harder on Brady. Belichick took away Hogan, Develin, Martellus Bennett, Malcolm Mitchell, and LeGarrette Blount, who combined for 19 of the 25 receptions in the first scrimmage. Still, Brady's team won 11–10 thanks to his game-clinching touchdown drive, and he completed passes to five players—three who were ultimately cut, one who was traded, and a special teamer in Bolden. Brady played behind the backup offensive line and against most of the starting defense. It was the ultimate, lighthearted "screw you" type of performance.

That level of energy is the norm, age be damned. Brady jumped on the back of D.J. Foster during a May 2017 organized team activity when the second-year running back made a big catch.

Keep in mind, this was about 10 weeks shy of the five-time Super Bowl champion's 40th birthday. For as often as his veteran teammates have seen the offseason exuberance, they're still struck by it. And for the newbies? That's when they start to understand it all.

Brady treats everyone the same way, and that extends off the field, whether it's the rookies and veterans in the locker room or a fan at a community event. His greatest work might be with the Best Buddies program, and he has become genuine friends with Chris Harrington and the family, spending time and conversing with them and others when there's no spotlight around. During his annual Best Buddies weekend with a football game at Harvard Stadium and a bike ride on Cape Cod, Brady speaks with anyone who approaches him. He was greeted in 2016 by Nicole Bjorkgren, a family friend of slain Auburn police officer Ronald Tarentino Jr. Bjorkgren asked Brady if he could help Tarentino's wife, Tricia, and three sons in their time of need. "I really want to help," Brady told her. Weeks later, Brady sent them an autographed jersey that the family auctioned off for $6,000 at a fundraiser. It's unimaginable how many families Brady has discreetly helped like this through the years.

And yet, he remains firmly committed to the Patriots. Brady usually beats the sun to Gillette Stadium, and he is tenacious about treatment for injury prevention and recovery. He saw first-hand that Drew Bledsoe nearly had to die on the field—that's not even an exaggeration—to win the starting job in 2001, so the array of shoulder sprains, cracked ribs, ankle sprains, knee tweaks, and bone bruises aren't going to keep him out for a week. Brady has been injured more than he has ever disclosed, but only a torn ACL took him off the field.

The Patriots run Brady's offense, not the other way around. Brady designed it with offensive coordinator Josh McDaniels, who has remained onboard longer than expected in his second stint to see it through with the greatest quarterback to ever grace a huddle. The line protections, the route tree that is dedicated to get the ball out within 2 to 2.5 seconds, the hot reads, they've all got Brady's imprint.

That's why Belichick turned it over to Brady during the 2014 playoff game against the Baltimore Ravens, who had leads of 14–0 and 28–14 before Brady was given the authority to call every play on the field. He didn't panic then, and he was practically unfazed in the face of a 28–3 deficit against the Falcons in Super Bowl LI. One thing Brady wanted to do then? Drag out the game because it was his seventh Super Bowl and many of the Falcons' first. Brady's opponents didn't appreciate the post-halftime exhaustion that comes with a longer game, so if he could wear them down, he knew the Patriots had a chance.

Every game is an experience, and every experience has stuck with Brady, whether he was playing for a buck in three-ball in his condo or a priceless fifth Super Bowl ring in Houston. He adapted to Tom Martinez's route tree at Serra High and refined McDaniels' Odyssey at Gillette. He captivated major-league ballplayers at Candlestick Park as a teenager and taught young Patriots how to act like kids as a 39-year-old.

There's no mystery why the Patriots have always tried to give Brady even more in return, as impossible of a task as it might always seem.

Tom's Boys

The emotional high never tapered from Tom Brady's return in 2016, and it was wild to witness. Obviously, since 2001 Brady's Patriots teammates have played hard for him, among other reasons, but this was different. There was a welcoming party for Brady's return to Gillette in Week 5 upon the completion of his suspension.

The Patriots then unleashed hell in the form of a 33–13 firestorm against the Browns in Cleveland. Before the game, when players are dressed in suits for the bus ride to the road stadium, defensive end Jabaal Sheard wore a Brady jersey, reversed so the quarterback's name flashed across his chest. Sheard wanted Brady to sign the jersey for good measure. After the game, Rob Gronkowski noted the intensity of the locker room and said, "Tom always brings the ampness." Yeah, Gronk made up a word. The party continued the following week for Brady's first home game against the Bengals—as if the "on to Cincinnati" week wasn't enough torture for the Bengals in 2014—and the Pats ripped off a 35–17 win amid a sea of season-long "Brady! Brady!" chants from the home crowd.

Fast forward to Week 12, when the Patriots beat the Jets 22–17 at MetLife Stadium. Brady orchestrated the 50th game-winning drive of his career to also notch his 200th win, which tied Peyton Manning for the most in history. Again, cue the locker-room celebration that centered on Brady. Martellus Bennett was impressed with Brady's steadiness throughout the tough game and fourth-quarter deficit. "It's nothing new to him. He just continues to build on his legacy," Bennett said.

Brady set the record with his 201st victory a week later with a 26–10 beating of the Rams at Gillette. It was surreal to hear

Brady's teammates gush over him. Malcolm Butler said, "We're in the locker room with a walking legend." Julian Edelman, who has been one of Brady's best friends for years, called it "an honor" to be his teammate and said Brady "should be the face of the league."

For some context, the Patriots were personally offended when the NFL put Brady through the ringer for two years over Deflategate. Rather than being the face of a mucked-up scandal, Brady should be marketed more aggressively as a guy who has proven that hard work can transform an underdog into a G.O.A.T. Every player who has walked through the Patriots' locker room since, say, 2005 has had that "holy crap" moment when they meet Brady, and then it subsides. But that stretch in 2016 freshened up those feelings again.

There was another element involved here, too. So many times each season, national reporters converge on Gillette Stadium with the intentions of producing an evergreen story about Brady's greatness. It's an easy topic, for sure, but there are only so many times Brady's teammates can sum up the quarterback's accomplishments without rolling their eyes and rattling off a cliché. (Related: "Can you tell me something no one else knows about Tom Brady?" is always everyone's favorite question. Because Brady has been intensely covered for a decade and a half, players usually react with a look like, *If I unveil his secrets now, I'll be off the team by dinnertime.*) But when asked about Brady during this stretch, his teammates opened the floodgates. They were in awe of the record-setting win total and humbled to play a part in it.

As the Patriots barreled toward Super Bowl LI against the Falcons, Brady's teammates were increasingly vocal in their desire to complete the redemption tour for him. The entire season led up to that point for them. "I think it's pretty obvious," Danny Amendola said as they prepped to win the Super Bowl for Brady.

There's more to it than that as well. Brady's teammates genuinely adore him because he treats them with a level of respect that they generally wouldn't expect out of a superstar.

"I think that's a little bit uncommon for a superstar like that to care about the special teams guys or the practice squad guys," Patriots special teams captain Matthew Slater said. "We're all equal in his eyes, and we really appreciate that about him."

Those weren't empty words from Slater. It's impossible to count the amount of practice squad players and rookies who have shuffled in and out of the locker room over the years who were taken aback when Brady walked up to them to introduce himself. They all laugh after the fact because if there's anyone at Gillette Stadium who doesn't need an introduction, it's Brady.

Rob Ninkovich will never forget the time when he walked by Brady and complimented his watch. On Christmas that season, Brady gave Ninkovich an identical version as a present. Dont'a Hightower was informed of Ninkovich's story and immediately cracked, "I'm about to go compliment that Escalade outside." Funny enough, it's not a huge stretch. Remember, Brady gave Malcolm Butler his ceremonious Super Bowl XLIX MVP truck.

Brady also sets up everyone with training and massage treatments at his TB12 facility at Patriot Place. There is always at least one shipment of UGG boots and slippers to every player on the team. And Brady hooked up everyone with his new line of Under Armour sleepwear when it was unveiled in 2017. Others have gotten headphones and other random tokens of appreciation.

"Tom is the heartbeat," Ninkovich said. "The guy is phenomenal, a competitor, the best quarterback ever. It's not just the way he is on the football field."

Of course, Brady has reached the age where most of his teammates were actually his fans while growing up watching the NFL. Brady was at least 10 years older than 43 of the Patriots on the 53-man roster for Super Bowl LI. Logan Ryan was among the group who admitted to owning a Brady jersey since he was about 10 years old.

The NFL picked the wrong guy to engage in a battle for power.

"I think a lot of guys grew up actually watching Tom Brady," Hightower said. "To actually play with him is one thing, but to see him shatter these goals and all of the things that he has done, it's very rewarding. As cliché as it sounds, it's crazy to come in and be able to see the guy work as hard as he does and to have all these things come up about him. It's great to see your teammate conquer goals and reach a milestone as big as that. It's 200-something wins, so it's really crazy. I'm proud to be able to say that I play with Tom Brady."

Since 2008 when Brady showed his mortality with a torn ACL, there's been this strangely incessant impulse to try to predict the end of his career. It's almost like people think they'll get a more passionate pat on the back years from now when they're sitting with their friends in a bar and can brag about that time they knew before anyone else Brady's career was over.

First, it was, *Can he perform at the same level after his knee injury?*

Then, it was, *Look, he's not winning Super Bowls anymore. He must not be as clutch. He can't win when he's getting hit.* But seriously, what quarterback performs well when he's getting hit?

More recently, it's been, *Brady can't play into his 40s because no one has played into their 40s.*

Before Brady, no quarterback had won more than four Super Bowls. No professional athlete has ditched tomatoes to prevent swelling or bragged about their lust over avocado ice cream. No one has ever been so maniacal about their health and conditioning. So the logic is Brady can't play into his 40s because Joe Montana and Joe Elway and Dan Marino and Brett Favre and Peyton Manning all broke down in their late 30s? Brady shouldn't be compared to them. They should be compared to him.

So again, what can't this guy do?

CHAPTER 8

DYNASTY: PART I (2001–04)

Nobody with a rational frame of mind wakes up one day and has visions of dynasties dancing in their heads. It'd be an even greater degree of lunacy if any members of the New England Patriots daydreamed of such success in August 2001, especially any holdovers from the 1990s. They lost six of their last eight games in 1999, fired head coach Pete Carroll, and were 5–11 in their first season with Bill Belichick in 2000.

"I would love to meet the guy who had that type of big-picture view in August of 2001," said linebacker and special teamer Matt Chatham, who won three Super Bowls with the Patriots during his tenure from 2000 to '05.

The Patriots prepared for the 2001 season with an intently narrow focus. With few exceptions, virtually every player on the roster was competing for his employment. They recognized Belichick was a rigidly strict coach who preferred his players to have some versatility and to go about their business with their heads down. Past performance carried no weight, which was expressed down the stretch in 2000 when a handful of younger players like Troy Brown were vaulted into more prominent roles than previously established veterans. Belichick experimented with different players in different situations, and those who shared Belichick's frame of mind could almost predict which personalities weren't going to make the team out of camp in 2001. Everyone was still trying to figure out Belichick, but they at least understood the requisite level of attention to succeed in his camp.

In retrospect, the 2001 Patriots were far more talented than anyone probably recognized at the time, especially on defense with cornerback Ty Law; safety Lawyer Milloy; linebackers Tedy Bruschi, Willie McGinest, Ted Johnson, and Mike Vrabel; and defensive lineman Richard Seymour, the sixth overall pick in that year's draft. Law, Milloy, and McGinest were in the prime of their careers while the others were still ascending. And then guys like cornerback Otis Smith, safety Tebucky Jones, linebackers Bryan Cox and Roman Phifer, and defensive linemen Anthony Pleasant and Bobby Hamilton were terrific role players.

Obviously, the turnaround began in Week 2 when Tom Brady replaced an injured Drew Bledsoe, but Brady wasn't singularly responsible. He didn't need to step in and display the natural leadership traits that were more prominently showcased over time. Offensive coordinator Charlie Weis was the true leader of the group, though Brady's teammates all believed in his capabilities due to a really strong training camp and preseason. Brady had help, as running back Antowain Smith (1,157 yards, 12 touchdowns) was a significant addition after a solid tenure with the Buffalo Bills. Kevin Faulk and J.R. Redmond also added value, while wide receivers Brown (101 catches, 1,199 yards, five touchdowns) and David Patten paced the passing attack.

And let's not forget about the importance of their special teams. Brown and kicker Adam Vinatieri were the stars, but Belichick has always viewed Larry Izzo as the best special teamer whom he has ever employed. Chatham was another key piece, and the pair of linebackers were the necessarily crazy components to leading the special teamers. Back in that era, when wedges were still legal on kickoffs, every team needed at least one guy who wasn't afraid to grab the smelling salts and kamikaze a wedge for the good of his teammates.

But look, they were all nuts. Willie McGinest used to crack up the locker room by running around like a madman wearing nothing but a wrestling mask. Izzo once got a game ball from Belichick for taking a shit on the sideline. Bruschi, long before becoming a great linebacker, was a tornado on special teams and at practice, even as veterans talked about the undersized rookie behind his back like he was a walk-on from junior varsity. That group was the heart of the defense on the field, and they would have bonded well with the 2004 Boston Red Sox, who were adored as lovable idiots.

"A lot of guys were crazy," Chatham laughed. "You have to have a screw loose to play linebacker in the NFL. We're all nuts."

(The linebackers weren't the only kings of the prank wars during that era. Left tackle Matt Light once had a friend show up to training camp and stand right underneath the play clock so all the coaches would have to see him. The friend was dressed up in daisy duke jean shorts, waving pom-poms, and holding signs that read I LOVE MAYO ON MY BUNS and TOMMY, HIT ME IN THE SLOT. Every coach thought it was hysterical, but Belichick never acknowledged it. Light also plastered pictures across the locker room of Brady's *GQ* magazine spread when he was holding a goat. And Brady once stripped the tires off Matt Cassel's car, stacked three in front of his locker, and sent him on a scavenger hunt for the fourth.)

The Patriots weren't thinking about Super Bowl XXXVI, though. Or the AFC Championship Game. Or probably even an AFC East title. From Week 10 in 1999 through Bledsoe's final start in Week 2 of 2001, the Patriots had lost 19 of 26 games. They weren't delusional.

Then, like a slow snap of a finger, it somehow came together. Another theme of that season was how a team named the Patriots rallied together in the wake of the 9/11 terror attacks. The team instantly converged to support offensive lineman Joe Andruzzi, whose three brothers were New York City firefighters who were dispatched to the World Trade Center. (The Andruzzi family's commitment to public service is expansive. Joe and his wife, Jen, helped launch the C.J. Buckley Brain Cancer Research Fund at Boston Children's Hospital in honor of a young boy and family friend who succumbed to a brain tumor. Andruzzi later overcame Burkitt's lymphoma and started the Joe Andruzzi Foundation in 2008 to help families of cancer patients pay their expenses. And in 2013, Andruzzi and Chatham were on Boylston Street in Boston for a JAF event during the Marathon bombings, and both helped victims of the explosion.)

Andruzzi got word of the attacks while sitting in the dentist's chair, and there were some tense moments that morning and the ensuing days during the firefighters' rescue efforts. The Patriots honored all three firefighters before their Week 2 game against the New York Jets, and Andruzzi ran onto the field with two American flags in his hands.

"It was a hair-on-the-back-of-your-neck situation," Chatham said. "We were all pretty distracted, especially for Joey, to see what was going on. We knew the emotions he was going through. He walked down with us and had the two flags with him, and all three of his brothers and his dad were out on the field. I remember standing with Lonie Paxton and Dave Nugent at the time. We knew the thing was going to happen with Joe. It was just tingles. You were thinking about stuff other than football, which isn't normal."

In an unexpected twist, that ceremony actually spooked the players due to an unannounced flyover. Before that, there was a security briefing that was designed to ease their concerns as the world changed around them. It wasn't uncommon for their imaginations to veer off course, recognizing a football stadium could be a target for a hijacked plane. So with that in mind, the Patriots were informed that all flyovers would be completely eliminated.

"We all stood on the side for the anthem," Chatham said. "I'm with Lonie and Dave, and the flyover happened. You could hear a rumble of a plane in the distance, and I remember looking to the guys to the left and right of me going, 'What the fuck?' Why is there a plane going over our stadium? We were told this shit wasn't going to happen. What do we do here? What the hell? There was the cool, American moment, but I think there was still some palpable nervousness over what was going on. I remember being distracted in that game. To this day, I don't remember a ton of details from it other than Drew getting injured."

Brady certainly stabilized the offense by limiting turnovers, and Weis and Belichick harped on the importance of complementary football. Law had two of their five defensive touchdowns, and Brown returned a pair of punts to the end zone in the regular season. Patten had an historic performance in a Week 6 win against the Colts with a 29-yard touchdown run, a 91-yard touchdown catch, and a 60-yard touchdown pass to Brown.

The Patriots, who were the sixth-ranked scoring offense and defense, won eight of their final nine games, and the lone loss, 24–17 against the Rams, carried as much weight as any performance. On Labor Day, the Patriots assembled a collection of 53 guys who were largely happy to accomplish the simple goal of gainful employment. By Thanksgiving, they believed something far greater could be in their future.

Title Run

The second-seeded Patriots were 11–5 in the regular season thanks to a six-game winning streak after the loss to the Rams, and they opened the postseason against the Raiders in a perfect winter evening at Foxboro Stadium. The Raiders, who trounced the Jets in the wild-card round, appeared to be a juggernaut before dropping their final three regular-season games. The Patriots were thrilled to welcome their visitors with a blizzard to add to the pageantry of such an improbable season.

And how's this for the evolution of roles? Tom Brady completed 32 of 52 passes for 312 yards in his playoff debut—in an insane snowstorm. It was his second-highest passing output of the season, and he threw for more yards that night than he did in the next two games combined. Oakland's Rich Gannon, who was in the middle of a string of four consecutive Pro Bowl appearances, was just 17 of 31 for 159 yards and a touchdown.

Tight end Jermaine Wiggins, who caught 14 passes all season, had 10 grabs in the Snow Bowl. And the typically dynamic Troy Brown fumbled two punts in the fourth quarter. Larry Izzo recovered both, and the Patriots scored on each drive to erase a 13–3 deficit. On that first touchdown drive, Brady was 9 of 9 for 61 yards, and he capped it with a tumbling, six-yard scoring run to make it 13–10 with 7:52 remaining in regulation.

Let's fast forward a few series for a moment to a first-and-10 with 1:50 to play. Charles Woodson strip-sacked his old Michigan teammate and Greg Biekert recovered the fumble. The Patriots used their three timeouts on the previous possession, so the game would have been over if referee Walt Coleman didn't review the play and overturn the ruling by citing the little-known Tuck Rule. To put it in context, Bill Belichick's Patriots have been the most prepared team on the planet for almost two decades, and you'd be hard-pressed to find any players who had ever heard of the Tuck Rule before that moment. It also mercifully served as a monumental break for a franchise that had some difficult playoff losses littered throughout its history, including a phantom flag against Ray "Sugar Bear" Hamilton to help the Raiders win a matchup between the teams in 1976. So for a fumble to end this ride? Say it ain't so.

The Tuck Rule has served as an obvious form of contention for those Raiders. The Patriots laugh it off every time they hear the Raiders complain about the enforcement of what was then an actual, legitimate rule. The Patriots also roll their eyes when the Raiders blame the loss on that singular play. After the Patriots made it 13–10, the Raiders moved the ball to the Patriots' 45-yard line but couldn't score. And when the teams exchanged punts and the Raiders recouped possession with 2:41 remaining, Charlie Garner's seven-yard run set up the Raiders with second-and-3. Tedy Bruschi then stopped Garner for two yards and 240-pound fullback Zack Crockett for no gain on third-and-1 to force the punt. In that era with a natural grass field that was blanketed in snow, the offense has a major advantage on short-yardage runs, but the Patriots made the decisive stops.

Then immediately after the Tuck Rule play, the Raiders gave David Patten too much of a cushion for an easy 13-yard completion. Three plays later, Brady's one-yard sneak might have been every bit as valuable because Adam Vinatieri's game-tying, 45-yard field goal through the snow miraculously crossed through the uprights. Brady then completed all eight of his overtime passes for 45 yards during the Pats' 15-play, 61-yard game-winning march that concluded with Vinatieri's 23-yard field goal. The Patriots converted twice on third down and once on fourth-and-4 before Vinatieri won the game.

So when the Raiders complain about the Tuck Rule, they're whistling past their own graveyard.

"The Tuck Rule? Never heard of it at all," Chatham said. "It's annoying to me that it's remembered as the difference. If you're Oakland and want to blame the loss on that and live with that shit for the next 20 years of your life, not being able to convert second-and-3 and third-and-1 there with two chances at it, that was huge. Then giving the ball up and not finishing the series. There were so many opportunities for them before and after the Tuck Rule to still keep us out of it where we could have reasonably pulled it off. I look at it with a Patriots lens, but their situational football was really bad. Yeah, the Tuck Rule happened, but there were several instances where they should have beaten us if they executed in those spots. I look back at it like, it'd be one thing if the Tuck Rule ended the game and we kicked it from that spot, but that's not what happened. A, they never should have given up the ball without points on the other end of it before the Tuck Rule series. B, there were a lot of yards that they had to give up after the Tuck Rule. I hadn't heard of the rule, but if I were part of that team, I'd think that was a pathetic excuse."

The Patriots then drew a date in Pittsburgh with the Steelers, who were publicly overlooking their opponents. Because the NFL postponed its Week 2 schedule for 9/11, there wasn't a bye week between the conference championship games and Super Bowl XXXVI. The Steelers were openly treating AFC championship week as their bye, saying they were setting up ticket requests and travel arrangements to New Orleans for the Super Bowl. The Patriots became famous in that era for drawing motivation from various sources, real or contrived, but they were genuinely offended by the Steelers that week.

It was another ultimate team win, by a 24–17 count, as Brown had a 55-yard punt return for a touchdown and recovered Brandon

Mitchell's blocked punt before lateralling it to Antwan Harris for a 49-yard score and 21–3 lead. In between, Drew Bledsoe replaced an injured Brady and delivered an 11-yard touchdown pass to Patten.

Brown enjoyed the best special teams performance of his Patriots Hall of Fame career, and it validated his prolonged rise. He was drafted in 1993 in the now-defunct eighth round, cut in 1994, and unemployed for two months before Bill Parcells re-signed him. Parcells and Pete Carroll were always looking for someone bigger or faster than Brown, but he cut his teeth in the kicking game and continuously displayed soft hands that Scott Zolak knew would be useful if he ever got his shot. Brown eventually enhanced offensive coordinator Charlie Weis' spread offense as one of the league's first great slot receivers.

The Patriots celebrated on the flight home from Pittsburgh on Sunday night, got their arrangements in order Monday morning, and immediately turned around for New Orleans. The absence of a bye week worked in Belichick's favor because the Patriots' attention on the Rams never waned. The team went out on their own for dinner Monday night—NOLA's was a popular spot—dealt with Media Day the following morning, and cracked down from there on out. The Patriots were 14-point underdogs, but they weren't daydreaming about the biggest upset in Super Bowl history. Per Belichick's culture, they obsessed over assignments. Like outsiders who never thought the Patriots had a chance, the Patriots weren't thinking, "Can we actually beat this team?" It was really about, "Who do I cover on this play?"

Ty Law always knew who to cover, and his coaches and teammates knew it, too. He became an elite man-coverage cornerback under Carroll's tutelage and with Otis Smith's guidance, and there was little need to deploy him in any other capacity.

Belichick's pregame meetings were always stressful, and Law's brashness provided a level of levity. Belichick would go around the room and ask players for their assignments on various plays, and he'd also want the players to know others' tasks. They'd get ripped for wrong answers, which wasn't exactly a common occurrence. These guys were well-equipped to rattle off the percentage of times their opponents would run a specific play on third-and-short. They were smart, studious, and accountable to each other.

Law was cocky in a great way, and he was beloved in that locker room. So for example, if Belichick asked Law a question during Bills week, Law would immediately reply, "Fuck Eric Moulds!" Colts week? "Fuck Marvin Harrison!" You get the idea. The room cracked up every single time.

"We just all knew Ty was one of the best in the game at what he did, and it was sort of a weird contrast to a Belichick room," Chatham said. "It was just, show me who to cover. It made for some comic relief. They try to get him with the quiz stuff or, 'What is Richard Seymour doing on this play?' He didn't give a fuck, but that was real. Ty had such a unique talent, could dominate his position, and was a huge asset to the team."

Law was always one of the funniest guys in the room, and he was definitely their most ruthless ball buster. When the Patriots would load the buses at the stadium to head to the airport for road trips, the first two buses were for the coaches and executives. They were serious buses. But Bus 3, that's where you don't fight the Law because the Law always wins. Those guys would rip the hell out of each other for the whole ride, and Law was the ringleader. You needed thick skin and great material for that ride because Law's delivery was like a Louisville Slugger to the melons. He'd know everything about your family, and no one was off limits. Or maybe your clothes were an easy target, or really anything else. If you accidentally got on Bus 3, you better keep your head down and pray Law didn't notice you, because there were tears.

Law earned his respect, though. He worked out as hard as anyone in that locker room, and players would look at his eight-pack of abs and wonder where he stored the Big Macs that he'd routinely demolish. The fact is the junk food never had a chance with Law. There'd be times after a cold, winter practice when guys couldn't wait to get off the field, watch some film, and get home. It'd be dark out, just about dinnertime, and teammates would walk past the weight room to find Law on the treadmill, dialed all the way up, wearing full gear and going hard for another half hour. He was the damn truth.

And so came Rams week: "Fuck Isaac Bruce!"

Law was a handful for the Rams' star receiver in Super Bowl XXXVI, and he plucked Kurt Warner's errant second-quarter pass in that direction, returned it up the sideline with his right hand raised, and gave the Patriots a 7–3 lead. Locals will never forget Law's three-pick performance against Peyton Manning in the 2003 AFC Championship Game, but it was Law's pick-six against Warner that solidified their early dominance with some points that propelled the Pats to victory.

The win was cemented yet again by the right foot of the most clutch kicker in NFL history, as Vinatieri became the first player to bang home a Super Bowl–winning field goal at the buzzer, just 15 days after his Snow Bowl heroics. He had a repeat effort in Super Bowl XXXVIII against the Panthers.

Vinatieri was always special, but there have been a lot of great kickers who have turned into puddles in crunch time. There's a naturally ingrained talent in some of the best, but don't discount the peripheral factors that propelled him. Parcells was always tough on his kickers—save for maybe Matt Bahr, who used to sit on an upside-down Gatorade bucket and read books during practice—and Vinatieri trained like crazy with strength coach Johnny Parker. He'd go through drills with linebackers and tight ends, and it was no coincidence Vinatieri ran down Cowboys star Herschel Walker on a kickoff in 1996.

Vinatieri earned that "football player" label from his coaches and teammates. There were times when Parcells would put the full onus on Vinatieri at the end of practice in training camp to make a kick that would give the players a night off. Parcells would put the spotlight right on him, squirt the ball with a water bottle, and tell him to make a 47-yarder from the left hash. No, that wasn't Super Bowl pressure, but kickers never want their teammates to look down on them like dispensable part-timers. The great thing about coaches like Parcells and Belichick is they ensure practices are treated like games, so by the time Sunday came it'd be second-nature to the players, especially from a mental perspective.

Vinatieri was admired, to the point where his teammates would wonder what the heck Parcells was doing when he'd work out other kickers during lunch, all while the players were on the Foxboro Stadium club section looking down on the game field. Ditto for 1998 when Carroll brought in Phil Dawson to push Vinatieri, who at that point shouldn't have had to compete for his job. Dawson had a heck of a camp, too.

Vinatieri's kickoffs were even a thing of beauty, and Izzo and Chatham genuinely appreciated the kicker's accuracy because it helped their coverage path. If Vinatieri was expected to put the ball

on the 3-yard line several paces off the sideline, Vinatieri would put the ball on the 3-yard line several paces off the sideline. He could kick a ball into a bucket more accurately than most could throw it.

Vinatieri was a chameleonic figure who could harness various environments. He was a country guy from South Dakota and liked hunting, fishing, and going on these wild offseason safaris. And when he arrived in Boston one offseason, he attended an event at a department store and wound up with a box of free FUBU gear. He basically got laughed out of the building the next day at Foxboro Stadium. More practically, Vinatieri was the first guy on the team to begin wearing a wet suit under his uniform to stay warm during extreme weather conditions. His teammates laughed at first, but they quickly adopted the idea. Brady took up the tactic for a while before the clothing technology caught up to speed.

For anyone who knew Vinatieri, there was no surprise that he delivered on his 48-yard kick from the right hash at the Superdome to finalize the Patriots' 20–17 victory against the Rams. And finally, with that concluding one of the most improbable title runs in history, the Patriots had no more assignments, no more quizzes. It was time to party.

"You don't have time to dream before the game," Chatham recalled. "It sounds corny as shit. I get that. When we did win, it was like, 'Holy shit, we won.' I hadn't even allowed myself to consider it, and it wasn't because I had just been happy to be there. It was because I hadn't gotten there yet. You could see the shot when Adam makes the kick, and there's a shot on the front page of the *Times-Picayune* the next morning of me leaping in the air, and I'm like at the shoulder level of the guy next to me. I have no idea how I got that high. I have a terrible vertical. I remember Bill busting my balls on the flight home. He had a copy of the *Times-Picayune* and gave me a hug and a high-five. He says, 'You see this, Chatham?' I'm like, 'Fuck yeah, let's go back and retest my vert!'

"We won and I remember that scene. Everyone is running onto the field and high-stepping and you see Antowain Smith on all the highlights. At that moment, it was finally okay to realize what really happened. That post-party at the Fairmont in New Orleans, you're just sitting there with a shit-eating grin, and Snoop Dogg is sitting there with his gold, diamond-bedazzled goblet, and I'm sitting there with my shit-eating grin because it just happened. I'm like, 'Does everyone around us understand what just happened?' That night was one of the coolest nights of your life. You spend the next three or four hours boozing at the hotel, and it was one of those moments when you really think about it and let it all set in."

Dynasty Driven

By 2003, Bill Belichick had his system in place, and he had a greater library of examples on film to show the team when they needed to make certain improvements. For a coach as demanding as Belichick, it always helps when he can show the players what to do, as opposed to citing past examples from other teams like the 1980s Giants or whoever. They had the talent, the full-team commitment, and the understanding of how to accomplish something great. They would have been out of their minds to dream about a Super Bowl in August 2001, but the 2003 Pats added safety Rodney Harrison and linebacker Rosevelt Colvin in free agency and knew they were good enough to make a playoff march.

They got embarrassed 31–0 in the opener against the Bills and former teammate Lawyer Milloy, who joined the AFC East rival after his shocking release when he wouldn't take a pay cut. The loss caused ESPN personality Tom Jackson to say the Patriots "hate their coach," and pundits hammered home the idea that 2001 was a fluke. This was all the perfect setup for Harrison, who loved playing the "us against the world" card.

The Patriots were 9–2 and prepping for their Week 13 trip to Indianapolis, and they showed some real fortitude with six wins by a single score at that point. Their defining moment was against the Colts, and it was crucial because the Patriots had blown a 31–10 lead to Peyton Manning. Clinging to a 38–34 advantage, the Patriots allowed the Colts to navigate to the cusp of the goal line, as the hosts had first-and-goal from the 2. On fourth-and-1, Willie McGinest raced around the edge and engulfed running back Edgerrin James for a one-yard loss with 11 seconds to play, and the Patriots had won their eighth consecutive game.

McGinest was the Patriots' leader for virtually his entire career, even as others got more attention on the field. But he was a physically imposing pass rusher when the lights were on and an intimidating force with a corner stall in the locker room. He learned how to lead from Andre Tippett, and McGinest already had a strong voice because he knew how to disseminate his message. He was smart and deliberate when he spoke, so when he decided to talk to the room, everyone stood at attention.

No one messed with McGinest, well, except for 6'7", 300-pound defensive end Ferric Collons. Maybe this late-1990s encounter served as a cautionary tale for future Patriots, or maybe it was an isolated, selfishly moronic slipup on the first day of training camp.

The entire team had to gather at 5:30 in the morning in the basement of Dorm 15 at Bryant University for drug testing, so they all drank a ton of water the night before to accelerate the pace of the line. And as a result, the players showed up as early as possible to avoid prematurely soaking their shorts. Their eyes were half shut and they were miserable, but that was the deal. They understood the situation and had to respect the process.

McGinest was the third guy in line, and Sam Gash and Scott Zolak were right behind him. Collons stormed from the back of the line to cut everyone and promptly ran into a wall.

"Willie told him to get the fuck back," Zolak said. "Ferric said, 'I've got to pee.' Willie said, 'I'll tell you one more time. Back the fuck up and get in line.' Ferric said, 'Fuck that.' Next thing you know, smack, and Ferric's right eye swells up right away. Willie clocked him. Ferric took a swing, and Willie ducked and went, boom, popped him in the other eye. Ferric starts swinging again, and Sam Gash picks him up and says, 'Dude, it's over.' We went out for the morning session of two-a-days and came back and Ferric was laid up in the training room with an IV. The trainer was Ron O'Neal, and he said he had a bad reaction to food. I said, 'Yeah, the bad reaction to Willie's two fucking fists in the piss line.' It was no-nonsense. You didn't fuck with Willie. It was his team."

Returning to 2003 in Indianapolis, McGinest's fourth-down stop was a monumentally important moment because they avoided a three-touchdown collapse against Manning's Colts and got a decisive play from the heart of their defense.

The Patriots closed their regular season with 12 consecutive wins and knocked off co-MVPs Steve McNair and Manning in their first two playoff games. And then it was time to stave off the Panthers in a wildly entertaining Super Bowl where there was plenty of drama that extended well beyond the wacky box score.

That's saying something, too. The Patriots and Panthers played a scoreless first quarter, and the Pats took a 14–10 lead at halftime with all 24 points coming in the final 3:05 of the second quarter. They were scoreless again in the third, and the Patriots escaped with a 32–29 nail-biting victory thanks to a pair of go-ahead drives in the last 2:51. (Mike Vrabel caught one of his 10 career touchdowns to make it 29–29, and Ricky Proehl, like he did with the Rams in Super Bowl XXXVI, tied the game in the final moments with a touchdown catch.)

Before it all unfolded, Matt Chatham added to his on-field résumé by becoming a folk hero. A streaker stormed the field as the teams were lining up for the second-half kickoff, and Chatham dropped a shoulder into the nude rube to end the charade. Chatham has retold the story a hundred times over, and he is still angrier about the ensuing kickoff than the naked guy who tried to get a rise out of the crowd.

"In context, the first Super Bowl happens just after 9/11," Chatham said. "The Iraq War is going on, and there's a lot of patriotism and security conversations. You go back to the time and talk about how much concern there was over protocols and Super Bowl security, halftime stuff, sideline stuff. We were being briefed about it a lot as a team. Part of the surprise initially was that it happened in that era of security. In my mind, it wasn't, 'What's this funny guy doing?' It was more, 'Is he out here to do something bad or just a joker?' You don't know. I'm looking at Larry Izzo. He is looking at me. His arms are thrown up. I'm turning to my right, and Tedy Bruschi is making some bizarre faces. There was a frozen moment like, 'What the fuck do we do? Is this real? Is this dangerous? Is it really just a streaker?'

"Finally, he broke and ran, and I remember being weirded out by it and just giving him a shoulder. After I hit him, he kind of flew like a trash bag of mashed potatoes. I gave him a shot, but then I quickly kind of scuttled out of the frame because it wasn't like, 'Lay on him. Celebrate over him.' It was more annoyance. It was a pretty knock-down, drag-out first half. We had just gone in all focused and thinking about what we've got to do in the second half. Then this distraction happens, and New England is so anti-distraction.

"I'll tell you this, to this day, the thing that annoys me most about it is coming down covering the kickoff that happened right after it, I didn't get my block. I was covering one of the toughest guys in the NFL, Kemp Rasmussen. I had done pretty good against him throughout the day. He's a huge dude, and there aren't a lot of guys my size on kickoffs. He was 6'3", 265 pounds, and a heavy dude on kickoffs. Those guys fucking suck because they get rolling with a good head of steam. Even though you can kind of buck him a little bit, you have to wall them off because it's really hard to stop a guy running at full speed.

"I had a fucked-up neck. I had tweaked it several times throughout the year and pinched it during the practice week. After I knocked down the streaker, I didn't get my block on the very next play. He had gone over to my right side where my neck was jacked up, and when you've got a big guy rolling down, you've really got to give him a nice shot. My neck was fucking killing me. I was wearing one of those collars, and I don't have much mobility, can't swing my head left and right, couldn't get in a stance so I had to stay in a two-point the whole time. I remember being more pissed off that you get the adulation for the streaker thing, but I didn't fucking make the block. That meant so much more to me. I did really good against him the rest of the game, but it was more concerning that he slipped off me the next play down the field and made the tackle. That means way more to me than the other shit."

The other side of the story to Super Bowl XXXVIII flew way under the radar for outsiders, but it was far more obtrusive to the Patriots than a bare-bodied stranger with a dad bod. Earlier in 2003, the Patriots lost the league's best long snapper, Lonie Paxton, to a season-ending knee injury. His replacement, Sean McDermott, then went down in his first game, so Belichick cracked open the glass for their Week 16 emergency. Belichick summoned Brian Kinchen for the job, despite the fact the 38-year-old hadn't played an NFL game since 2000 and had been working as a teacher in Louisiana. Kinchen was a solid tight end during Belichick's five-year tenure with the Cleveland Browns, and he became a fulltime long snapper with the Panthers in 1999. He had experience, was respected in the league, and was familiar to Belichick, which is always important in dire situations.

Kinchen was fine for his pair of regular-season appearances but bounced a snap and floated a couple others in the ice-cold play-off opener against the Titans. He was then catching heat from the coaches at practice, and that furthered his anguish. His teammates became well-aware of the issues, especially punter and holder Ken Walter, who was tasked with catching every one of Kinchen's wayward wobblers. But no one realized the true depths of Kinchen's instability until he shared his story with *Sports Illustrated* in 2017, as he said he even tried to retire three days before Super Bowl XXXVIII because he had such an unsolvable case of the yips. Personnel director Scott Pioli wouldn't let Kinchen quit, so the long snapper tried to get over his issues in his hotel room. Decked out in full uniform, Kinchen was firing snaps into a wall of pillows to try to get his act together.

His teammates didn't know what to do, and they really became mortified the day of the Super Bowl when Kinchen sliced open his right index finger with a steak knife while trying to cut a roll of bread. There can be a bit of a comedic element to a specialist's struggles, but that gets tossed out the window when the Super Bowl is on the line, particularly for those who knew how they won it in 2001, and they recognize there's no way to help the poor dude.

"Brian is the nicest guy in the world, a really nice dude," Chatham said. "But cutting himself was just a 'what the fuck' kind of thing. You know he's in a volatile position, and you don't want to pile on. You don't want to be a source of stress for him. You want to be encouraging. It would always exist as a side conversation."

It all led to another hellish moment on the sidelines prior to Vinatieri's winning kick against the Panthers. As Brady led his squadron down the field for the winning score, the defensive players and offensive subs were mirroring them down the sideline. That's when they all noticed something many, if any, had never seen before. Kinchen was trying to snap the ball into the kicking net, which is normally reserved for Vinatieri's warmups in such a situation, and it wasn't exactly going so well. Chatham and Izzo couldn't believe what they were seeing.

"Brian was over there trying to snap it into the net. He was fucking bouncing them," Chatham said. "It was terrible. I remember Izzo and I giving each other looks like, 'What in the fuck?' You're giving each other bug eyes and shaking your head, but you don't want to contribute to it. You don't want to go over and if you pat him on the shoulder and say something encouraging, you're highlighting it. That makes it worse. If you go over and give him a speech like, 'Get your head out of your ass. We need you.' Then that makes it worse, too.

"It's like a reverse no-hitter. If he keeps fucking up, don't talk to him and maybe he'll get it right this time. It's not like you're dealing with a rookie or some guy who hasn't done it. He was a long-tenured guy who Bill previously had a ton of faith in to bring him in. In the back of your head, you know this guy is capable, so there's no reason to pile on or contribute in any way. You just have those side conversations, cross your fingers, and hope he pulls it off. I read about all the stress and mental anguish he was having. I didn't know that. He wasn't sharing it with anyone. You look back on it like, 'Thank God it all worked out.'"

With a dose of divine intervention, Kinchen delivered a perfect snap to Walter, and Vinatieri's 41-yard boot split the uprights with four seconds remaining. The Patriots' second Super Bowl party was under way.

Despite the Pats' penchant to squash outside distractions, they couldn't ignore their drive for their place in history, so they embraced it internally. They established an NFL record with their 21st consecutive victory in Week 7 of the 2004 season, and it was doubly nice to come against the New York Jets. They also set their sights toward becoming the second team in history (Dallas Cowboys: 1992–95)—and the first of the salary cap era—to win three Super Bowls in four years. That's when the "dynasty" word began getting thrown around, and the players were jacked up about it.

"It was like, 'Fuck yeah, let's do something special,'" Chatham said.

The 2004 Patriots encountered minimal on-field adversity on their way to their second straight 14–2 record in the regular season. The only storyline to cling to that season was the rise of the Pittsburgh Steelers with rookie quarterback Ben Roethlisberger, whose 13–0 regular-season record included the victory that halted the Patriots' winning streak. There was little drama in the AFC Championship Game rematch in Pittsburgh, as the Pats won easily 41–27 after building a 24–3 lead in the first half.

The achievement of their dynasty was the carrot at the end of the season-long stick, but it was still a challenge to meet Belichick's high standards on a weekly basis. The 2004 Patriots were as talented as any team in history, but there's a reason why talented teams sometimes fall short. It's exhausting to keep it together mentally long enough to be successful. It's even more taxing to do it when the success is rooted in past seasons, and that's the type of recipe that sometimes leads to shocking defeats such as the 29–28 fall to the Dolphins on Monday night in Week 15.

Belichick worked his magic on the eve of Super Bowl XXXIX against the Philadelphia Eagles, who were overmatched yet undeniably talented with a 13–3 record, a fifth consecutive season with at least 11 wins, and a fourth straight postseason with an NFC Championship Game appearance. Belichick could have stoked the fire with any number of talking points, including the bizarre trash talk from Eagles backup receiver Freddie Mitchell, but he opted for two key subjects during their Saturday night team meeting. Belichick has always been terrific at delivering a message to all 53 guys, so he addressed Harrison's "us against the world" types by disclosing the Eagles' plans for their Super Bowl parade route.

The most important element of the meeting sounds so simple, but it was incredibly effective. Belichick was scrolling through film like any other night before a game when he walked to the center of the room where the projector sat on a table with a white tablecloth. He cut the film much earlier than usual to pique the team's interest, turned on the lights and reached underneath the table to pull out both of the Patriots' Lombardi Trophies, and then returned to the front of the room to place the hardware on his podium. The way Belichick transfixed his room that night, it's not a stretch to think the Patriots won the Super Bowl before even going to bed.

"I've been in a thousand meetings, night before Super Bowls, big games, whatever," Chatham said. "That was the most captivated room I ever remember because it's so much different to talk about stuff than to be able to candidly show someone what they're working toward. I just remember chills upon chills upon chills. I remember making my own guys go around the room, look at Bruschi, look at Troy, look at Tom, guys who had seen it before. And they've got the big grin. Then you can also look around the room at Tyrone Poole, Vince Wilfork. You've got a blend of people who have been there, done that, some who are new to it, and no matter which tier you were in, you had a shit-eating grin, frozen with hair standing up on the back of your neck, on your arms, the goosebumps. It was like, 'That's why we're doing this shit.' I was overwhelmed by it.

"I remember thinking, 'We're going to get another fucking ring.' After four years, like a lot of guys, I was tired. Winning three in four was hard to do. It's really hard to stay focused. It's really hard to keep driving. The fourth year was hard for me. Been there, done that. It wasn't like I wasn't still trying to be a pro or trying to do my best. I was. But it loses some of its luster. I remember my own attention waning a little bit but still having a good season, still playing pretty good. It was just trying to find that emotional motivation that year. I remember it all coming back that night, like this is special."

The Patriots clipped the Eagles 24–21 in Super Bowl XXXIX. Still in their grass-stained white jerseys and blue game pants, they celebrated on the field at Alltel Stadium while holding up three fingers on one hand and clutching copies of *Patriots Football Weekly* in the other. It was headlined, DYNASTY!!! with three Lombardi Trophies against a faded blue background.

Twenty-two players won their third Super Bowl with the Patriots on February 6, 2005, including a half dozen who spent at least one on the practice squad or injured reserve. Amazingly, another 39 players won their second Super Bowl, including practice squadders and injured reserve residents, so 51 Patriots got to experience a Duck Boat parade through Boston after the 2003 and 2004 championships.

They were a dynasty by design. A collection of individuals with untapped talent and a burning desire to master their roles had shocked the football universe on their trek to Super Bowl XXXVI. They tweaked their flaws after missing the playoffs in 2002 and became dominant as back-to-back champs in 2003 and '04. Even though it was the Patriots' last Super Bowl win for a decade, they remained among the class of the NFL and set the stage for the longest-running and most successful dynasty in NFL history.

"It really gives me a pleasure and honor to say I was part of the Patriots organization, the dynasty and legacy of what they have built and continue to do out there," Colvin said. "I look forward to seeing how far they can stretch it."

CHAPTER 9
DYNASTY: PART II (2014–?)

Relative to past decades, when futility would have been an upgrade for the New England Patriots, their extended title drought was hardly a cause to ring the alarms off the lighthouse at Gillette Stadium. But when the taste of success is still so fresh, the shortcomings are incrementally bitter. That's a significant reason why their ascension back to the top of the mountain was so glorious in 2014 and again in 2016. Of course, there were other factors in play at the time, namely the unparalleled feeling of redemption against commissioner Roger Goodell and the NFL for its Deflategate-related witch hunt against their credibility.

The premise often gets lost on outsiders, but winning is hard, as quarterback Tom Brady frequently offers as a reminder. Everyone became so spoiled with the banners and the crowded trophy case from 2001–04, and the Super Bowls seemed so easy because they were claimed during the dawn of the partnership between Brady and head coach Bill Belichick. So fast forward through a bannerless decade, and New Englanders were wondering what in the world had gone wrong.

Plus, the Patriots were close during almost every single one of their shortened journeys from 2005 to '13, and they were dominant throughout that stretch as a whole. They led the NFL with 110 regular-season victories (11 more than the second-place Indianapolis Colts and 20 more than the third-place Pittsburgh Steelers during that time), and their nine playoff wins was tied for the most with the Steelers, Baltimore Ravens, and Seattle Seahawks, who all won Super Bowls over that period.

None of those wins did much to temper the pain of coming up short. The Patriots blew a 21–3 advantage and three fourth-quarter leads against the Colts in the 2006 AFC Championship Game.

They then suffered quite possibly the most agonizing defeat in sports history in Super Bowl XLII when the New York Giants executed a miraculous game-winning drive to stain the Patriots' perfect record. With a roster that was nearly as loaded in 2008, Brady tore his ACL in the regular-season opener. They still won 11 games but missed the playoffs due to a tiebreaker.

The 2009 Patriots, similar to the 2005 team, simply weren't good enough. They were clearly rebuilding in 2010 but still went 14–2 and grabbed the AFC's No. 1 seed—only to be embarrassed by the New York Jets in their playoff opener at Gillette Stadium, where they had beaten the Jets 45–3 just six weeks earlier. Cue up another Eli Manning comeback in a second Super Bowl loss to the Giants in 2011, when it was downright crazy that the Patriots even made it that far in the first place because of injuries on defense. (Wide receiver Julian Edelman was playing cornerback against Ravens stud receiver Anquan Boldin during the final drive of the AFC Championship Game.) And the Ravens and Denver Broncos bullied the Patriots in the 2012 and 2013 AFC title games, respectively.

Consider the themes of the circumstances, too. One theory is they were cursed—remember, this market also houses the Boston Red Sox—because of a couple of insane catches by Giants wideouts David Tyree and Mario Manningham, a season-ending injury to Brady, a high ankle sprain that hobbled superstar tight end Rob Gronkowski in Super Bowl XLII among his series of ailments, and back-to-back AFC Championship Game–turning injuries to lockdown cornerback Aqib Talib in 2012 and 2013. The helpless feeling of a decisive injury also lent credence to the critics who wanted to believe the Patriots were a product of Spygate. The only way to silence such a blanket statement would be to win, but that process ultimately took more patience than they realized.

Another theory is there was a clear map to knock off the Patriots by beating them up, and that was certainly part of the equation during their playoff losses. It became almost cliché that Brady could be taken down when he was continuously hit. But really, isn't that true for every quarterback? But nonetheless, the Patriots won those street fights from 2001 to '04, and they were on the receiving end during the drought.

All legitimate factors, to be sure, but to circle back to the initial point, it's tough winning a Super Bowl. The Patriots wouldn't have won their first if Adam Vinatieri didn't have the greatest postseason in history for a kicker. Their second was aided by John Kasay's kickoff out of bounds. And for their third, they got the game-winning defensive stand against the Philadelphia Eagles that they couldn't execute either time against the Giants. And even through all of that, it'd be borderline hyperbolic to restrict the successes and failures to a few highlights. Belichick frequently notes most games are decided by a few plays, and that's an undeniable point for nearly every Super Bowl of the current millennium, regardless of the Patriots' involvement in that game.

The relaunch of the Patriots' dynasty fortified their reputations. Brady won a fifth Super Bowl that set him apart from Hall of Famer Joe Montana and for all intents and purposes solidified his status as the greatest of all-time. Belichick's in-game coaching has essentially been beyond reproach, but the fourth and fifth Super Bowls strengthened his status in roster construction. Aside from Brady, the roster completely turned over during the gap in Super Bowl wins, and that process also included the departures of key personnel executives who are now scattered across NFL front offices. And for owner Robert Kraft and the Patriots' franchise in its entirety, they have a solid argument to be known as the greatest dynasty of all-time.

Oh, and don't forget about the critics, because the Patriots surely didn't. They won Super Bowl XLIX under an unforgiving microscope in the immediate aftermath of Deflategate. And after Brady served his four-game suspension in 2016, officially laying to rest an exhausting process, and getting through the season unscathed, Goodell's Lombardi Trophy presentation was as anticipated as a ceremony will ever be. Kraft, Belichick, and most of all Brady recognized the fifth was "unequivocally the sweetest."

Island Life

The lack of Lombardis likely led to the angst among the fan base upon the dawn of free agency in March 2014. The Patriots accelerated their rebuilding process in 2010 and had gotten close to ending the longest-running championship drought during New England's comically successful run of dominance on the professional sports landscape. They knew they didn't play well when they fell to the Denver Broncos in the 2013 AFC Championship Game, but a roster tweak and a healthy Rob Gronkowski could have been the difference. But the clock was again ticking in 2014, as the Red Sox had just won the World Series and the Bruins (2011) and Celtics (2008) weren't far removed from their most recent Duck Boat parades in Boston. For the Patriots, 2004 seemed like ages ago.

Panic struck on the first night of free agency when cornerback Aqib Talib landed a six-year, $57 million contract from the

Broncos. Anybody but the AFC champs, right? But less than 24 hours after Talib's departure, Bill Belichick dropped a bomb by reeling in the most high-profile free agent in franchise history. They netted cornerback Darrelle Revis on a deal that was structured to look like a two-year, $24 million pact, but it was obviously designed to pay him $12 million for 2014 alone. Revis said 26 teams showed interest in the five hours between his release from the Tampa Bay Buccaneers and his agreement with the Patriots.

The unlikely marriage between Revis and the Patriots was mutually beneficial. The Pats managed to upgrade their cornerback depth chart despite losing Talib, and they didn't have to commit huge money over the long haul to do it. For Revis, the New York Jets' first-round pick in 2007 who had been the premier corner in the game from 2008 until he tore his ACL in 2012, he had the chance to solidify his legacy with a Super Bowl after only making two career playoff appearances. And after disappearing for a year in Tampa, the 29-year-old would be back in the spotlight with the Patriots and could play himself into one more massive payday.

What's more, Revis' addition enticed cornerback Brandon Browner to join the Pats. The 6'4", 221-pound physical brute had interest from other teams but traveled to Gillette Stadium and had no intention of leaving without a deal. Browner left Gillette in the afternoon, and reports swirled that he'd leave town for other meetings. But Browner merely sat in his hotel room across the parking lot waiting to sign his three-year, $17 million contract.

Those moves shook the NFL, particularly Browner's former partner in crime and defending Super Bowl champion Richard Sherman.

"Man, I think they improved tremendously. They knew what they wanted to do and went out and got the best players available," Sherman said at the time. "I think they're going to have specific roles for each one of them, a specific role for Darrelle and specific role for Brandon that is going to allow their talent to shine. I think they'll definitely be a top-two, top-three secondary in football."

The Patriots turned out to be better than that, and it ultimately came at Sherman's expense. But before they got there, Revis' ruthlessness at practice was absolutely astounding. It was a joy to watch him compete, and his intensity was unique for a defensive player. (The rules have a lot to do with that because minimal-contact practices strip the front-seven defenders from making a lot of noise.)

Usually, practices served as a Tom Brady clinic, but Revis altered that dynamic. Their battle during the first padded practice of training camp offered the most memorable workout of the past decade. Revis intercepted Brady twice and broke up two other passes. Revis undercut an out route to Julian Edelman in one-on-ones, and he caught up to Edelman's go route to pluck his second pass in full-team drills. Brady, Edelman, and Brandon LaFell got their revenge against Revis in the two-minute drill to close down practice, and the session offered a glimpse of the rest of the season.

It wasn't always utopic on the practice field, though, that's for sure. At one point during the season, Revis and Browner were barking back and forth at each other from the locker room to the practice field, and it ultimately spilled over into the workout. Browner blew a coverage during team drills, so Revis let him know about it. Browner didn't always grasp the play calls as capably as the Patriots' other veteran defensive backs, so it probably struck a nerve when Revis drove home that point, especially after their earlier words. So Browner punched Revis in the face, knocking him to the ground in the middle of practice.

They both looked at each other, almost in disbelief that it got to that, shook hands, and continued with their business. The pair basically realized they screwed up and it was time to get their act together before Belichick kicked them off the field, which is his usual policy for practice fights. Belichick handled them after practice, believed to be in the form of sprints. The fight had no lasting effects in the locker room, but it showed how friends and competitors can lose their cool even as they work together toward a Super Bowl.

Revis was special on game days in 2014, and it was the last great one of his career. Quarterbacks targeting Revis in the regular season completed 33 of 76 passes (43.4 percent) for 523 yards, two touchdowns, and four interceptions (two picks by Revis, two that wound up in a teammate's hands) for a 53.8 passer rating. He was anything but perfect in the season's first seven weeks, as Miami Dolphins wide receiver Mike Wallace easily beat Revis for a 14-yard touchdown in the opener and Oakland Raiders rookie quarterback Derek Carr completed five passes for 63 yards against Revis in Week 3.

The corner transformed from Clark Kent to Superman at the right time. The Patriots were facing a gauntlet of quarterbacks from Weeks 8 to 14 with Jay Cutler, Peyton Manning, Andrew Luck, Matthew Stafford, Aaron Rodgers, and Philip Rivers in succession. And from Week 8 through the end of the regular season, quarterbacks were a paltry 15 of 45 (33.3 percent) for 240 yards, one touchdown, three interceptions (one for Revis), and a 31.7 rating. During that stretch, Revis matched up against wide receivers Brandon Marshall, Alshon Jeffery, Emmanuel Sanders, Demaryius Thomas, Reggie Wayne, Golden Tate, Calvin Johnson, Jordy Nelson, Randall Cobb, Keenan Allen, and Sammy Watkins.

Revis was the best corner in the NFL in 2014, and that's not an opinion. He led all cornerbacks with 42 of 50 All-Pro votes for the fourth First Team honor of his career. Revis was both entertaining and insightful, as he'd take time to reveal the things that motivate him as well as the intricacies of certain plays. He didn't celebrate his own breakups or interceptions on the field because he called it "wasted energy," but he bought into the team culture that embraced the work that yielded victories.

A couple answers stuck out with Revis from late in that season. He was open and genuine about everything, for better and worse really, and Revis dismissed the impressiveness about his coverage stats.

"I don't look at stats," Revis said. "I stopped looking at stats probably four years [earlier] because I don't get balls thrown to my side that much. That's how I look at it. My thing is to play team ball. As long as we get the win, that's what I'm most excited about."

And for a guy who fully embraced the "Revis Island" moniker during his time with the Jets, Revis also wasn't all that absorbed with the All-Pro voting. Cornerbacks like Sherman, Patrick Peterson, Joe Haden, and even Talib had challenged his perch as the game's best, but the elder statesman shrugged off the importance of being considered the top dog as a 29-year-old.

"I'm over that," Revis said. "Everybody has got their own opinions. The world is full of opinions. You don't know which one is right. You don't know which one is wrong. I don't get into that whole opinion thing. Guys have opinions and feel a certain way, and that's how it is. I'm all about team ball and just winning. That's the main goal, just winning. When you win, it eliminates a lot of things."

Revis was an indispensable piece during the Patriots' Super Bowl run, and that might solidify his bid for the Pro Football Hall of Fame, even if critics rail on his lack of interceptions. His legacy is mildly complicated on the whole, but Revis helped the Patriots in more ways than one. The Pats were legitimately interested in keeping Revis beyond the 2014 season, but they had to void the second year of his contract either way. A day before that deadline, the Revis camp informed the Patriots that the Jets had an offer that was set to blow away the Pats' best proposal, so Belichick bowed out. Still, the Patriots leaked information over the next 24 hours to make it appear they were still in on the Revis bidding, which caused the Jets to up their offer to a five-year, $70 million pact. Revis was average in 2015 and terrible in 2016 before the Jets released him, having paid out $39 million for two regrettable seasons. They fell short of the playoffs twice and had to blow it up after 2016 with a series of high-profile cap casualties.

In 2016, Revis surrendered a pair of touchdowns to Patriots rookie Malcolm Mitchell, marking the first time in his career he'd been beaten for two scores by one player in a game. So while the Revis brand took a hit, there's no denying his worth to the Patriots, during the Super Bowl march and then thereafter.

Last Hurrah

There was a moment in March 2014 when it seemed certain Vince Wilfork had played his last snap for the Patriots. The captain of the defensive line realized he'd have to take a pay cut after coming back from a torn Achilles, but the Patriots' initial contract proposal was so infuriating that he ripped the name plate off his locker amid a tirade at Gillette Stadium. Cooler heads prevailed later that offseason, and Wilfork inked a deal that helped him earn $8 million in 2014 while the Patriots saved about $5 million in cap space.

Wilfork was the subject of perhaps the most underrated storyline as the Patriots prepared for Super Bowl XLIX against the Seattle Seahawks. His teammates really wanted to win the ring for Wilfork, knowing everything he had given the organization for 11 seasons, and that this would almost certainly be his final game in a Patriots uniform. Wilfork, a first-round pick in 2004, had an important role for the Super Bowl XXXIX champions as a rookie, but his presence for the 2014 team was far greater.

Wilfork was the unquestioned leader of the defense, a big brother, an advocate for his teammates' charitable endeavors, a grill master for summer cookouts, and so much more.

"He has done so much for me as far as teaching me along the way," linebacker Dont'a Hightower said.

Longtime captain Jerod Mayo was on injured reserve but wanted to see a longtime family friend go out on a high note, summing up the team mentality before kickoff: "Definitely want to see it for Vince.... I think it would be huge to get him a ring. It would be a great feeling for everyone."

The responses were interesting because I was polling Patriots veterans to get their thoughts on joining other Patriots greats with a Super Bowl ring of their own. Unprompted, they all immediately turned their attention to Wilfork, clearly shining a light on a topic from the locker room. And Wilfork had no idea. He was completely taken aback when informed of the sentiment.

"It's amazing," Wilfork said. "I have a great group of guys. I'll tell you that I'm blessed to be at the level I'm at, and I'm very fortunate to have the teammates I have. It's been a special bunch all year. When things are down, when things were tough, nobody put their head down.

"It's a true team. The way they feel toward me is the same way I feel toward them. I'm happy that they're here now. I hope I can get them one."

Wilfork joined the Houston Texans in 2015 and played at a high level for two seasons. He was every bit the leader they needed, too. Before signing, Wilfork said he'd only join the Texans if they'd assure him that defensive end Jadeveon Clowney would be fully committed to following his lead. As it turned out, Clowney was in the weight room at the time, so Wilfork met him face to face and asked the first pick of the 2014 draft if he was truly serious about becoming a great player. Clowney responded accordingly and ultimately dedicated himself to the team, finally showing a stretch of dominance in 2016.

Wilfork will undoubtedly be a Patriots Hall of Famer in the early 2020s. The only question is whether or not he'll get the call from Canton.

Out to Pasture

Physically, Logan Mankins had been kicked much harder on the farm. But physical pain often disappears quicker than the emotional toll of getting the heave ho from the wolf pack, and it's even less fun when you can see it coming. Still, it was a stunner when they pulled the trigger on the training camp trade, shuttling off Mankins to the Tampa Bay Buccaneers for tight end Tim Wright and the 2015 draft pick that turned into defensive lineman Trey Flowers.

Like so many before him, the Patriots wanted Mankins to take a pay cut, but he refused to budge. It's hard to fault his decision, but it's too bad it couldn't have been resolved more amicably. Mankins was a first-round pick in 2005, selected less than three months after the Patriots won their third Super Bowl. And he was ousted two weeks before the 2014 opener. No Patriot in the 2000s had a longer career without a Super Bowl than Mankins.

Mankins was tougher than nails thanks to a childhood on his family's cattle farm in Catheys Valley, California. It was a way of life to get kicked or stomped on by a cow, and there were no sick days on the ranch. When reminiscing about the beef cattle, he even cracked, "You may have ate one someday. You never know." How tough was Mankins, though? He played much of the 2011 season on a torn ACL, and no one knew about it until the following offseason. Mankins shrugged it off by saying he'd "tape an aspirin to it and go."

But 2014 was a different kind of tough. Mankins' ensuing $10.5 million cap hit stuck out like a broken car alarm. He was on the verge of becoming the ninth offensive lineman in Patriots history to play 10 seasons with the team. He had been to five consecutive Pro Bowls and had been a captain since 2011. Among other accomplishments, Mankins was Brady's personal body guard, protecting the superstar like a fourth liner on a hockey team, and Mankins was also largely credited with the development of left tackle Nate Solder.

As camp opened, Mankins was asked July 23, 2014, how much longer he thought he could keep playing. It was an innocent question, but it revealed his outlook for the first time.

"I don't know," Mankins responded. "That's a good question. It depends on health, I think, and if they want to keep me around here still. We'll see."

A month and three days later, Bill Belichick traded him. Mankins was conspicuously absent from practice before the trade, and word quietly spread between the players before Belichick's announcement. The news spread even quicker afterward in the locker room, and Belichick addressed the team at some point soon after, stunning the team in a way that few had witnessed since the Richard Seymour trade in 2009. By sending Mankins to Tampa, the Patriots freed up $6.25 million in cap space in 2014, $11 million in 2015, and $7 million in 2016, and Flowers became a major return on the back end of the deal. Belichick called Mankins "the best guard I ever coached" the day after the trade, further confusing veterans like Brady and offensive linemen Dan Connolly and Ryan Wendell who were particularly close with Mankins.

But Mankins was hardly the only hit the Patriots took on the offensive line that season. Legendary coach Dante Scarnecchia retired from his fulltime role, and Dave DeGuglielmo took over. The Patriots were reworking their line that season, but the Mankins trade didn't make DeGuglielmo's job any easier. DeGuglielmo was a popular guy in the locker room, but he was quietly criticized at times for adjusting some of Scarnecchia's techniques. DeGuglielmo didn't have his linemen lean as far forward and instructed them to almost let the defenders get into their bodies, rather than coaching the offensive linemen to attack.

There were also issues with DeGuglielmo's rotations. To open the 2014 season, the Patriots started Marcus Cannon at left guard, Connolly at center, and Jordan Devey at right guard. Cannon's best work in the NFL has come at right tackle, and Devey looked overmatched from the beginning so it was unclear why he was starting. Brady was absolutely assaulted in the opener in Miami against the Dolphins, who harassed him 25 times on 60 drop-backs, including 17 hits and 12 times he was knocked to the ground. All the while, Bryan Stork and Josh Kline were healthy scratches, and DeGuglielmo shuffled Wendell to center and Connolly to right guard during Brady's battering. The Patriots were smoked 33–20 and blew a 20–10 lead.

Stork got his first start at center in Week 4 against the Kansas City Chiefs, and tackle Cameron Fleming was inserted at right guard. Brady got his tail kicked again, fumbling twice and throwing two interceptions in the wretched 41–14 loss. Worse, when Brady was knocked to the ground, there were a handful of examples when none of the linemen went over to pick him up. In the days after the loss, DeGuglielmo read newspaper articles to his room of offensive linemen to let them know how heavily criticized they'd been in the media.

By Week 8, he finally settled on a permanent rotation with Connolly at left guard, Stork at center, and Wendell at right guard.

They were flanked by left tackle Nate Solder and right tackle Sebastian Vollmer, and Kline became the top backup interior lineman. The combination seemed so obvious from the beginning of the season, as it added important veteran presences and some nastiness that they lacked in September.

Stork wasn't exactly the most popular teammate to ever reside in Foxboro, but he made up for it with his physicality on the field. Brady commonly got frustrated with Stork's inability to get on the same page with the pre-snap reads, checks, and calls, and it came to a head in the week before Super Bowl XLIX when Stork missed an assignment in practice. Brady went berserk on Stork, and DeGuglielmo stepped in to protect his rookie, screaming back at Brady to not forget the line had been much better with Stork in the lineup to protect him. Stork's temper eventually got the best of him, though. He head-butted Denver Broncos defensive lineman Vance Walker to draw a crucial flag during the 2015 AFC Championship Game loss, when Stork was also criticized for tipping the snap count, and tossed from two practices for fighting in the spring and summer of 2016 before his release. It also didn't help Stork's cause that he had a growing concussion history, and David Andrews quickly became Brady's preferred center.

DeGuglielmo's final season was overrun by strange, almost series-by-series rotations on the line in 2015. During their loss to the Broncos, Brady was hit—not just harassed—on 25 of 60 dropbacks, and Cannon had the worst game of his career by allowing eight hits, including 2.5 sacks. DeGuglielmo was fired for failing to make enough progress with his group, but the Patriots caught a franchise-altering break.

Scarnecchia didn't know how to properly retire. He spent 2014 and 2015 scouting college prospects for the Patriots, and he traveled to pro days and the combine to do it right. He also checked in at Gillette Stadium about once per week during the season as an advisor. But Scarnecchia didn't have any long-term goals of returning on a fulltime basis. Belichick seemed to feel him out during the 2015 season to see if Scarnecchia would come back, but if Scarnecchia was intrigued, he didn't tip his hand. He had too much respect for his friend DeGuglielmo to put him on the hot seat like that. When DeGuglielmo was fired, three people close to Scarnecchia said he offered no indication that he wanted to return to the sidelines. One person even said there was "no fucking way" Scarnecchia would return. But when the offer was on the table, Scarnecchia couldn't help himself. He's a football coach, and he doesn't know anything else.

Among Scarnecchia's greatest accomplishments in 2016, he turned Cannon into a right tackle who earned a five-year, $32.5 million contract extension. Scarnecchia also immediately shrugged off the idea of a rotation, and the line was as strong as it had been in more than a decade.

Quarterback Evaluation

Bill Belichick caused New England's collective heart to skip a beat late at night on May 9, 2014, when he hinted at Tom Brady's mortality. The Patriots drafted quarterback Jimmy Garoppolo in the second round, and Belichick's explanation was highlighted by nine words: "We know what Tom's age and contract situation is." Brady was turning 37 three months later and he was under contract through 2017 at the time, so Belichick effectively tipped over the hourglass.

Hell, maybe Belichick just wanted to stoke a fire up Brady's ass with the Garoppolo pick, and if it also turned out the Patriots would upgrade their backup quarterback, so be it. But it created a dynamic straight out of the *Twilight Zone* that season when the Patriots lost two of their first four games, and in a weird, round-about way, the selection of Garoppolo might have actually pro-pelled the Pats to Super Bowl XLIX.

Garoppolo was a relative unknown from Eastern Illinois University, and the Patriots rookie was downright abysmal in prac-tice during his first few months. By comparison, Tim Tebow had been more functional during his cup of coffee with the Pats in 2013. Garoppolo was regularly running laps during the first two weeks of training camp because he was botching snaps and fumbling hand-offs. His signature throw occurred during the annual in-stadium practice that followed Ty Law's induction into the Patriots Hall of Fame. Law was standing on the sideline watching the session, and the best cornerback in franchise history was easy to spot in his freshly pressed red Hall of Fame jacket. Garoppolo completed a single pass on nine attempts that night, and one of his misfires sailed deep into the sideline and was caught by a surprised Law.

Garoppolo's first impression wasn't promising. He was also 1 of 8 a few days later during a joint practice with the Washington Redskins in Richmond, Virginia, with the only completion thanks to a leaping, turnaround catch from soon-to-be-released tight end Justin Jones. But Garoppolo was shockingly capable during the preseason opener against the Redskins, leading to the notion that he was simply better in games than practices. That game catapulted

Garoppolo's summer, and his teammates saw a changed man, both on the field and off.

The young quarterback really won over the room during the rookie skits in front of about 100 teammates and coaches inside a Gillette Stadium auditorium. And the 22-year-old unleashed a spot-on impression of special teams coach Scott O'Brien. Garoppolo, who practiced his routine frequently in his hotel room, wore a visor and fake mustache, stuffed a play sheet into his khakis, and marched back and forth swearing like a sailor. Every player and coach was buckled over watching the most hilarious skit of the summer.

Garoppolo's big-time August was enough to beat out backup quarterback Ryan Mallett, who was traded to the Houston Texans for a seventh-round pick in the 2016 draft. (The Patriots took a loss here. The Denver Broncos offered a second-round pick and Tebow to the Patriots for Mallett in 2012. When the Pats declined, the Broncos used that pick on Brock Osweiler.) Garoppolo's unpredictable rise after his poor start turned every head in the building, and one teammate observed, "Jimmy is going to be fucking cold-blooded."

Brady was getting beaten like a drum in the opening month of the regular season, and those issues came to a head during the 41–14 loss to the Chiefs on *Monday Night Football*. Brady was ultimately benched in garbage time, and Garoppolo led a meaningless touchdown drive. The performance punctuated Brady's tough stretch, which also featured a calf injury that popped up during a Week 1 practice.

Belichick dismissed a question that night about possibly reevaluating the quarterback competition, but it took on a new life that week. Some in the media wondered if it was time for a change, and fans filled up radio stations with calls about playing the kid and trading Brady after the season. The illogical logic was that a Super Bowl champion would never get blown out in such a fashion, so the Patriots should start the rebuilding process right away. It was Bizzaro World. But the following week against the Cincinnati Bengals, the Gillette crowd erupted in continuous "Brady! Brady!" chants during the Pats' 43–17 victory. Tight end Rob Gronkowski was emotional afterward to the point where he looked to be on the verge of crying.

"I told my brother before we came to the game, 'I'm going to make 12 look like Tom Brady,'" Gronkowski said, with the pitch of his voice rising. "And I went out there with my teammates, and we made Tom Brady look like Tom Brady after you guys were criticizing him all week—the fans, everything. And it feels so good."

Naturally, Belichick never considered benching Brady, and the head coach went so far as to defuse any perceived controversies in 2016 when the veteran was suspended. Belichick pointed out in camp Brady would be the starter upon his return in Week 5 and mocked any questions to the contrary in the ensuing two months. And despite some attention-starved speculation that Brady couldn't stand Garoppolo, just know the two have always enjoyed a solid relationship.

Finding Motivation

The quarterback drama was overblown, but the Patriots' warts most certainly were not in the fallout of the blowout in Kansas City. The Pats had three turnovers against a defense that hadn't forced any to that point in the season. The offensive line had been a mess. Tight end Rob Gronkowski didn't look like himself, which was understandable considering he was less than 10 months removed from tearing his ACL. The defense was decent but not yet dominant. So the Patriots knew there were corrections in order before becoming the sixth team in history to overcome a 27-point regular-season loss before winning the Super Bowl.

"This was probably the most embarrassing game I've been a part of," safety Devin McCourty said. "We lost on every aspect."

Defensive lineman Vince Wilfork added, "Am I worried? I'm always worried when we go out and put up a performance like we did tonight because that's not us."

So could the second-worst loss ever under Bill Belichick be a rallying cry, like the way they woke up after the 31–0 shellacking against the Buffalo Bills in the 2003 season opener? Or would it be a sign of things to come, like the 38–13 defeat to the Miami Dolphins and the Wildcat offense in 2008, or the lethargic 38–17 drubbing by the New Orleans Saints in 2009?

Of course, the master of handling distractions changed the tenor of the conversation the following week. Anytime a reporter questioned the quarterbacks, or the adversity or the character in the locker room, Belichick retorted, "We're on to Cincinnati," or some variation. It spiraled out of control from there. On to Buffalo. On to the Jets. And eventually: on to the White House.

The message was obvious, and Belichick relayed it all the same to his players. Past results didn't matter. Two weeks from now didn't matter. Contracts didn't matter. That week's game was the only thing that mattered. A decade and a half later, Belichick had his new "one game at a time."

Gronkowski's postgame emotion against the Bengals was striking, but the Patriots were fighters again between the whistles. Gronk, Wilfork, running backs Stevan Ridley and Brandon Bolden, left tackle Nate Solder, and defensive lineman Dominique Easley all started skirmishes with the Bengals during the game. The Patriots found their emotion against the last remaining undefeated team in the NFL.

They couldn't lose that focus, either. Captain Jerod Mayo tore his patella, and Ridley tore his ACL against the Buffalo Bills in Week 6. Defensive end Chandler Jones went down for two months with a hip injury in Week 7. Brady tweaked his ankle in October, too. And the Pats had that vaunted gauntlet of quarterbacks from Week 8 to 14.

The 2014 Patriots were reminiscent of the groups from the early 2000s in that they were able to manufacture motivation by any means necessary. The best example was undoubtedly in Week 12 when they beat the Detroit Lions 34–9 at home to improve to 9–2. The Lions had the top-ranked defense in the NFL at that point, and guys like McCourty, Darrelle Revis, and Brandon Browner didn't like hearing the Lions brag about it. So members of the defense plastered the Lions' quotes throughout their meeting rooms. Even though the rankings validated the Lions' feelings, the Patriots believed they had a better defense and wanted to prove it. And not just that, but the Patriots were genuinely mad about it.

"We took that as a challenge," Browner said. "You guys think you're the best, but we're confident that we can compete with the top defenses across the league."

Revis was even more expansive.

"I think a lot of us kind of viewed it as trash talk, too, of how they were just coming out of nowhere," Revis said. "I mean, they're the No. 1 defense. You've got to give them credit, too.

"At the same time, we know we've got a great defense, and we've got to continue to keep on pushing and working. We feel like we can match up with anybody across the board, and we feel like we can out-execute them."

The Patriots proved they could be chameleons, as their 34 points were the most against the Lions all season. A week earlier against the Indianapolis Colts and the NFL's highest-scoring offense, the Pats held them to a low of 20 points to that stage of the season.

The players built on each of these experiences. They leaned on each other in the divisional round of the playoffs when they knocked off the Baltimore Ravens 35–31, becoming the first team in postseason history to overcome a pair of 14-point deficits. The Patriots relied on trick plays, including a trio of formations with just four offensive linemen and a 51-yard touchdown pass from Danny Amendola to Julian Edelman. And when Ravens coach John Harbaugh criticized the Patriots' tactics, Brady barked back that he should learn the playbook. Brady was the leader in the intestinal fortitude department.

The next week spawned Deflategate, as the Colts cried foul after their embarrassing 45–7 loss in the AFC title game. Brady pledged to his bosses and friends that he'd go to his grave believing he didn't do anything wrong. Publicly, he was the face of a contrived controversy that somehow led national news broadcasts, and he fielded 61 questions over 31 minutes in his first news conference of the week. One reporter even asked Brady what parents were supposed to tell their children.

Belichick flipped the script again, as media in attendance at Gillette that Saturday—eight days before Super Bowl XLIX— were encouraged to stick around later than usual. It wasn't initially indicated why. A couple hours later, Belichick passionately hit the podium and said he was "embarrassed" over how much time he spent researching air pressure in footballs that week. He watched field tests, science experiments, and conducted his own exhaustive investigation rather than preparing for the Seattle Seahawks. Belichick was agitated enough to drop a *My Cousin Vinny* reference.

"I'm not a scientist," a frustrated Belichick said. "I'm not an expert in football measurements. I'm just telling you what I know. I would not say that I'm Mona Lisa Vito of the football world as she was in the car expertise area, all right?

"It sounds simple, and I'm not trying to say that we're trying to land a guy on the moon, but there are a lot of things here that are a little hard to get a handle on. There is a variance in so many of these things."

Patriots owner Robert Kraft also shockingly addressed the situation upon the team's arrival in Arizona, as he sent a message to the NFL office to say he expected an apology when Ted Wells' investigation cleared the organization.

All the while, the Patriots were tasked with taking down the Seahawks, the defending champions who entertained the possibility of being known as the greatest defense in history. Interestingly, the players felt prepared for the game before they even got on the plane. Brady had the game plan down pat three days after they beat the Colts, and his teammates on offense were oozing with confidence throughout the week in Arizona. Belichick even canceled the walkthrough the day before the Super Bowl because the week had gone so well. Amazingly, every distraction caused the Patriots to focus that much more in those two weeks.

The Patriots beat the Seahawks 28–24 and erased a 10-point fourth-quarter deficit for the first time in Super Bowl history. And to think, the Seahawks were the fourth team in history to lead the NFL in both points and yards allowed in back-to-back seasons, and they had surrendered 13 total fourth-quarter points against their previous eight opponents. Brady closed the game with two touchdown drives, completing 13 of 15 passes for 124 yards and scores to Amendola and Edelman to win his fourth Super Bowl.

Brady was ultimately suspended for Deflategate, but his best defense is in the numbers. In Brady's 34 games from Super Bowl XLIX to Super Bowl LI, he went 28–6 (.824 winning percentage) and completed 65.2 percent of his passes for 10,401 yards (305.9 per game), 78 touchdowns (2.3 per game), and 16 interceptions (0.47 per game). With the NFL's overly burdensome eye zeroed in on Brady for two years, the quarterback had better splits than his previous 15 seasons in the league.

Malcolm, Go!

Cornerback Malcolm Butler was an unlikely hero, but his game-winning interception in Super Bowl XLIX wasn't uncharacteristic. On a grand scale, Butler was practically anonymous. The University of West Alabama product was undrafted in 2014 and didn't get any guaranteed money when he signed with the Patriots, signifying almost no competition for his services as a free agent. He was a healthy scratch four times as a rookie, including as late as a two-game stretch in Weeks 12–13. And Butler played the 19th-most snaps on defense and the 37th-most on special teams, so he had virtually no role in 2014. The only reason he played 18 defensive snaps in the Super Bowl was because cornerbacks Kyle Arrington and Logan Ryan struggled so badly, and that was a surprise from Arrington's standpoint because he had the best season of his career up to that night.

Rewind the clock to training camp, though, and Butler's big play was anything but a surprise. Butler consistently stood out for his ability to be around the ball and then make plays on it in the air. There was no question early in camp Butler was going to make the team, even on a roster that had cornerbacks with starting experience like Darrelle Revis, Brandon Browner, Arrington, Ryan, and Alfonzo Dennard. Bill Belichick rarely keeps six corners, especially when four have almost no value on special teams, but there was no chance Butler was getting axed.

Butler was summoned late onto the field when safeties coach Brian Flores yelled, "Malcolm, go!" The Patriots used a goal-line personnel package with four defensive tackles, two defensive ends, two linebackers, and three cornerbacks. In comparison to the previous play, a four-yard run from Marshawn Lynch, the Pats removed safeties Devin McCourty and Patrick Chung and defensive end Akeem Ayers in favor of Butler and defensive tackles Alan Branch and Chris Jones. The heavy inside presence was meant to deter the Seahawks from running with Lynch, who had been stuffed twice earlier in the game in similar situations.

From there, the Patriots recognized the Seahawks' play based on prior tendencies to use pick routes in clutch passing situations, although they were already on alert based on Browner's first-down jam in front of Revis on the prior play. On second-and-goal, Browner immediately jammed wide receiver Jermaine Kearse, who was supposed to clog Butler's avenue to the ball, and Butler read the route as soon as intended receiver Ricardo Lockette shuffled his feet. Butler learned two days earlier in practice that he had to sell out for the pick route, and that's why he won the race to Russell Wilson's pass.

"That's why people know me—because of that play," Butler said in a moment of reflection. "I can't do anything but accept it when they bring that up because that's how they know me. But you know me, high standards, and I'm well past that play. I'm trying to do other things.

"It's going to be there forever. That's the best play I'll ever make in my life, period, no matter what else I do. So it's going to be there."

Butler's immortal act, perhaps the immaculate interception, was turned into a bobblehead doll. He got his own parade in his hometown of Vicksburg, Mississippi. And when the Patriots decided to duck out of the Revis bidding during the 2015 offseason, it's partly because they hoped Butler could seize the starting job. Butler was elected to his first Pro Bowl in 2015, though he couldn't play due to a minor knee injury, and he was even better in 2016 when he allowed two or fewer catches in 11 games. He shut down Steelers star Antonio Brown twice, including the AFC Championship Game, among his biggest performances.

While Butler made the best play during their Super Bowl XLIX march, he was undoubtedly one of the Patriots' best players throughout 2016 to signify his surge to stardom. Even as Butler recognized and embraced the historical significance of his Super Bowl interception, he wants even more to have a long career that lives up to the immeasurable hype from such a play.

"I belong here," Butler said. "That's without a question even before that Super Bowl play. I think I've proven a little bit, but it's not about me. It's about the whole team. I've still got plenty more to show, so I'll be ready."

Get Gronk'd

Rob Gronkowski has been everything the Patriots could want in a superstar, aside from the injuries of course. By the conclusion of his second season in 2011, when he set a tight end record with 18 touchdowns, there was already a debate that he was the greatest talent to ever play the position. The 6'6", 265-pounder plays with punishing physicality and reckless abandon, once nearly breaking his neck to score a touchdown against the Kansas Chiefs in 2011 and offering no regrets afterward. And he is a genuine goofball who has done the impossible by making adults think "69" jokes are funny again.

Gronk embarrassed six Colts on his way to a 26-yard touchdown in Week 11 of 2014, and he stormed back to the sideline like a real-life Tasmanian devil. His eyes were bulging. He was out of breath. And he was rattling off a bunch of questions to his teammates in the high-pitched voice of a crazy man.

"How did I do that?"

"Did you guys just see what I did?"

"Did it look cool?"

Everyone thought it was hilarious. It's amazing. Gronk is always on, and no one can get enough of him because they know it's real and not an act. *Why does he party so hard?* he was asked prior to Super Bowl XLIX. "Because I'm a baller," he instantly replied. The quote immediately consumed the Patriots' team hotel just like one of his impromptu dance parties. His teammates often jokingly wonder what music is playing in Club Gronk—the space between his ears—because he'll dance to the beat in his own head.

Gronkowski works out as hard as anyone in the building. After a rare earthquake in Massachusetts, a few Patriots quipped Gronk must have thrown a dumbbell across the weight room. But he holds himself accountable and produces on the field and in the meeting room, where he's been known to apologize to coaches and teammates for dropping a pass. Or he'll just laugh at himself for his mistakes, which don't come often.

It's also better to work with him than against him. Gronk famously kicked Colts safety Sergio Brown "out of the club" with a dominant block, and he has steamrolled others for yapping too much.

"When he gets angry, it's scary," wide receiver Julian Edelman said. "He is a big guy that is strong, powerful. He is like a big old baby. But once you tick him off, get out of the way."

Gronk's injuries can't be ignored, though he finally got over the hump with six catches for 68 yards and a touchdown in Super Bowl XLIX. It solidified his importance to the Patriots after he was a decoy in Super Bowl XLVI due to a high ankle sprain, broke his arm in the 2012 playoffs, and missed the 2013 postseason due to a torn ACL. Gronkowski was also a spectator during the Super Bowl LI run because of back surgery, which was his ninth known procedure since 2009.

As long as Gronkowski doesn't suffer a catastrophic injury that leads to an early retirement, future Hall of Famer Tony Gonzalez predicted Gronk would break his record of 111 touchdowns for a tight end. But considering Gonzalez only missed two games in 17 years, it's inconceivable to think Gronk would catch his other marks.

"That'll go down," Gonzalez said of the touchdown record. "But the career catches and yardage, that's 17 years of me being awful damn lucky of never getting hurt and being able to play full seasons. I only missed two games. It's tough and that's just the nature of the beast. It's a lot of luck. Gronkowski is running down the field and a guy takes his knee out on a cheap shot [from then-Browns safety T.J. Ward] as far as I'm concerned, but that's just how it goes. That could happen again. Hopefully not."

Pro Football Hall of Famer Shannon Sharpe said "there's no debating" Gronk is "the best tight end in football." Mark Bavaro, one of Bill Belichick's favorite players with the Giants, marveled over Gronkowski's ability to produce even when defenses treat him like Jerry Rice and Randy Moss. Gronkowski was humbled to hear their praise.

"I appreciate their comments and what they think," Gronkowski said. "I've got much respect for all those players. I've looked up to them my whole career. I'm just focused on what I've got to do right now as a player and not really focused on what can happen in the future. I'm just trying to be the best player I can be."

The other cool element of the Gronk experience is his dedication to the community because, not to sound like a broken record, everything he does is genuine. When his knee was healthy enough to run around again in the 2014 offseason, Gronk returned to Gillette Stadium and asked the director of community affairs how he could help again. In just one week during the 2015 season, Gronk played football at Gillette with a 16-year-old from the Make-A-Wish Foundation and sent a personalized video to Medway High School as they coped with the death of 17-year-old senior Madeline Lamson.

Gronk annually shaves his head at One Mission Kids Cancer Buzz-Off at Gillette, and his attendance has helped the cause's popularity explode. The event raised more than $5.7 million in its first seven years. He also attends many teammates' charitable events, hosts a summer football camp, has dressed up like a Christmas tree at the Patriots' holiday party for kids, passes out turkey baskets to families at Goodwill, and has helped build a school playground. He loves the times when he meets a kid at a hospital and they ask him to do a Gronk spike and then recognize him out at dinner down the road.

"A lot of times, you always see a kid saying, 'Do a Gronk spike for me.' Or they do it right there in the hospital with the football you give them right there," Gronk said. "That's definitely cool when they bring that up."

So when Gronk cuts loose, it's crazy to think twice about it. The guy does it all in front and behind the cameras, and the traveling frat party comes along with the package. Some of his best work has come at the Super Bowl parades, where he has shotgunned and spiked beers from the crowd, worn a Patriots jersey with the No. 69, gone with no shirt at all, and twerked on the bow of the Duck Boats.

He surely causes some eyes to roll, but Gronk is well-intentioned. The big goofball even called out President Barack Obama in April 2015 during the White House ceremony. Obama, who spent some time with Gronk in the State Room before his eight-minute speech on the South Lawn, made a Deflategate crack. "I usually tell a bunch of jokes at these events, but with the Patriots in town, I was worried that 11 out of 12 of them would fall flat," Obama smirked. "All right, all right. That whole story got blown a little out of proportion."

Gronk was in his element afterward, so someone jokingly asked him if he was drinking that morning.

"No, there was no drinking," Gronk replied before acting as the team spokesman in regard to their ever-growing frustrating over the Deflategate investigation. "Maybe the President was wasted from his deflate joke. We're still wondering as an organization about that, right?"

Obama also cracked that he advised Gronk to keep his shirt on at the White House because the Secret Service might not be thrilled. Gronk's response? "What could they do to me?"

Fair point. Gronk might actually engage them in a dance-off. And who wouldn't be up for that?

Edelmania's Arrival

Surprisingly, it took a while for Bill Belichick to know what he had in Julian Edelman. Sure, the athletically gifted wide receiver with squirrellike elusiveness showcased his talent in spurts from 2009 to '12 while he backed up slot machine Wes Welker, but Edelman was often held back by a lack of opportunities or an abundance of injuries. And even after Belichick split with Welker during the 2013 offseason, he initially turned to Danny Amendola with a five-year, $31 million offer and let Edelman dangle for a month in free agency. (Amendola ultimately earned $17.8 million during the deal due to three pay cuts.)

After visiting with the Giants in 2013, Edelman returned to the Patriots on a one-year deal that was worth $1.015 million through earned incentives. Through an explosion to Edelman's own credit and Amendola's torn groin, Edelman turned into the Welker replacement with the best season of his career: 105 catches, 1,056 yards, and six touchdowns. But Belichick still gave him a hard time in free agency, as Edelman needed a two-day visit to his hometown San Francisco 49ers before the Pats bit with a four-year, $17 million offer.

Edelman has helped Tom Brady as much as anyone over the past decade, and it's no fluke. They've spent an incalculable amount of hours in the offseason pacing up and down football fields and running through the route tree, from Foxboro to Montana to California. As Edelman rehabbed from foot surgery in 2015, the pair disappeared into the field house behind Gillette Stadium after practice to keep their timing in sync for Edelman's playoff return. Edelman's work during practice has been legendary as well, as he forces cornerbacks to hate him rep by rep, especially during joint workouts with other teams.

Edelman is clutch in crunch time, and that will be his legacy. Yeah, he caught the game-winning touchdown in Super Bowl XLIX, but don't stop there. He did it by beating cornerback Tharold Simon with the exact same route that he ran a series earlier, though Brady misfired. Edelman also caught a pair of third-down passes on the drive that cut the Seahawks' deficit to 24–21, and he withstood a head-rattling hit from supersized safety Kam Chancellor for a 21-yard gain on third-and-14.

Fast forward to Super Bowl LI, and Edelman made a helicopter, gravity-defying catch against the Falcons that could best be described as a video-game glitch. Brady delivered a pass that should have been intercepted, and as Edelman and the ball pinballed between a pair of Falcons on their way to the ground, he magically corralled it for a 23-yard gain. Four plays later, James White (touchdown) and Amendola (two-point conversion) tied the game.

Edelman had 80 catches for 949 yards and three touchdowns in 10 playoff games from 2013 to '16, and he had a case for Super Bowl XLIX MVP. During that stretch, he had twice as many receptions as anyone in the league except Doug Baldwin (52) and twice as many yards as all but five players. Under what logic is he not a No. 1 receiver?

New Englanders love clutch, blue-collar underdogs, and Edelman has endeared himself to the fan base in a major way. Former Boston Bruins forward Milan Lucic was among the city's sports champions who called Edelman to welcome him to the club in February 2015. Edelman has been as big of a star as any Patriot during the Super Bowl parades, drawing massive roars from the crowd by jumping off the Duck Boats to take pictures, sign autographs, and wave a gigantic Patriots flag. Edelman's signature moment during the February 2015 parade came when he delivered a knockout punch to a Richard Sherman sign.

"I definitely feel the love and respect from the fans around here," Edelman said. "I think that's because we can reflect from one another. Boston is a blue-collar town that is a tough town. I like to try to play my game like that, coming from nothing and keep on trying to get better and do your job. That's kind of what New England is about. I'm thankful to be with a team, an area, a region that relates how people think I play."

You know what's really amazing? Belichick actually had Edelman pegged from the start. He didn't lazily pigeonhole Edelman as the next Wes Welker at all. Patriots Hall of Famer Troy Brown, a playoff hero in his own right, was surprised to hear Belichick's scouting report during Edelman's rookie training camp in 2009. Belichick was fawning over Edelman, which led to the following exchange.

"Oh, is he the next Welker?" Brown asked.

"No way, he's the next you. He reminds me more of you," Belichick replied.

"Okay, all right."

Right, indeed.

Numbers Game

It was a big deal in 2012 when Tedy Bruschi wanted Dont'a Hightower to wear his No. 54. It was just as big of a deal in 2016 when Bill Belichick shifted Hightower to the all-important corner stall in the locker room, which is perched next to the door that all players must traverse on their way to full-team meetings. That locker had previously been occupied by respected leaders Willie McGinest and Jerod Mayo. The purpose? If a player was ever out of line, he couldn't avoid McGinest, Mayo, or Hightower.

Some of the greatest Patriots of their dynasty have been unquestionable leaders off the field and unparalleled performers on it, and that's why Hightower's legacy is soaring. The linebacker put himself into contention for the Patriots Hall of Fame in 2017 when he signed a four-year extension worth up to $43.5 million. With two defining Super Bowl plays under his belt already, the new deal offered an avenue to become one of the greatest defensive players in franchise history.

The first play was Herculean. Hightower played through a torn shoulder labrum down the stretch in 2014, fought through a squared-up Russell Okung block, and made a one-armed tackle to stuff Seahawks running back Marshawn Lynch at the 1-yard line on the play before Malcolm Butler's game-winning pick in Super Bowl XLIX.

"I want to be known as a smart, aggressive, tough, physical football player," Hightower said when asked about his potential legacy. "In my mind, I feel like those are all the words I would use to describe myself. That's part of it. I do what my coaches ask me to do and try to live by what my teammates expect me to do, either as a team captain or as the toughest son of a bitch out there on the field. I want people, whenever they think of Hightower, I want them to think, yeah, he tackled Marshawn Lynch on the 1-yard line, which was a great play, but he was a tough son of a bitch. That's kind of been my legacy, just doing what I can for my teammates."

Hightower's second act was just as significant to a Super Bowl victory, as the Patriots needed every break necessary to erase a 28–3 third-quarter deficit against the Falcons. A minute and a half after Stephen Gostkowski's 33-yard, fourth-quarter field goal trimmed the margin to 28–12, Hightower rushed off the front side and was surprised when running back Devonta Freeman offered him little attention, noting it's a blitz the Patriots had just called earlier. Hightower, who loves to blitz as much as he loves to breathe, used his left hand to dislodge the ball from quarterback Matt Ryan, and defensive tackle Alan Branch recovered it. The Patriots were desperately crunched for time, so a takeaway was a mandatory ingredient in the comeback.

Hightower also offered a tremendously giddy and casual description of the play.

"I saw Matt Ryan with the ball in his hands, and I wanted it," Hightower said. "So I went and took it from him."

Hightower earned the locker and captaincy before the Patriots even got to the Super Bowl. Linebacker Jamie Collins was one of his best friends on the team, and he was stung more than anyone in the locker room after the Week 9 trade. After curbing those emotions, Hightower rallied the group to focus more on the big picture, noting they were far too talented to let the season go off the rails. His teammates responded well by realizing if Hightower can get past it, no one else had an excuse not to do the same. He backed it up by watching extra film with his less-experienced teammates, sometimes deep into the night.

Hightower had an immediate grasp of the playbook as a rookie in 2012, and he felt truly comfortable on the field in the system by late in the 2013 season. Every defensive teammate, regardless of position, asks the self-proclaimed football nerd questions about the game plan because Hightower always has the answers. Without Collins, the Patriots relied on Shea McClellin, Kyle Van Noy, and Elandon Roberts in an assortment of linebacker roles, and consider Hightower's challenge. McClellin, who joined the Patriots in free agency in 2016, opened camp as a defensive end. Van Noy, a trade acquisition from the Lions, hadn't played a game for the Patriots at the time of the Collins trade. Roberts, a sixth-round pick, was a healthy scratch twice in the opening month of his rookie season. And Hightower got the committee to fill Collins' void in a variety of ways.

Hightower, a two-time national champion at Alabama, is a winner and a warrior. He played through a torn meniscus in 2016 and a sprained MCL in 2015 after enduring the torn labrum in 2014. And as much as he hoped to return to the Patriots in free agency following Super Bowl LI, he wanted to find his true value on the open market. A week later, the Patriots gave him the deal that he coveted.

Hightower has made Patriots teammates and legends alike proud of his work, and that's the singular driving force.

"No disrespect, I don't care what anybody outside the New England Patriots organization thinks about me," Hightower said. "I don't care if you think I'm tough. I don't care if you think I'm too slow. None of that matters. As long as those guys that I go out to battle with and I go out to practice with, as long as they respect me and I'm able to help us win, that's all I really care about. I'm here for my teammates. That's all I'm really worried about."

One for the Fifth Finger

The fifth ring is usually termed "one for the thumb." With the 2016 Patriots, they probably had the middle finger in mind.

They were saddled with adversity from the jump, as Tom Brady was sidelined for his four-game Deflategate suspension. The players treated it appropriately, though, because they used the ban to refuel their Scorched Earth tour that was derailed by injuries in 2015.

Nate Solder, Ryan Wendell, Jerod Mayo, Dion Lewis, LeGarrette Blount, Trey Flowers, and Dominique Easley headlined the group of 18 players who were placed on season-ending injured lists. And then add missed games due to Julian Edelman's broken foot, Jamie Collins' virus, Jabaal Sheard's ankle, Danny Amendola's knee and ankle, Rob Gronkowski's knee, Dont'a Hightower's knee, Devin McCourty's ankle, Chandler Jones' toe, and Sebastian Vollmer's ankle. It got so bad that if Rob Ninkovich didn't take a commercial flight to Miami in Week 17, they wouldn't have been able to dress 46 players. Oh, and Brady sprained his ankle that day, too.

Jones was then involved in a bizarre incident during the play-off bye week when he showed up shirtless to the Foxboro Police Station seeking help due to a medical emergency. The fallout from the episode spiraled out of control, and the Patriots ultimately decided they wouldn't extend Jones' contract following the 2016 season, which led to his trade to the Arizona Cardinals. The Pats used assets from that trade to draft left guard Joe Thuney and wide receiver Malcolm Mitchell.

Bill Belichick made a string of terrific roster decisions during the 2016 offseason. The Pats pried restricted free agent Chris Hogan from the Bills with a three-year, $12 million contract that was so aggressive it shocked both Hogan and the NFLPA. Hogan solidified the receiver depth chart after Brady was forced to throw to a bunch of nobodies when Edelman and Amendola were injured. Martellus Bennett was a godsend from start to finish, but he was particularly helpful after Gronk's back surgery. Bennett was finally the answer as a second-string tight end after Tim Wright and Scott Chandler failed in the fallout of Aaron Hernandez's arrest.

Defensive end Chris Long boosted the pass rush, and he made several winning plays that didn't get the spotlight on the stat sheet. The greatest example was the drawn holding penalty that forced the Falcons out of field-goal range in the fourth quarter of the Super Bowl. Another under-the-radar moment—and there were a lot—occurred when he pushed the pocket into Matt Ryan's face to cause the quarterback to lean back and prolong his throwing motion during Hightower's strip sack. Trade acquisitions Kyle Van Noy and Eric Rowe also fortified unforeseen issues at the position with the Collins trade and top pick Cyrus Jones' struggles.

There were roadblocks, like always. Quarterback Jimmy Garoppolo got off to a blistering start for Brady, but he suffered a Grade 2 sprain of his AC joint in the second quarter of his second start. Rookie third-stringer Jacoby Brissett was a complementary piece during the Pats' 27–0 win against the Texans in Week 3, but he had to play through a sprained thumb ligament for his final start because Vince Wilfork landed on him.

Things got a bit weirder from there, as Sheard was kept home during a trip to play the 49ers in San Francisco, which led to questions over Belichick's control of the locker room in the wake of the Collins trade. In Week 16, Malcom Brown was benched for the first half against the Jets for being late to a team meeting. Pundits wondered if this was 2009 all over again.

The Patriots defense drew the public's wrath throughout the season. It's been a common criticism over the years because Brady's play has largely been beyond reproach, but this example was stranger than most. There's no question the defense played poorly in a 31–24 loss to the Seahawks in Week 10, which doubled as their first game without Collins, but personnel and schematic improvements down the stretch yielded a superior defensive product. Logan Ryan was reinserted as a starting corner with Malcolm Butler and Rowe. Shea McClellin and Van Noy split linebacker duties on passing downs, with Van Noy better used as a pass rusher, and Elandon Roberts harnessed a running-down role. And Flowers' seven sacks in the final nine weeks propelled the pass rush.

On the whole, the Patriots allowed 15.6 points per game, the best mark in the NFL in three seasons, so they knew how to fight back against the critics. Then they just threw up their hands when the counterpoint involved their lack of prolific opponents. It came to a head after their 16–3 victory against the Broncos in Week 15 when Devin McCourty yelled over to Ryan in the locker room to "Remind [the media] they said we sucked!"

Ryan was surrounded by the media after notching his first interception of the season and had fun with McCourty. "We were doubted all year," Ryan said. "They said we sucked. And we heard about [the Broncos'] secondary and their defense, and we wanted to come out here and prove something."

McCourty and Ryan later clarified they didn't take the outside criticism to heart, especially compared to the way Belichick hounded them earlier that season. But McCourty had been the face of the defense since taking over for Vince Wilfork in 2015, thanks to a five-year, $47.5 million contract extension, and he wanted to have his teammates' backs. Ryan cited the 2014 calls for Brady's benching and laughed that people can hammer him all they want because if they're willing to call out Brady, they'll do it to anyone. Hightower relayed a similar opinion. He didn't care about the criticism, but he got sick of hearing the repetitive questions about the defense even as they allowed an average of 14.8 points during their 10-game winning streak to close the year.

Every Super Bowl champion needs to learn something about itself along the journey. The 2016 Patriots recognized they needed to believe in themselves when the world crashed down around them, whether it involved Brady's suspension, Collins' trade, Gronk's surgery, or the merciless criticism of the defense.

So when the Patriots faced a 21–3 halftime deficit against the Falcons and Duron Harmon calmly told his teammates they were about to record the greatest comeback in Super Bowl history, there was actual meaning and belief behind his words. During their Super Bowl prep, the Patriots discussed the Falcons' penchant for building big leads in the playoffs, and the Pats watched in disbelief as the Seahawks and Packers both quit.

The Patriots knew they weren't quitters. Not only that, they even got cocky. A couple defensive players joked—or, hell, maybe they were serious—they began to untie their cleats after they won the overtime coin toss to give Brady the ball and the means to a 34–28 win. A champion's script doesn't just play out in one night. It's months in the making.

So NFL commissioner Roger Goodell handed the Lombardi Trophy to Robert Kraft and the Super Bowl MVP award to Brady; the beneficiaries showed class upon receipt. If they chose to show more vitriol during a private ceremony at Kraft's house that summer, well, the new rings had to find a home on one of their fingers.

CHAPTER 10
HISTORY UN-REPEATED

On February 7, 2017, Boston's 10th championship parade in 15 years was certainly its most raucous, as the vitriolic, frat-house crowd cheered Tom Brady and jeered NFL commissioner Roger Goodell, whose two-year rage against the Patriots machine culminated with the quarterback's four-game suspension for his role in the controversial Deflategate. Brady—donned in all black—the Patriots, and their region responded during their Duck Boat ride through the Back Bay. Rob Gronkowski caught beers from the crowd, opened them with his teeth, and spiked them on the pavement, and Danny Amendola wore a "Fire Goodell" hat.

Their venom was real, and it carried through the ensuing offseason. Even on that rain-soaked ride through Boston, it was impossible to ignore the 2017 season, when the Patriots had their second chance to win three Super Bowls in four years. They were equipped with $65 million in cap space that they used to sign cornerback Stephon Gilmore, trade for wide receiver Brandin Cooks, retain linebacker Dont'a Hightower, and double Gronkowski's pay, among a flurry of other deals that sparked the debate over their potential to go undefeated.

Yet, it was a move the Patriots didn't make that yielded a season-long storm. Cornerback Malcolm Butler, a restricted free agent on a $3.91 million tender, was miffed by Bill Belichick's decision to grant Gilmore a five-year, $65 million pact after the Patriots failed to offer Butler more than $7 million annually. Butler's teammates raised their eyebrows as well, considering Gilmore landed a contract that was worth the most total dollars that Belichick had ever given a defensive player. Butler was the hero of Super Bowl XLIX, a Pro Bowler in 2015 who played at an elite level down the stretch in 2016 when the Patriots won Super Bowl LI, so he was rightfully ticked that negotiations over a new deal had never gotten close. He then visited the Saints, who, unwilling to sacrifice the 11th pick in the draft as the required compensation to sign the restricted free agent, offered a four-year deal in excess of $50 million that was contingent upon a trade with the Patriots. But the Saints balked at the trade during the draft. Butler then reported to Gillette Stadium during the third week of voluntary offseason workouts.

Butler had the worst of his four seasons as a pro in 2017, and he admitted early in the season that his contract status was on his mind, though his teammates pledged that he was still his same, hardworking, dependable self during the workweek. The issues were with inconsistencies, most notably as he was demoted behind Eric Rowe in Week 2 against the Saints, which marked the only time in a stretch of 55 games that Butler didn't start. He responded well in Week 3, limiting Texans star wideout DeAndre Hopkins to a pair of catches for 10 yards when the two matched up. Midway through the season, however, he had a strange stretch during which he would play well for most of the game but would suffer a lapse for a critical play or two. It's largely why he surrendered a career-worst nine touchdowns during the year.

Then, things got weird when Belichick benched Butler in Super Bowl LII. Butler led the Patriots in defensive snaps in 2015 and 2017 and never left the field in their playoff victories against the Titans and Jaguars. And despite his inconsistent play, Butler was better in the AFC Championship Game against the Jaguars than the week earlier, so his performance was trending upward. On the Sunday before the Super Bowl, Butler went to a Boston hospital to get treated for flu-like symptoms, and he missed the team flight to Minneapolis the following day. Butler arrived Tuesday and finally started to kick the bug by Thursday. For context, Gronkowski (twice), running back Dion Lewis, cornerback Johnson Bademosi, and linebacker Marquis Flowers all missed practice time due to related illnesses earlier in the season and regained their typical role during that week's game.

Whatever led to Butler's benching, the players were livid with the decision. They felt badly for their teammate, who bawled during the national anthem and cried later on the sideline. Beyond that, the players didn't believe the coaching staff put them in the best position to beat the Eagles, who scored on eight of their 10 possessions in Super Bowl LII and frequently attacked lesser-used defensive backs Rowe, Bademosi, and Jordan Richards. Related, the Patriots were also curious why Lewis and defensive end Deatrich Wise weren't as featured in the game plan, while a former player noted linebacker James Harrison "looked old" in his most extensive work of the season. Belichick's judgment has been questioned in-house plenty of times before, as recently as the Jamie Collins trade in 2016, but the fallout from the loss to the Eagles was stranger than usual.

Parallel to the Butler conundrum, Gilmore was outstanding later in the season. He experienced a September learning curve due to the Patriots' revolving game plans that altered defensive philosophies and assignments on a weekly basis, according to teammates who have grown to expect these issues with new players. Gilmore spent his first five seasons with the Buffalo Bills, who ran straightforward systems and didn't stress their players nearly as mercilessly. At one point during organized team activities during the spring of 2017, Gilmore told his teammates it was the hardest practice he'd ever endured, and they weren't even in pads.

So when Gilmore struggled during the first four weeks of the season, the Patriots didn't panic, and his teammates had his back during a breakout performance against the Buccaneers in Week 5 when he shut down wideout Mike Evans. Safeties Devin McCourty and Duron Harmon vocalized their trust in Gilmore, while other players swore at the media for criticizing Gilmore, who actually played the majority of the game with a concussion. Gilmore kept it up after a three-game absence, but he reached his pinnacle in the playoffs when he allowed only four catches on 15 targets for 55 yards, and he broke up six passes, all of which yielded greater excitement about his potential for the following season.

Drama Club

It seemed as though there were more subplots than usual during the Patriots' 2017 season. And because they're the Patriots, who are essentially dissected with the Hubble Telescope by the national audience, subplots are treated with the vigor of a political scandal. It's true that there was friction between Bill Belichick and Tom Brady over the case of Alex Guerrero, Brady's personal trainer who began to treat a major segment of the team, but the discord wasn't a divide. Belichick restricted Guerrero's privileged access with the team by removing him from the sideline during games and team flights.

The fact of the matter is Belichick and Brady have always had a typical coach-quarterback relationship. They occasionally butt heads as they work toward the same goal, and every now and again Belichick isn't keen on the idea that Brady is portrayed as someone who is bigger than the team, which is understandable on multiple fronts. But to suggest a rift was irreparable and would spark an abrupt end to the dynasty? Everyone around the team rolled their eyes at that idea.

It was inarguably a transitive season, though. Defensive coordinator Matt Patricia's 14-season tenure closed after Super Bowl LII when he became the head coach of the Detroit Lions, though the damage to the coaching staff was mitigated when offensive coordinator Josh McDaniels reneged on his agreement with the Indianapolis Colts. That decision, thanks in part to a nice pay raise from owner Robert Kraft, might have also been a determining factor in the Patriots' ability to retain assistant quarterback coach Jerry Schuplinski and special teams coordinator Joe Judge, and maybe even more assistants. And the Patriots were lucky the

Arizona Cardinals chose to hire Steve Wilks as their head coach, rather than Pats linebackers coach Brian Flores. The purge was avoided.

The search for Brady's successor, however, forged ahead because the quarterback became the first 40-year-old MVP in league history. Though Belichick wanted to keep Garoppolo on team-friendly terms, it would have been financially reckless to use the franchise tag on him after the season, so they traded Garoppolo to the 49ers on October 30 for a second-round pick in the 2018 draft. Garoppolo never intended to sign an extension with the Patriots to remain as a backup, and that hardline stance paid off in February 2018 when the 49ers handed him a record-setting, five-year, $137.5 million contract.

Belichick likely could have exceeded the return on Garoppolo if he created an auction, which is a decision worthy of criticism, but the quick trade trigger at least helped the Patriots control the quarterback's landing spot. The Pats won't see the 49ers until the 2020 regular season, barring an epic Super Bowl showdown. And while the Browns relentlessly tried to pry away Garoppolo during the spring of 2017, Belichick would have only surrendered him for a laughably one-sided ransom. There's logic behind that, as Belichick wanted to ensure his 40-year-old quarterback wouldn't resemble a 40-year-old quarterback. So Belichick's choice at the deadline was to trade Garoppolo for a high second-rounder or lose him in free agency for, at best, the top compensatory pick (No. 97 overall) in the 2019 draft.

The trade was second-guessed again when Brady collided with running back Rex Burkhead during the Wednesday practice prior to the AFC Championship Game against the Jaguars. Brady needed 12 stitches on his throwing hand and sat out Thursday's practice before returning Friday, when he began to look like himself again, and had the ninth-best passer rating (108.4) of his playoff career against the top-ranked pass defense in the NFL in a 24–20 comeback victory.

After throwing for a Super Bowl–record 505 yards against the Eagles, Brady reiterated his stance to return for the 2018 season. Belichick previously reached the same conclusion as well. And Kraft called a season-ending meeting for the triumphant triumvirate to ensure they'd squashed their differences. Some of the issues were already detailed, but it was also believed the meeting would help them hash out the fallout from a highly refuted ESPN article that slammed Brady and predicted the fall of the dynasty. If there had been a high-ranking organizational mole, or moles, it behooved Kraft to get the pair's takes on that subject and anything else that may have lingered.

Beyond that, the Patriots had to figure out tight end Rob Gronkowski's status. Gronk admitted after the Super Bowl that he was considering retirement, and this wasn't a heat-of-the-moment reaction. The thought weighed on Gronk's mind late during the season, and he stated it wasn't related to health concerns.

What's on Tap

The Patriots spent time stewing over their 41–33 loss to the Philadelphia Eagles, but they've got too much talent and veteran leadership to crumble like other Super Bowl losers of the past. They scored the second-most points in the league despite losing receiver Julian Edelman to a torn ACL, and they surrendered the fifth-fewest points in the league without linebacker Dont'a Hightower (torn pectoral muscle). Those are essentially two of the Patriots' four most indispensable players.

Right tackle Marcus Cannon, tight end Martellus Bennett, wide receiver Malcolm Mitchell, cornerbacks Jonathan Jones and Cyrus Jones, linebacker Shea McClellin, defensive end Derek Rivers, defensive tackle Vincent Valentine, and valued special teamer Nate Ebner also hit injured reserve, while receiver Chris Hogan, special teams captain Matthew Slater, and cornerback Eric Rowe each missed about half the season with injuries.

During the dynasty, they've overcome far more gut-wrenching defeats and far greater adversity regarding restocks and rebuilds. The integral characters remain in place, and Tom Brady is coming off a historically remarkable year for a quarterback of any age. The reinforcements will arrive, as they always do. And the Patriots will contend for every Super Bowl for as long as this partnership remains in place.

A quarter century earlier, the dream of such a stability of excellence had been more unrealistic than the hope for a warm shower in the Foxboro Stadium locker room. Now, the Patriots' unparalleled journey remains intact, as much of their history as it is their future.

ACKNOWLEDGMENTS

Caitlin, as if we weren't already busy enough, I remember coming home after a long day at training camp and telling you, almost in disbelief myself, that I thought I had an opportunity to write this book. Avery had just turned one and we had grand plans for Taylor, and the 2016 season had just begun, which spun a low-stress summer into a high-octane adventure that culminated with Super Bowl LI. I should've known how you'd react to the possibility of a book and whatever endless amount of work it'd entail in the ensuing months, but even I didn't know if it was worth pursuing at that point. Your reaction, like it has always been, pushed me to go for it. No matter how wild of an idea I've ever had, you've always been the rock who solidified my decision to chase a dream.

You put up with me for three years when I lived at home with my parents and scooped ice cream while trying to figure out how to make it in this business. After I got laid off and passed over for a job I deserved, you didn't hesitate when I joined NESN in 2009 to make $25 a week to write a Patriots column. (Everyone laughs at Bill Belichick making $25 a week during his first year in the NFL in 1975. I made that on the wrong side of 34 years' of inflation.) And I'll never forget that Friday night, May 4, 2012, when I was hired by the *Boston Herald* and we celebrated at the condo. I knew you always believed in me and I always needed that, but that night just sort of validated why that part of the journey had been worth it. It was similar in February 2018 when you were on overdrive to keep me level before The Athletic called with the offer of a lifetime, our lifetime.

You know I've told this story before, but when I interviewed at the *Herald* and they asked how you felt about my work hours, I said you'd be the most valuable person in the newsroom. You've proven that to be true a million times over with every job I've taken, and I cited that point again with The Athletic. You knew how interested I had been in writing a book, and you were willing once again to make a sacrifice in order for me to see this through. I wouldn't have accomplished this or much of anything if it weren't for you. I appreciate everything you do—taking care of the girls' dinners or handling our accounting, painting a room or not complaining too loudly when I take over the TV, just being there when I need you or making sure I'm not perpetually sunburnt. Being a great mom can't always be easy when you've got an extra fully grown toddler running around the house, too.

And far more importantly, I wouldn't have grown this much as a person without you, Avery, and Taylor. We laugh about it, but my goodness, these two little angels have changed our whole world. Avery and Taylor, you're bound to hear some stories about a dad you might not recognize. You've turned me into a softie, and I love it. Thankfully, I don't bawl anymore, or at least not too recently anyway—I could've ended a drought that first day of daycare—but you don't have to look hard to see swollen eyes or a quivering cheek at every sign that you're growing up: crawling, walking, wearing a backpack, making a Halloween painting with your feet, saying something adorable, or, okay, basically anything. I'm not sure there's a more amazingly satisfying feeling than coming home from a road trip and having Avery run to meet me at the door while Taylor lights up in the background. (By the time this book is out, Taylor will be running with you, Avery. And your mom will laugh as I recycle a joke about allergies.) It'd be impossible for us to be any more in love with you two.

To Mom and Dad, I'd need space for another book for all the ways I could thank you for raising me the right way and giving me every opportunity to succeed in life. Beyond words, with the way Caitlin and I have raised Avery and Taylor, know it's because we've each had amazing parents who showed us how to guide a family.

After things went—to put it kindly—south at UNH, Dad gave me the—to put it kindly—motivational speech I needed to get back on track. And Mom, when I wanted to take that semester off, you were the reason why I stayed the course. You made the calls, drove me around to college interviews, and helped me make the best of a tough stretch that ultimately defined my professional life. I know I went to UNH and all you got was that lousy T-shirt, but I'm not sure I'd be where I am today or you'd have this book in your hands if I didn't learn how to respond to failure, not just with one or two decisions but with a rededication to the work ethic that is demanded to create and then reach a goal. Thank you for passing along those qualities, even if they took me a little longer to apply them than most of the others.

I've been so blessed to have such an amazing family, from generation to generation. Alyssa, I'm so proud of who you've become. Grandma, my goodness, we've had some unbelievably fun times together. Karen, Brendan (we know you're watching over us), and Kellen, thank you for welcoming me into your home. Jamie, if we kept it out of the best-man speeches, it sure isn't getting mentioned here.

I wouldn't be who I am without all of you, plus too many more to mention. Thank you.

Caitlin, Avery, and Taylor, this is still just our beginning. I love you.

—Jeff Howe